GREGORY J. L

PAUL RICOEUR
&
LIVING
HERMENEUTICS

Exploring Ricoeur's Contribution
to Biblical Interpretation

destinēe

© 2016 Gregory J. Laughery

Without limiting the rights under copyright reserved above, no part of this publication may be reproduced, stored in, or introduced into a retrieval system, or transmitted in any form or by any means (electronic, mechanical, photocopying, or otherwise), without the prior written permission from the publisher, except where permitted by law, and except in the case of brief quotations embodied in critical articles and reviews. For information, write: info@destinee.ch

Reasonable care has been taken to trace original sources and copyright holders for any quotations appearing in this book. Should any attribution be found to be incorrect or incomplete, the publisher welcomes written documentation supporting correction for subsequent printing.

Some Scripture quotations are taken from the Holy Bible, New International Version®. NIV®. Copyright ©1973, 1978, 1984 by International Bible Society. Used by permission of Zondervan. All rights reserved. Other Scripture quotations are taken from New Revised Standard Version of the Bible, copyright © 1989 by the Division of Christian Education of the National Council of the Churches of Christ in the USA. Used by permission. All rights reserved. ISBN: 978-1-938367-24-3

Published by Destinée S.A. destineemedia.com
Cover and interior by Art Director Per Ole Lind
    Set with Doves, Akzidenz and Garamond
Copy editing by Susanna Young
All rights reserved by the author.

destinée

ACKNOWLEDGEMENTS

The author wishes to thank the following for their permission to use copyright material:

Temps et récit, t. 1, L'intrigue et le récit historique, Paul Ricoeur, © Editions du Seuil, 1983.

Temps et récit, t. 3. Le temps raconté, Paul Ricoeur, © Editions du Seuil, 1985.

Du texte á l'action. Essais d'herméneutique II, Paul Ricoeur, © Editions du Seuil, 1986.

Le Confilit des interprétations. Essais herméneutique, Paul Ricoeur, © Editions du Seuil, 1969.

Préface de P. Ricoeur *Jésus, mythologie et démythologisation*, Rudolf Bultmann, Paul Ricoeur, © Editions du Seuil, 1968.

"Biblical Hermeneutics," Paul Ricoeur, *Semeia* 4 (1975), 29-148 © Society of Biblical Literature.

CONTENTS

Acknowledgements   III
Preface   VI

PREFIGURATION

1.	**Introduction**	1
1.1.	Setting the Scene	1
1.2.	The Aim of the Study	16
2.	**Life and Work**	18

CONFIGURATION

3.	**Text, Interpretation Theory, Biblical Hermeneutics**	37
3.1.	Why the "Text"?	37
3.1.1.	Explanation and Understanding	38
3.1.2.	Discourse and Dialectic of Event and Meaning	46
3.1.2.1.	Sense and Reference	51
3.1.2.2.	From Speaking to Writing	52
3.1.3.	The Text	56
3.2.	Consequences for Biblical Hermeneutics	61
3.2.1.	Philosophical and Biblical Hermeneutics	62
3.2.1.1.	Ricoeur-Bultmann: Reading the Biblical Text	71
3.2.2.	Methodology: Its Concerns and Limits	81
3.2.2.1.	Historical Criticism	81
3.2.2.2.	Structuralism	90
3.2.2.3.	Hermeneutical	104
3.2.3.	Application to Biblical Parables	113
3.2.3.1.	Parables: Crossan - Ricoeur	114

3.2.3.2.	Methodology for Parable Interpretation: Complementarity in Tension	128
3.2.3.2.1.	Reading Parables: A Historical-Critical View	129
3.2.3.2.2.	An Evaluation of a Structural Rendering of Matthew 13: The Parable of the Sower	132
3.2.3.2.3.	Parables: A Hermeneutic Trajectory	140
3.3.	Narrative	154
3.3.1.	Why Narrative?	154
3.3.2.	Decoding: What is Narrative?	162
3.3.2.1.	History and Fiction	169
3.3.2.2.	A "Re-decoding" of Narrative	179
3.3.3.	An Evaluation for Biblical Hermeneutics	186

REFIGURATION

4.	**Trajectories Towards Closure**	**193**
4.1.	Authors, Readers, and Texts	193
4.2.	Refiguration and Beyond	210
5.	**Conclusion**	**221**
	Select Bibliography	228
	Index	244

PREFACE

A reading of and interest in the writings of Paul Ricoeur, I believe, has become crucial for a better understanding of our current philosophical and theological landscape. Hermeneutical considerations are so much a part of all we do, whether in general as human beings or more specifically as exegetes, theologians, or philosophers. As an exegete, my own orientation has always been, moderately at least, philosophical, and Ricoeur's writings combine a rare mixture of hermeneutics, philosophy, biblical hermeneutics, and theology that merit further exploration.

When I began my research it became evident that a fair amount of work had already been done on Ricoeur's philosophy and hermeneutics, but very little on the *theological* dimension of his trajectory and its connection to biblical hermeneutics. In one sense, this made the research more arduous, as a proliferation of secondary sources was lacking. In another sense, however, it made the journey more stimulating and thought provoking, as some of the ground now covered in this work, to my knowledge, has not been dealt with elsewhere. Confronted with what, at least some argue, is a modern - post-modern interpretative context, I was interested in ascertaining if Ricoeur's work could offer an alternative perspective.

Ricoeur's enterprise was a continual challenge. The formidable task of deciphering his theological overtures and his ventures into biblical hermeneutics presented numerous *detours* daring the Ricoeur reader to dig ever deeper into the text, mining both insights and ambiguities. In my opinion, this is likely to be the way Ricoeur would have it. This book is entitled *Living Hermeneutics*, as it was this perspective of biblical interpretation that emerged into a growing conviction along the way.

I'm grateful to a number of people who helped make the completion of this book possible. Many thanks go to my mother, Margaret Rivette. I must also mention the unflagging support and friendship of George and Eileen Diepstra. Susanna Young edited this work and contributed remarkable insights. Per-Ole Lind and his creative insights produced the cover and interior.

A special thanks goes to Professor Paul Ricoeur who met with me, answered correspondence, and several phone calls in a gracious way. His legacy, no doubt has, and will continue to impact many for years to come.

My debt to my wife Elisabeth (Lisby) and our three grown children, Vincent, Alexander, and Lawrence, transcends anything I could ever write here. They have expressed, through a shared life together, the reality of God's love and grace.

PREFIGURATION

1. Introduction

1.1. Setting the Scene

We readily acknowledge that any study of hermeneutics today is a complex undertaking. In regards to such subject matter, the literature is vast and arduous. The word "hermeneutics" itself is given different meanings by various protagonists and it is difficult, nigh impossible, to imagine that we all understand the same thing when we use the word. While a consensus, therefore, is unlikely to be easily established, it is nevertheless important to situate the contemporary context for hermeneutics, which will set out the parameters for the following discussion. Paul Ricoeur states:

> I see the recent history of hermeneutics as dominated by two pre-occupations. The first tends progressively to enlarge the aim of hermeneutics, in such a way that all *regional* hermeneutics are incorporated into one general hermeneutics. But the movement of *deregionalization* cannot be pressed to the end unless at the same time the properly *epistemological* concerns of hermeneutics – its efforts to achieve a scientific status – are subordinated to *ontological* preoccupations, whereby *understanding* ceases to appear as a simple *mode of knowing* in order to become a way of being and a way of relating to beings and

to being. The movement of *deregionalization* is thus accompanied by a movement of *radicalization*, by which hermeneutics becomes not only general but *fundamental*.¹

As Ricoeur sees it, the recent history of hermeneutics, suggests we are engaging with something regional and with something general. Regional hermeneutics deals with specifics, let's say the interpretation of texts (Old and New Testaments for example), whereas general hermeneutics is concerned with interpreting and understanding ourselves.² Ricoeur is convinced that all regional hermeneutics are being subsumed to or overcome by general hermeneutical considerations, and his term for this is deregionalization. Another way of articulating this, following Ricoeur's assessment, is to point out that he believes that ontology (being) has displaced epistemology (knowledge) at the heart of the hermeneutical enterprise. What configuration these two preoccupations are to have remains an open question that will be taken up later, but for the moment it is important to underline that one of Ricoeur's main interests is to move hermeneutics, through language and texts, in the direction of re-regionalization.³

Our motivations in this study are to decipher this Ricoeurian project and to assess its potential contribution to the question-problem-issue of hermeneutics and its relationship to language and the text, notably the biblical text. As we increasingly find ourselves in what some refer to as a post-structuralist, post-modern, post-meaning cultural context, two of the major problems we face are the role of language and

---

1 Ricoeur, "The Task of Hermeneutics," *Philosophy Today* 17 (1973), 112-128 ("La tâche de l'herméneutique," reprinted in: F. Bovon et G. Rouiller, éds., *Exegesis. Problèmes de méthode et exercices de lecture*, Neuchâtel: Delachaux, 1975, 179) and in: *From Text to Action, Essays in Hermeneutics II*, trans. K. Blamey and J. B. Thompson, Evanston: Northwestern University Press, 1991, cited 54, ET. (*Italics* his).

2 Ibid., 55-63. Ricoeur argues that a restrictively general emphasis may tend to over-subjectivize hermeneutics, leaving out an epistemological moment in the movement of interpretation. The subject of interpretation becomes primarily subjectivity or the process of understanding itself. This suggestion merits further investigation, which we shall undertake below.

3 For a fuller discussion of this paragraph see Part 3 below.

how to interpret texts.⁴ Does language communicate something viable and have the capacity to refer outside of itself? What is a text? Are we to understand the biblical text as a compilation of facts that are absolutely and objectively clear? Or, is it a text that one approaches simply to satisfy the subjective desires of interpretative interest?⁵ How does a text, if at all, mean anything?⁶

Today, for example, the Scriptural text often undergoes a severe form of theological *de-materialization* (spiritualizing) on the one hand, while it is frequently diluted historico-theologically (literary, socio-pragmatic, or a maze of other concerns) on the other.⁷ We become aware of the recent plethora of books and articles on the literary or spiritual dimension, attend various symposiums on the artistic dimension, and read readers accounts of the reader's dimension. Scripture, it is argued, is multi-dimensional.⁸ This may well be a true and relevant conclusion, but is there not room to question whether this textual multi-dimensionality, conceivably, is often reduced to a readerly one-dimensionality?⁹ In other words, does this supposed "multi-dimension-

---

4   See S. D. Moore, *Poststructuralism and the New Testament*, Minneapolis: Fortress, 1994. E. V. McKnight, *Postmodern Use of the Bible: The Emergence of Reader-Orientated Criticism,* Nashville: Abingdon, 1988. R. Barthes, "The Death of the Author," in: *Image-Music-Text*, London: Fontana, 1984, 142-147. T. Eagleton, "Capitalism, Modernism, and Postmodernism," *New Left Review* 152 (1985), 70-71.

5   S. E. Fowl, "The Ethics of Interpretation or What's Left Over After the Elimination of Meaning," 379-398, in: D. J. A. Clines, S. E. Fowl, and S. E. Porter, eds., *The Bible in Three Dimensions*, Sheffield: Sheffield Academic Press, 1990. Fowl argues that it is futile to discuss textual meaning because there are no criteria for doing so. Those of us in biblical studies should give up our meaning discussions and start to work in the direction of interpretive interests, 380. But see A. C. Thiselton, *New Horizons in Hermeneutics*, Grand Rapids: Zondervan, 1992, 602-603. "If interests determine how we read a text, and if any interest represents as good a candidate as another, how can biblical texts do more than instrumentally serve interests rather than shape, determine, and evaluate them? How can they unmask oppressive interests if the status of a socio-critical reading is ranked no higher than a socio-pragmatic reading, which serves the interests of the oppressor?"

6   See J. Stout, "What is the Meaning of a Text?" *New Literary History* 14 (1982), 1-12. "If interpretation is a matter of discovering meaning, and is therefore bound to run amuck when informed by mistaken assumptions about what meaning is, then literary criticism, religious studies, classics, history [biblical studies] - in short, all disciplines involving the interpretation of texts - will consist largely in failure to deliver the goods."

7   D. A. Carson, *The Gagging of God*, Leicester: InterVarsity Press, 1996, 57-92. F. Watson, *Text, Church and World: Biblical Interpretation in Theological Perspective*, Edinburgh: T & T Clark, 1994, 33-93.

8   This is said to be the case because there are no facts, only interpretations, which tends to signify readerly interpretative licence, rather than a textual multi-dimensionality. For no facts, only interpretations see Moore, *Poststructuralism* , 1-9, 89. For readerly interpretative licence, see Thiselton, *Interpreting God and the Postmodern Self*, Edinburgh: T & T Clark, 62-66.

9   R. Morgan, in: R. Morgan and J. Barton, *Biblical Interpretation*, Oxford: Oxford University Press, 1988, 7. "Texts, like dead men and women, have no rights, no aims, no interests." Also R. Lundin, The *Responsibility of*

ality" fuel an interpretive free for all? Should readers just pick a dimension that they prefer and go with it?

So, on the one hand, to center on a single dimension of Scripture, such as the literary one, will be reductionistic and in danger of leaving the reader *outside* a holistically meaningful text, which comprises more dimensions; theological and historical to mention just two.[10] But, on the other hand, an overemphasis on the pluralistic nature of the text can leave us *inside* a Scripture made up solely of an intra-linguistic series of signs, symbols, and events. This would make Scripture a text that can only refer to itself and therefore render it unable to adequately address or instruct the reader with its content.[11]

In regard to the first example of being left outside the text, the literary critic Stanley Fish argues that a text is always subject to the meaning that a reader imposes upon it. Readers are left "outside" the text because meaning is reduced to residing only in readers. This is considered to be consensus or ideology reading in opposition to critical reading. Text meaning then, for Fish, is always a product of readerly construction and never a question of textual discovery.[12] In Fish's view there is no way to speak of meaning residing "within" a text.[13] According to Fish, the text has no capacity to resist a reader's domination; it is always subject to, and controlled by a reader's own ideology.

With reference to the second example of being trapped inside the

---

Hermeneutics, Grand Rapids: Eerdmans, 1985, 18. When referring to Emerson's romantico-Cartesian views, "the text becomes a pretext for the dance of the imaginative spirit upon the grave of the dead letter."

10   What we have in mind here is those who argue that the text lacks the capacity to inform interpreters of its meaning. S. Fish, *Is There a Text in this Class? The Authority of Interpretive Communities,* Cambridge: Harvard University Press, 1980, 3, for example, argues, "the readers response is not *to* the meaning; it *is* the meaning." (Italics his).

11   This perspective is argued for by structuralists, artists, and scholars of "play." The text is viewed as an intricate web of interconnections related to other interconnections. Texts do not have the capacity to refer to anything other than themselves. J. D. Crossan, *The Dark Interval. Towards a Theology of Story,* Niles: Argus, 1975, 20-42; M. C. Taylor, *Deconstructing Theology,* New York: Crossroad, Chico: Scholars, 1982, 99.

12   C. Norris, *What's Wrong with Postmodernism? Critical Theory and the Ends of Philosophy,* Baltimore: Johns Hopkins University Press, 1990, 129-131. "Thinkers such as Fish urge us to accept the total obsolescence of all binary distinctions such as true/false, science/ideology, real/imaginary, history/fiction. Reality is now defined through and through only by belief systems, cultural codes and consensus. All disciplines merely do what comes naturally - accept consensus - it is both where we start and end up - this means no discoveries."

13   See Fish, "Why No One's Afraid of Wolfgang Iser," in: *Doing What Comes Naturally, Change, Rhetoric, and the Practice of Theory in Literary and Legal Studies,* Oxford: Clarendon Press, 1987, 68-86.

text, the biblical interpreter J. D. Crossan and the literary critics Roland Barthes and Mark Taylor argue that instead of searching for the meaning of the text, it is more appropriate for readers to play with its words.[14] This is because a text is in unlimited play, which is its greatest virtue.[15] Readers are allowed entry into a text, but are left "inside" the text to play with its words, as these words are only able to refer to one another. The prospect of textual meaning is always and forever undecidable and irresolvable, which in turn leads to an endless erring.[16] For Crossan, Barthes, and Taylor, readers are stranded "inside" the text because it can only pluralistically—given any number of interpretations—refer back to itself in a ceaseless flux that incessantly defers meaning.

These two examples, the first of readers being excluded from a text, and the second of readers being forever caught within it, have the same conclusion. Whether readers are left "outside" or "inside" the text, it has no meaning in and of itself. It is either unable to resist a ruling readerly imposition, or it spirals off into an endless spin of non-meaning. In light of these options, an accelerating cultural scream confronts us. Where is meaning? Does such a being-concept-thing-experience-reality exist? As the teacher says:

Meaningless! Meaningless! Utterly Meaningless!
Everything is meaningless![17]

---

14 See Crossan, *Cliffs of Fall: Paradox and Polyvalence in the Parables*, New York: Seabury, 1980, 9-10. Barthes, "Death," 148. Taylor, *Erring. A Postmodern A/Theology*, Chicago: University of Chicago Press, 1984, 121-148.

15 Barthes argues in "Death," 154, "In the multiplicity of writing, everything is to be disentangled, nothing deciphered; the structure can be followed, 'run' (like the thread of a stocking) at every point and at every level, but there is nothing: writing ceaselessly posits meaning ceaselessly to evaporate it, carrying out a systematic exemption of meaning."

16 Taylor, *Erring*, 11-13. "Ideas are never fixed but are always in transition; thus they are irrepressibly transitory. For this reason [....] (this) might be labelled Nomad Thought. The erring nomad neither looks back to an absolute beginning nor ahead to an ultimate end. His writing, therefore, remains unfinished. His work less a complete book than an open (perhaps broken) text that never really begins or actually ends." Also, 179 and 182, "Texts forever cross and crisscross in a perpetual process of interweaving. Rather than stable and static, texts are insubstantial and transitory." "The unending erring of scripture is the eternal play of the divine milieu."

17 Ecclesiastes 1: 2.

This could well describe, in some circles, our current cultural / theological malaise.[18] Is this the end of the story? It may well be! If so, we are left numb and instructed to create our own meaning. Yet, how is it then, that the proponents of such interpretive orientations (Fish, Taylor, and Crossan), still dogmatically expect us to concretely understand the meaning of each of their texts?

What we have just briefly outlined above is a *central* issue for hermeneutics, which we will say more about later. But this specific problematic of hermeneutics now needs to situated within a broader horizon. Our aim in doing so is to continue setting the scene, while also introducing a subject that has a wider relevance for the question of text interpretation. We shall refer to this subject as: modernism and post-modernism.

It is important at the outset, to acknowledge that these are *vast* and often *disputed* concepts currently used to describe sweeping cultural movements. There is no question that there are different views and positions concerning modernism and post-modernism.[19] Our intention is not to resolve the issue of a precise definition of either movement, but rather to more narrowly focus on what some scholars argue is a distinction between them with respect to their over-riding perspectives.[20] In building off these arguments, we will next look at how these broad cultural phases have generally influenced hermeneutics, and then explore how those influences specifically affect the area of biblical hermeneutics.

---

18   B. D. Ingraffia, *Postmodern Theory and Biblical Theology*, Cambridge: Cambridge University Press, 1995, 1-15.

19   P. Lakeland, *Postmodernity*, Minneapolis: Fortress, 1997, ix-xi.

20   N. Mercer, "Postmodernity and Rationality: the Final Credits or just a Commercial Break?" in: A. Billington, T. Lane, and M. Turner, eds., *Mission and Meaning*, Carlilse: Paternoster, 1995, 319-338, esp. 319-320. In regards to post-modernism for example, Mercer remarks: "Postmodernity is a delightfully slippery word; a lexicographer's nightmare." However, in spite of this, Mercer draws out a plausible scenario in terms of a broad definition that would have some agreement (see below). "Postmodernity passes the death sentence on the Cartesian project [....] and it marks the final abandonment of the Enlightenment (modernist) promise." J-F. Lyotard, "A Conversation," in: *Flash Art*, 921, 1985, 32-35, esp. 33 states, "Even though the field of post-modernism is very very vast [....] it is based fundamentally upon the perception of the existence of the modern era that dates from the time of the Enlightenment and that has now run its course." Also, Thiselton, *Interpreting God*, 11-17 and P. Sampson, "The Rise of Postmodernity," in: V. Samuel and C. Sugden, eds., *Faith and Modernity*, Oxford: Regnum Books, 1994, 29-57. See below for a fuller discussion and clarification.

For some today, as we have seen, all texts (including the biblical one) are said to be in play without a referent.[21] Any hope for a coherent textual meaning is amputated.[22] For others, readers cannot help but rule over a text that is helpless to resist their conquests.[23] This state of affairs, it is argued, is merely the shift away from the modern world with its emphasis on facts, rationality, the myth of the neutral observer, and an absolutely precise universal textual meaning. It is a shift toward the postmodern world, which rejects such hubris.[24] Any post-modern should know better than to assume that a text has a fixed sense and referent, or for that matter that anything is fixed.[25]

Modernism it seems, according to this perspective, has indeed fallen on hard times. Its proposal of transparent clarity between the interpreter and the interpreted, exact definitions of the world, and absolutely accurate total clarity in textual interpretation has not been achieved. Some argue that the advance of what is referred to as post-modernism is that it suggests a move from the necessity of interpreting texts to that of interpreting interpretation.[26]

Others counsel us to abandon modernist attempts to speak of a meta-narrative which would give sense to the whole of reality, affirming that the business of postmodernism "is not to supply reality, but to

---

21   Taylor, *Erring*, 184, argues that textual meaning revolves around in a ceaseless flux without boundaries, "as the play of the word never stops." Also Crossan, *Raid on the Articulate*, New York: Harper & Row, 1976, 23. All language is in play. Any quest for meaning is "an eternal game of hide and seek."

22   Watson, *The Open Text*, London: SCM, 1993, 5. "Deconstruction challenges all claims to textual coherence or unified meaning, bringing to light the repression on which they are founded."

23   Fish, *Is There a Text?* 326-327, "Interpretation is not the art of construing but the art of construction. Interpreters do not decode poems, they make them."

24   S. J. Grenz, *A Primer on Postmodernism*, Cambridge: Eerdmans, 1996, 81. "The modern mind assumes that knowledge is certain, objective, and good. It presupposes that the rational, dispassionate self can obtain such knowledge. It presupposes that the knowing self peers at the mechanistic world as a neutral observer armed with the scientific method." There was a "modern explosion of knowledge under the banner of the Enlightenment project. Whatever else postmodernism may be, it embodies a rejection of the Enlightenment project, the modern ideal, and the philosophical assumptions upon which modernism was built."

25   Watson, *Text, Church and World: Biblical Interpretation in Theological Perspective*, 90. "Freed from the burdens of reference and meaning and from the linear temporality they create, postmodernism celebrates the pure and random play of signifiers."

26   See Taylor, *Deconstructing*, 81. Moore, "The 'Post'Age Stamp: Does it Stick?" *JAAR* 57/3 (1989), 543-559, esp. 548, "Taylor [....] sends rip(ple)s through the traditions of theological and biblical reflection inherited from the Enlightenment."

invent allusions which cannot be presented."[27] Hence, the post-modernist virtue is trumpeted as the privileged experience of heterogeneity, an unlimited allusiveness that rejects the rules of rationality or hermeneutic interpretation.[28]

While it is clearly true that for some scholars the modern project led to the post-modern, they question whether we should so willingly embrace the failures of one project for the false success of another.[29] But perhaps we have proceeded a little too quickly in our discussion of modernism and post-modernism. We need to re-trace our steps in order to clarify. What follows is a brief, but adequate analysis of both projects.

The *modern* project is delineated as an attempt to offer a comprehensive account of reality and the interpretation of texts on the basis of its meta-narrative of reason.[30] Human reason is often considered as the grounding principle for everything else. In Hans-Georg Gadamer's words:

> There can be no doubt.... the real consequence of the Enlightenment was the subjection of all authority to reason.[31]

René Descartes (1596-1650), within a theistic framework, set the modern world in motion in aspiring to ground all knowledge in reason.[32] John Locke (1632-1704), writing from a Christian perspective,[33] follows

---

27 J-F. Lyotard, *The Postmodern Condition: A Report on Knowledge*, Manchester: Manchester University Press, 1984, 82.

28 R. Kearney, *The Wake of the Imagination*, London: Hutchinson, 1988, 377.

29 Ibid., 20-33, 251-358. Also C. Norris, *What's Wrong with Postmodernism?* Carson, *The Gagging of God*, and Thiselton, *Interpreting God*.

30 It is not our intention to develop either modernism or post-modernism in detail, but only to show what is argued to be their general orientations and their effects on (textual) biblical interpretation. For further reading see, E. Gellner, *Legitimation of Belief*, Cambridge: Cambridge University Press, 1974; T. Docherty, ed., *Postmodernism: A Reader*, New York: Columbia University Press, 1993; J. Breech, *Jesus and Postmodernism*, Minneapolis: Fortress, 1989; F. W. Burnett, "Postmodern Biblical Exegesis: The Eve of Historical Criticism," *Semeia* 51 (1990); P. Gisel and P. Evrard, *La théologie en postmodernité*, Genève: Labor et Fides, 1996.

31 H. G. Gadamer, *Wahrheit und Methode*, Tübingen: Mohr, 1960. *Truth and Method*, trans. J. Weinsheimer and D. Marshall, 2nd edition, New York: Continiuum, 1989, 278.

32 Carson, *The Gagging of God*, 58-59. Also R. C. Solomon, *Continental Philosophy since 1750: The Rise and Fall of the Self*, Oxford: Oxford University Press, 1988, for a perspective of the influence of Descartes.

33 N. Wolterstorff, "John Locke's Epistemological Piety: Reason is the Candle of the Lord," *Faith and Philosophy* 11/4 (1994), 572-591.

Descartes in a number of ways, while also breaking with his rationalist perspective of innate ideas. Locke argues there is no idea that is universally held and therefore we should understand the mind as receiving and constructing universals. He develops empiricism, the attempt to trace all ideas to their origin in experience, but never abandons the efficacy of human reason. Locke points out:

> If he (God) would have us assent to the truth of any proposition, he either evidences that truth by the usual methods of natural reason, or else makes it known to be a truth, which he would have us assent to, by his authority, and convinces us that it is from him, by some marks which Reason cannot be mistaken in. Reason must be our last judge and guide in everything.[34]

Immanuel Kant's (1724-1804) perspective is another example of a modernist viewpoint. For Kant, the great cultural movement of the Enlightenment contained the promise of human independence from the constraints of outside authority. Kant states:

> The Enlightenment {was} man's leaving his self-caused immaturity. Immaturity is the incapacity to use one's intelligence without the guidance of another. Have the courage to use your own intelligence is therefore the motto of the enlightenment.[35]

Kant, following on from the skepticism of David Hume (1711-1776), renews the optimism and vigor of reason, breaking away from Hume, but also radically re-formulating his religious tradition in the light of these new discoveries. Gunton remarks:

---

34   J. Locke, *An Essay Concerning Human Understanding*, New York: Dover, 1690/1959, Book IV, xix, 14.

35   I. Kant, "What is Enlightenment?" in: C. J. Friedrich, ed., *The Philosophy of Kant*, New York: Modern Library, 1949, 132, 137.

Where Kant differs decisively from the tradition to which he is so closely related is in his view of what redemption is and how it takes place. Moving through one hundred and eighty degrees in relation to the Lutheranism in his past, he ascribes it not to God through faith in the justifying death of Christ, but to God operating through human moral reason.[36]

For better or worse, these movements (combined with the rise of a scientific methodology organizing knowledge into hard facts) and a reframing of the medieval view of the cosmos, led to a new paradigm. Human beings and their reason were elevated to the position of possessing a pristine objectivity, neutrally concocted, and scientifically sure.[37] Whatever was not known about the Bible or the world would ultimately become known on the confident grounds of reason.[38] "Certainty, absolute certainty" became the catalyst of the modern perspective.

In radical contrast however, some now argue that the Enlightenment's claim to enlighten failed to produce the results its meta-narrative so enticingly proposed.[39] This in turn became one of the central channels giving birth to *post-modernism*.[40] A.C. Thiselton, G.B. Madison, and B.D.

---

36   C. E. Gunton, *The Actuality of Atonement*, Edinburgh: T&T Clark, 1989, 5. Kant, *Religion within the Limits of Reason Alone*, 1794/1960, Greene and Hudson, New York: Harper, 46-56, ET.

37   V. Poythress, *Science and Hermeneutics*, Grand Rapids: Zondervan, 1988, 18-20.

38   V. P. Furnish, "Historical Criticism and the New Testament: A Survey of Origins," *BJRL* 56 (1974), 368, comments, "Now the Bible itself is on the way to being viewed as a datum of world history, as first of all an object, not to be believed, but to be observed, investigated and rationally understood." In our opinion, this seems to have been played out in two ways, both of which are based on the hermeneutical certainty of human reason and a precise scientific methodology rendering the interpreter a neutral observer. Some modernist interpreters overplay the historical-theological character of the biblical text, while others underplay its historical-theological character. Some seek to explain everything, while others seek to explain everything away. See T. D. Bozeman, *Protestants in an Age of Science*, Chapel Hill: University of North Carolina Press, 1977, 135-155. H. W. Frei, *The Eclipse of Biblical Narrative: A Study in Eighteenth and Nineteenth Century Hermeneutics*, New Haven: Yale University Press, 1974.

39   J. W. Cooper, "Reformed Apologetics and the Challenge of Post-Modern Relativism," *Calvin Theological Journal* 28 (1993), 108-120, esp. 108-109. "Times are changing. Modernism is dying, though its strength is not completely spent. By now the announcement of a new outlook, something called 'post-modernism,' has become a cliché [...]. At the heart of the new mood are a principled pluralism and a radical relativism."

40   Thiselton, *Interpreting God*, 11-12, argues that the postmodernist claims to shatter the innocent confidence of modernist rationality. "The modern retained a basic optimism about the capacities of human reason, governmental or social strategies and scientific achievement, to shape the world for the general advancement of human society. But such optimism omits too many factors to provide hope for the postmodern." Following Nietzsche and Freud postmodernism announces, "Disguise covers everything. Hence a culture of distrust and suspicion emerges."

Ingraffia argue that Friedrich Nietzsche's (1844-1900) trenchant critique of Christianity is closely related to the overall post-modern critique of reason and its singular ability to produce certainty.[41] Nietzsche states:

> The end of Christianity - at the hands of its own morality (which cannot be replaced), which turns against the Christian God (the sense of truthfulness, developed highly by Christianity, is nauseated by the falseness and mendaciousness of all Christian interpretations of the world and of history; rebound from 'God is truth' to the fanatical faith 'All is false').[42]

Nietzsche is understood by some commentators on post-modernism to be at the forefront of this movement.[43] It is argued that he is one who paved the way for the rejection of modern thought, instigating a different view of the world. Ingraffia points out:

> Nietzsche posits the psychological origin of the belief in another world beyond the physical. To protect oneself against the fearful reality of the world, one posits another world which, in antithesis to the real world, is void of these fearful qualities. According to Nietzsche, this is the basis of all philosophical, moral, and religious denigration of this world or reality. Although he follows the Enlightenment tradition of defining faith as the belief in an illusion, as an enemy of knowledge, he also criticizes reason as a form of faith, i.e. an illusion. It is in this broadening of the hermeneutics of suspicion to include reason and metaphysics that Nietzsche inaugurates postmodern theory.[44]

---

41 Ibid., 3-17. Also G. B. Madison, *The Hermeneutics of Postmodernity*, Bloomington: Indiana University Press, 1988, x. Ingraffia, *Postmodern Theory and Biblical Theology*, 19-45.

42 F. Nietzsche, *The Will to Power*, W. Kaufmann, ed., New York: Vintage, 1968, 1.

43 Taylor, *Erring*. 3. "Standing at the threshold of the twentieth century, Nietzsche, one of the greatest prophets of postmodernism, declared: 'God remains dead. And we have killed him.' "

44 Ingraffia, *Postmodern Theory*, 35. Thiselton, *Interpreting God*, who cites Nietzsche, 5. "All that exists consists of interpretations (no facts). Truths are illusions we have forgotten are illusions." See above footnote 26 and the similarity with Taylor's conclusions.

The movement away from the old ways of doing and thinking (modernism) was now coming to have a pervasive affect on language, hermeneutics, epistemology, the object - subject distinction, and the differentiation between fact and opinion.[45] Sharp boundaries, it is argued, were an illusion of the modern mind and now unmasked for what they were. Madison writes:

> The two great theoretical by-products of modern, epistemologically centered philosophy which places all the emphasis on method are the notions of subjectivity and a fully objective, determinate world - the essential business of the 'knowing subject' (man) being that of forming true 'representations' of so-called objective reality (sharp boundaries). The end of modernism means, accordingly, the end of epistemologically centered philosophy. It means the end of what modernism understood as 'the subject,' and it means as well the end of the objective world.[46]

Postmodernism,[47] has been declared by some scholars to be the end of metanarratives, the end of philosophy, the end of metaphysics, and the end of hermeneutics.[48] But, by contrast, some suggest its radical move away from anything sharp is nothing less than sharp. G. Himmelfarb argues:

---

45 Kearney, *The Wake of the Imagination*, 6, 252-253. "The mirror of the postmodern paradigm reflects neither the outer world of nature nor the inner world of subjectivity; it reflects only itself - a mirror within a mirror within a mirror [....] ." Also, "Language as an open - ended play of signifiers, is no longer thought to refer to some 'real' meaning." See also R. Rorty, *Philosophy and the Mirror of Nature*, New Jersey: Princeton University Press, 1979, 325, who claims, "Hermeneutics does not need a new epistemological paradigm. Hermeneutics, rather, is what we get when we are no longer epistemological."

46 Madison, *The Hermeneutics of Postmodernity*, x, (second parenthesis mine).

47 Ibid., x. "Nietzsche's 'death of God' - is what postmodernism is all about."

48 Lyotard, *The Postmodern Condition*: xxiii-xxiv, who speaks of our postmodern condition as "incredulity toward metanarratives." In addition, Lyotard argues that postmodernism is the development of the state of our culture after the nineteenth century in the light of the transformations which have altered the rules for how we do science, literature, and the arts. Madison, *Postmodernity*, xiv. Madison, in alluding to Barthes speaks of the day when language speaks only of itself, "which is dense and opaque, which expresses neither 'facts' nor 'thoughts' nor 'truth.' " He adds, "after the end of metaphysics, the end of 'the end of philosophy.' " Also Frei, "The 'Literal Reading' of Biblical Narrative in the Christian Tradition," in: F. McConnell, ed., *The Bible and the Narrative Tradition*, Oxford: Oxford University Press, 1986, 43, who argues that the destruction of normative reading "means an end, among other things, to the enterprise called 'hermeneutics.' "

The mainspring of postmodernism is a radical - absolute, one might say - relativism, skepticism, and subjectivism. For the postmodernist, there is no truth, no knowledge, no objectivity, no reason, and, ultimately, no reality. Nothing is fixed, nothing is permanent, nothing is transcendent. There is no correspondence between language and reality; indeed no essential reality.[49]

A. Huyssen writes:

Postmodernism at its deepest level represents not just another crisis within the perpetual cycle of boom and bust, exhaustion and renewal, which has characterized the trajectory of modernist culture. It rather represents a new type of crisis *of* that modernist culture itself. We are beginning to explore its contradictions and contingencies[....].[50]

It is clear, at least in the minds of some, that what is referred to as postmodernism has a de-stabilizing effect on what preceded it. This in turn has influenced the question of textual interpretation and meaning. According to Himmelfarb, Madison, and others, post-modernism is construed as the final end of philosophy, metaphysics, and hermeneutics. According to some interpreters, this perspective affirms a radical interpretive indeterminacy, showing that texts are void of meaning.[51]

It is argued, with the rise of technology (as with the rise of science for the modernist) and the attempted overthrow of Enlightenment notions of rationality, stability, objectivity, and sharp boundaries, that

---

49 G. Himmelfarb, "Revolution in the Library," *The Key Reporter* 62 (1997), 4.

50 A. Huyssen, *After the Great Divide: Modernism, Mass Culture, Postmodernism,* Bloomington: Indiana University Press, 1986, 217, (Italics his).

51 For Crossan, *Raid*, 34, textual interpretation is radically indeterminate. The biblical text, for example, is "freeplay, that is to say, a field of infinite substitutions." Also *The Dark Interval*, 40-41, where Crossan argues there is nothing out there apart from what is storied and if there is only one story, God language is either inside my story (a self-creation - idol) or outside my story (completely unknowable). Language about God becomes both indirect and non-referential. Language fails to refer beyond itself. Fish and Taylor can also be considered here. See discussion above.

another paradigm has now come into play.[52] Human beings and their reason are now held to be in no position to come to fixed conclusions about the world or its texts. With a lack of objectivity and the loss of a contrived neutral observer, nothing is sure. Whatever was known previously about the Bible or the world is now called into question and open to radical revision. "Uncertainty, absolute uncertainty" has become the mantra of the post-modern perspective.[53]

This brings us, hermeneutically speaking, to a major issue with two parts: First, from the modern perspective, as it has been suggested, human reason and the apparent certainty it produced claimed to be able to infallibly elucidate the content of texts, notably the biblical text. A modernist tendency, therefore, is to over-read the text. Second, the post-modern viewpoint counter-claims that no such modernist textual clarity is possible. Consequently, the orientation of postmodern interpreters is to under-read the text. Over-reading produces *sharp edges* and tight definitive interpretations. Under-reading leaves matters *wide open* and entirely fluid. If the interpretation of Scripture is constrained to either of these extreme archetypes, perhaps the hermeneutical result of such counter-reading is eventually silence.[54] Thus, the modernist failure to produce a complete textual sense leaves us with a post-modernist textual non-sense.

Having re-traced our steps, in what we have referred to as a broadening of the horizon of the hermeneutical discussion, we now wish to retain a few elements of our re-tracing concerning modernism and post-modernism. These elements play into the remainder of our study.

Hermeneutical *modernism* has a number of factors and components, a certain concreteness, which we do not intend to fully explain.

---

52 Himmelfarb, "Revolution," 5. Also one example of this in the contemporary scene might be understood as the incessant lure to "surf" books rather than "read" them. This, says Himmelfarb, relates to the post-modern influence of "virtual reality" as in opposition to the modern appreciation of the "hard copy." Also, Mercer, "Postmodernity and Rationality": 319-338, esp. 324. "A colleague ended up doing some bereavement counselling with someone he met in cyberspace (the internet) from [...] who knows where they are from - in virtual reality anyone is from anywhere."

53 E. Jabès, *The Book of Yukel,* Return to the Book, Middletown: Wesleyan University Press, 1977, 105. "Certainty is the region of death, uncertainty the valley of life."

54 Both modernist and post-modernist hermeneutical perspectives counter-read the "text."

For our purposes, in regard to hermeneutics, the concept of modernism is to be understood in the following ways: First, "sharp boundaries" in regard to matters of textual interpretation. Second, the text itself gives a "certain" knowledge. Third, absolute unlimited precision and pristine clarity based on human reason provide access to the sense and referent of the text.

Hermeneutical *post-modernism* also has an abundance of ingredients, including an uncertain nebulosity and flexibility (as Mercer has stated: "Postmodernity is a delightfully slippery word; a lexicographer's nightmare"),[55] which we do not plan to entirely account for here. In our opinion, and for our hermeneutical interests, the concept of post-modernism is to be understood in the following ways: First, "radical indeterminacy" concerning the interpretation of texts. Second, the text itself is impoverished and destitute of sense and referent. Texts are sense-and-referent-less. Third, the text is always in play with no boundaries, revolving around in a "ceaseless flux."

Now that we have described the over-arching perspectives of modernism and post-modernism and their restrictive effects on hermeneutics, we return to the specific questions this raises for biblical hermeneutics. Where are we today as biblical interpreters?[56] Where and on what, if anything at all, do we stand? Do we simply accept, as some suggest, the de-throning of modernism with its text interpretative naïveté in the quest of certainty grounded in human reason, and welcome the reign of post-modernism with its new interpretative strategies and its lack of concern for referents, meaning, history, or facts? Is there an alternative road ahead between what has been argued to be modernist "sharp boundaries" and post-modernist "radical indeterminacy"?[57]

---

55 See footnote 20 and the important discussion concerning hermeneutics, 1-8.

56 This same type of question is posed by Moore, *Poststructuralism*, 113.

57 Our intention is to develop this in greater detail in Part 3.

1.2. The Aim of the Study

The present study will center on the writings of Paul Ricoeur. Our task is to investigate Ricoeur's work for the ultimate purpose of elucidating any potential benefits for biblical hermeneutics in relation to the problematic posed in our "setting the scene" section. Does Ricoeur contribute to the paving of an alternative road ahead? We shall argue that a deciphering of the richly sedimented and hermeneutically complex orientation of Ricoeur's work has the potential to debunk modernist - post-modernist perspectives of biblical interpretation and offer us a way forward.

It is possible, in our opinion, to situate Ricoeur in two worlds, while at the same time, avoiding the extremes that each archetype produces.[58] Ricoeur argues for interpretative limits (against modernism), while not abandoning sense and reference (against post-modernism).[59] Our aim is to show, by what we refer to as a "living hermeneutics," that Ricoeur's ability to dynamically integrate what other interpretation theories keep apart, can point biblical hermeneutics past the polarities of *monologues*, which are in place at several levels.

One implicit Ricoeurian critique (among others) of the modernist-post-modernist extremes is to be found in his opposition to an historical - theological absolute certainty of sense or non-sense. Specifically, he relates this to the existential, historical, and theological aspects of "hope."[60] He refers to all history as sacred, imbued with meaning, and in this sense, "sur-rationnel."[61] Ricoeur's meaning filled theological hope

---

58 Ricoeur, "Herméneutique des symboles et réflexion philosophique I," *Archivio di Filosofia* 31 (1961), 51-73, reprinted – cited, ("The Hermeneutics of Symbols: 1," in: *The Conflict of Interpretations, Essays in Hermeneutics*, D. Ihde, ed., trans. D. Savage, K. McLaughlin, and others, Evanston: Northwestern University Press, 1974, 296). "[...] I do not in the least abandon the tradition of rationality that has animated philosophy since the Greeks." *(Le conflit des interprétations: Essais d'herméneutique,* Paris: Seuil, 1969, 292). Ricoeur sees a place for and is not willing to give up on reflective philosophy (modern), however, he recognizes that such philosophy has its limits (post-modern). See also *Talking Liberties*, London: Channel 4 Television, 1992, 40.

59 Ricoeur, "Biblical Hermeneutics," *Semeia* 4 (1975), 107-108.

60 Ricoeur, "Le Christianisme et le sens de l'histoire. Progrès, ambiguité espérance," *Christianisme social* 59 (1951), 261-274, reprinted in: *Histoire et vérité*, Paris: Seuil 1955, 81-98, reprinted - cited in: (*History and Truth*, trans. C. A. Kelbley, Evanston: Northwestern University Press, 1965, 92, ET).

61 Ricoeur, *Histoire et vérité*, 95, (*History and Truth*, 94).

for history critiques and hermeneutically surpasses both the modernist reign of certainty (sharp boundaries) and the post-modernist reign of uncertainty (radical indeterminacy), confirming the limitedness, yet meaningfulness of the whole interpretive process. For Ricoeur, limits do not necessarily connote a loss of meaning.

Ricoeur's work, therefore, is clearly a fitting one for our interests. Over the years, he has dealt with a number of issues concerning Scripture and its interpretation, the definition of hermeneutics, texts, and meaning.[62] His expeditions into history, theology, truth, symbol, interpretation theory, metaphor, narrative, and the self, render his writings eminently appropriate for exploration and direction. And we believe strongly that they can make a useful contribution to biblical hermeneutics. We are interested in discovering where Ricoeur situates himself as an interpreter of the biblical text, with how he does this, and why. In coming to understand his hermeneutical theory and trajectory, a study of Ricoeur's work may lead us to *new* and *creative* insights concerning the hermeneutical task.

There has been a good deal written on Ricoeur's philosophy to date, but relatively little by comparison, concerning the theological overtones in much of his work.[63] Our view is that the "theological" is part of the "deep structure" of Ricoeur's enterprise and indeed a pivotal, although often neglected, dimension of his hermeneutics. What is the last word for Ricoeur, if it is not, as in existentialism, ambiguity?[64] It is our contention that Ricoeur has long been concerned with the question of human knowing, willing, acting, feeling, with human existence itself and

---

62 For example, *Histoire et vérité. History and Truth.* "From Proclamation to Narrative," *Journal of Religion* 64 (1984), 501-512. *Essays on Biblical Interpretation*, L. Mudge, ed., Philadelphia: Fortress, 1980. "Sur l'exégèse de Genèse 1, 1-2, 4a," in: *Exégèse et herméneutique*, X. Léon-Dufour, éd., Paris: Seuil, 1971, 239-265. "Le 'Royaume' dans les paraboles de Jésus," *Etudes théologiques et religieuses* 51 (1976), 15-20. *Figuring the Sacred: Religion, Narrative, and Imagination*, M. I. Wallace, ed., Minneapolis: Fortress, 1995.

63 As the previous footnote points out, such overtones are unmistakable in Ricoeur's writings. There are a number of other texts that could be cited in support of this. Also see K. J. Vanhoozer, *Biblical Narrative in the Philosophy of Paul Ricoeur*, Cambridge: Cambridge University Press, 1990, 3. "[...] it is somewhat surprising that few book length studies have explored Ricoeur's 'theological sophistication,' and this despite Ricoeur's many forays into matters biblical and theological. Indeed, many commentators pass over this aspect of Ricoeur in silence, even though it is arguably fundamental to his whole enterprise."

64 Ricoeur, *Histoire et vérité*, 96, (*History and Truth*, 95).

that Scripture is not irrelevant to this unfolding hermeneutical task.[65]

In order to effectively carry out our mission it is imperative to devote a breviary part of our research to Ricoeur's life and work. This is important, as it will show his profound theological interests and hermeneutical concerns. Following on from this overview, the heart of the book, which intends to focus on Ricoeur's perspective of the text, interpretation theory, and narrative, will be developed. Ricoeur's theologically oriented writings on hermeneutics and biblical hermeneutics will serve as the catalyst for our examination, however, we will also include his other work with its diversity of resonances applicable to our investigation.[66]

2. Life And Work

We shall now further our study of Paul Ricoeur's contribution to biblical hermeneutics with a sketch of his life and work. We are concerned to show, albeit selectively, that Ricoeur's work is theologically sensitive, hermeneutically centered, and directly related to the problematics of biblical hermeneutics already established above. In addition to this, a *detour* at this stage into Ricoeur's life and work sets the context for the following movements of our presentation and therefore is not unrelated to the project as a whole.

Paul Ricoeur is heralded as one of the most important and versatile thinkers of the post-war period.[67] His work has been analyzed by a diversity of disciplinarians: philosophers, psychologists, hermeneu-

---

65 D. E. Klemm even refers to Ricoeur's hermeneutics as a "hermeneutics of existence." *Hermeneutical Inquiry* 2, D. E. Klemm, ed., Atlanta: Scholars, 1986, 178.

66 Some examples in addition to those already noted in footnote 62: *Le conflit, (The Conflict);* "Philosophy and Religious Language," *Journal of Religion* 54 (1974), 1, 71-85; *La métaphore vive,* Paris: Seuil, 1975 *(The Rule of Metaphor,* trans. R. Czerny, Toronto: University of Toronto Press, 1977, ET); *Interpretation Theory: Discourse and the Surplus of Meaning,* Fort Worth: Texas Christian University Press, 1976; *Temps et récit,* 3 tomes. Paris: Seuil, 1983-1985 *(Time and Narrative,* 3 Vols., trans. K. McLaughlin and D. Pellauer, vol. 1&2; K. Blamey and D. Pellauer, vol. 3, Chicago: University of Chicago Press, 1984-1987, ET); *Du texte à l'action: Essais d'herméneutique II,* Paris: Seuil, 1986, *(From Text to Action, Essays in Hermeneutics II,* Evanston: Northwestern University Press, 1991); *Soi-même comme un autre,* Paris: Seuil, 1990 *(Oneself as Another,* trans. K. Blamey, Chicago: University of Chicago Press, 1992, ET).

67 S. H. Clark, *Paul Ricoeur,* London: Routledge, 1990, 2.

ticists, but to lesser extent by theologians.[68] In spite of this however, Ricoeur's writings in France have been viewed as suspect. His theological overtures and his arduous engagement, not altogether favorable, with French structuralism often made him an unpopular voice in his home country. The French cultural context (rationalist philosophically and Nietzschean religiously)[69] appeared unable to appreciate a thinker of Ricoeur's breadth, refusing to acknowledge the valid place of a theological perspective in the wider world of scholarship and academia. It is entirely ironic that the value of Ricoeur's work in France was so late in coming, since his recognition elsewhere is striking: a member of nine academies and a doctor honoris causa of thirty-one Universities. But the tide turned in France with the writings of *Temps et récit* (1983-1985) and *Du texte à l'action* (1986) and Ricoeur finally received due acclaim for the vast contribution he made to contemporary thought.[70]

Ricoeur was born in Valence, France in 1913 and died in Chatenay-Malabry in 2005. He was an orphan, raised in the Christian Protestant tradition by his grandparents. Ricoeur points out this religious heritage

> [...] guided me toward a feeling that I identified much later upon reading Schleiermacher as a feeling of "absolute dependence"; the notions of sin and forgiveness played an important role, certainly, but they were far from the only ones. More profound, stronger than the feeling of guilt was the conviction that the word of man had been preceded by the "word of God."[71]

Educated in the 1930's at the Sorbonne, Ricoeur developed a strong

---

68 Ibid., 1. "Ricoeur is a genuinely interdisciplinary thinker, with distinguished and original contributions in a host of different areas - in addition to those listed above (human sciences, epistemology, philosophy of language, interpretation theory), hermeneutics, historiography, literary criticism, phenomenology, political theory, semiotics, structuralism, theology."

69 O. Mongin, *Paul Ricoeur*, Paris: Seuil, 1994, 206.

70 Ibid., 15.

71 Ricoeur, "Intellectual Autobiography," *The Philosophy of Paul Ricoeur*, trans. K. Blamey, L. E. Hahn, ed., Chicago: Open Court, 1995, ET, 5. *Réflexion faite: Autobiographie intellectuelle*, Paris: Seuil, 1995, 14.

interest in philosophy. Early influences were Gabriel Marcel and Karl Jaspers, both of whom Ricoeur later published books on.[72] In 1935 Ricoeur contributed several essays to the review Terre Nouvelle, which he had co-founded in frustration over the writings of Emmanuel Mounier and what some describe as the anti-Marxist polemics of the review *Esprit*, founded by Mounier.[73]

Taken as a prisoner in the Second World War, Ricoeur had the opportunity to study German philosophy and devoted a major part of this time to Edmund Husserl's phenomenology. He both commented on and translated the work of Husserl, whose philosophy has had an enduring effect on his own.[74] In addition to this, Ricoeur has been referred to as, "the best informed French historian of phenomenology."[75] There is no question then that *phenomenology* has been and continues to be an influence in his thought. Ricoeur states:

> Le précepte initial de la phénoménologie a été pour moi une sorte de guide. Aller aux choses même, c'était le mot d'ordre de Husserl.

> The initial precept of phenomenology was a sort of guide for me. To the things themselves, was the marching order of Husserl.[76]

After the war, Ricoeur, back in Paris, continued to wrestle with the philosophies of existence and began to publish a number of works that

---

72 P. Ricoeur et M. Dufrenne, *Karl Jaspers et la philosophie de l'existence,* Paris, 1947; Ricoeur, *Gabriel Marcel et Karl Jaspers*, Paris: Temps Présent, 1948.

73 M. Gerhart, "Paul Ricoeur," in: *A Handbook of Christian Theologians*, M. Marty and D. Peerman, eds., Cambridge: Lutterworth, 1984, 611. "In 1935, [.....] Ricoeur became cofounder of Terre Nouvelle, a monthly review. He and his colleagues, described as 'fiery young Christians,' were impatient with the anti-Marxist polemics of *Esprit*, a journal founded in 1932 by Emmanuel Mounier."

74 Ricoeur translated Husserl's *Ideen* as *Idées directrices pour une phenomenology*. He also published a work specifically on Husserl with *Husserl: An Analysis of his Phenomenology*, 1967, a series of essays. In this venture, Ricoeur analyzes Husserl's work from the beginning, through the Ideas, and the *Cartesian Meditations*, to a statement of his own philosophy, critiquing Husserl's idealism in the last chapters.

75 H. Spiegleberg, *The Phenomenological Movement*, The Hague: Nijhoff, 1982, 595.

76 Entretien avec Paul Ricoeur, *Bulletin du Centre Protestant d'Etudes*, 43, 1991, 22. (My translation).

set forth his own philosophy.⁷⁷ As Ricoeur has over three hundred bibliographical entries, it is impossible to give a comprehensive account of his writings in this study. We intend to limit ourselves to a brief presentation of Ricoeur's "theological" component, a tracking of something of his hermeneutical development, and a condensed foray into a number of his major studies related to biblical hermeneutics.

An important collection of essays entitled *Histoire et vérité* (*History and Truth*, ET), published in 1955, clearly shows Ricoeur's theological sensitivity. Purposefully excluded in this collection were essays deemed too philosophically technical, chronicles of criticism of recent philosophical work, and writings on *Finitude and Guilt* (the second part of the *Philosophy of the Will*). However, Ricoeur includes essays that explicitly attempt to show the link between the historian's craft and the mystery of eschatology, arguing that the methodological rigor of a history of philosophy need not exclude a theological perspective.⁷⁸ He deals primarily with two inseparable domains: method and ethics. The first domain is devoted to history—the skill needed for a historian responding to a demand for objectivity; as well as the theological and philosophical problematic of a comprehensive significance for history. The second domain deals with a critical view of civilization and its present expressions.

Ricoeur views humans as *broken* but *unified* beings, torn between objectivity and subjectivity, theory and practice, life and death. These essays express a certain longing for reconciliation, while avoiding an embryonic synthesis. The positive possibilities of language are left intact; the reflectively dynamic "parole" still possesses the power to transform actions. Ricoeur's notable self-transparency and theological acumen is expressed in the following way:

---

77 It is intriguing to discover that at this time the Ricoeur family took up residence as the only Protestants of six or seven families in the personalist community of Mounier, and Ricoeur became a regular contributor to *Esprit*.

78 Ricoeur, *History and Truth*, 6-8.

I believe in the efficacy of reflection because I believe that man's greatness lies in the dialectic of work and the spoken word. Saying and doing, signifying and making are intermingled to such an extent that it is impossible to set up a lasting and deep opposition between "theoria" and "praxis." The word is my kingdom and I am not ashamed of it. To be more precise, I am ashamed of it to the extent that my speaking shares in the guilt of an unjust society which exploits work. I am not ashamed of it primordially, that is, with respect to its destination. As a university professor, I believe in the efficacy of instructive speech; in teaching the history of philosophy, I believe in the enlightening power, even for a system of politics, of speaking devoted to elaborating our philosophical memory. As a member of the team of *Esprit*, I believe in the efficacy of speech which thoughtfully elucidates the generating themes of an advancing civilization. As a listener to the Christian message, I believe that words may change the "heart," that is, the refulgent core of our preferences and the positions which we embrace. In a sense, all of these essays are in praise of the word which reflects efficaciously and acts thoughtfully.[79]

Ricoeur's explicit hermeneutical development can be traced in the following manner.[80] *Philosophie de la volonté: Le volontaire et l'involontaire* (*Freedom and Nature: The Voluntary and the Involuntary*, ET) was Ricoeur's first volume in his *Philosophy of the Will* series (1950). By choosing the grand theme of the relation between the voluntary and the involuntary, Ricoeur developed a two-fold task:

> First, it allowed me to widen the eidetic analysis of the operations of consciousness to the spheres of affection and volition, an analysis that

---

79 Ibid., 5.

80 We are well aware of the debate about Ricoeur's "hermeneutical turn" or lack thereof. D. Ihde, *Hermeneutic Phenomenology: The Philosophy of Paul Ricoeur*, Evanston: Northwestern Univ. Press, 1971. P. L. Bourgeois, *Extension of Ricoeur's Hermeneutic*, The Hague: Nijhoff, 1973. Explicitly, it seems better to speak of a movement towards hermeneutics or a hermeneutics in motion arising in Ricoeur's work. Ricoeur refers to Ihde's terminology and his agreement with it. *Essays on Biblical Interpretation*, 43.

Husserl had confined to perception and more generally to "representative" acts. [...]

A second consideration tied my investigation to the work of Gabriel Marcel and to the field of existential philosophy. Under the title of the *Voluntary and the Involuntary,* the eidetic analyses, rich in subtle distinctions, were infused with a dynamism by the encompassing dialectic of activity and passivity, to which corresponded an ethics that was implicit and as yet unexplored, one marked by the dialectic of mastery and consent.[81]

In this study, Ricoeur applies Husserl's phenomenological method of the eidetic reduction – the attempt to get at the essences of things – and brackets the perception of both Fault and Transcendence, while at the same time being painstakingly aware of the incarnated subject of mystery (via Marcel). This is all done with the aim of giving a *pure* description of the will (choice, action, consent) and expressing the reciprocity of the voluntary and the involuntary (requirement, obligation). The subject's "I will" is primitively (prior to a consciousness of it) intertwined in both the voluntary and the involuntary, which in the final analysis of human freedom, affirms a dependent independence in human nature.

Ricoeur's next book length venture, the second volume of the *Philosophy of the Will,* appeared in 1960. *Finitude et culpabilité (Finitude and Guilt* ET) contains two parts: *L'homme faillible (Fallible Man,* ET) and *La symbolique du mal (The Symbolism of Evil,* ET). *Fallible Man* now leads Ricoeur in the direction of exploring the broken-ness of human beings. Existence, in reality, shows a disfigured or guilty will. Consequently, Ricoeur moves from a *bracketed* eidetic description of the structure of the will (le volontaire et l'involontaire) to a new *de-bracketed* approach leading to an empirics of the will. Ricoeur writes:

---

81 Ricoeur, "Intellectual Autobiography," The Philosophy of Paul Ricoeur, 11-12. *Réflexion faite: Autobiographie intellectuelle,* Paris: Seuil, 1995, 22-24.

[....] the fault is not a trait of fundamental ontology that is homogeneous with other factors that pure description discovers : motives, abilities, conditions and limits; it remains an anomaly in the eidetic of man.[82]

In the second part of this volume, *The Symbolism of Evil*, Ricoeur makes an essential move from one mode to another. Instead of merely describing the will, consciousness (Husserl), and fault phenomenologically, Ricoeur begins to actively interpret the *symbols*, and eventually, the *texts* in which such fault is specifically expressed.[83] Ricoeur's question then becomes: why the use of *symbolic language* to express evil and guilt? No pure reflection on fault or one's experience was possible without first considering evil – fault's expression in language. Such indirect *symbolic language* indicated, for Ricoeur, that direct reflection on oneself could neither explain the symbols, nor account for how they came to be. It is at this point that Ricoeur explicitly awakens to the necessity of a detour into hermeneutics.[84] Symbols, he suggests, are imbued with double – meaning, giving rise to thought and therefore, require interpretation.

Ricoeur argues that in order to better understand human beings, it is now necessary to take a *long detour* via the symbols, myths, and texts of religion and culture.[85] In this turn to the indirect, he critiques and surpasses both Husserl and Descartes and their common modernist presupposition of an immediate access to the Cogito. In seeing the problems of modernism, Ricoeur moves out of a structural phenomenology towards a hermeneutics, without abandoning phenomenology altogether.

---

82 Ricoeur, *Philosophie de la volonté* II, Paris: Aubier, 1960, 10. (My translation).

83 Ricoeur, Philosophie de la volonté. *Finitude et culpabilité II, La symbolique du mal,* Paris: Aubier, 1960, 173-186, (*The Symbolism of Evil*, trans. E. Buchanan, New York: Harper & Row, 1967, 10-24, ET). *Essays on Biblical Interpretation*, 41. "Thus the Symbolism of Evil proceeded from the inability of a 'pure' phenomenology of will to give an account of 'bad' will."

84 Ricoeur, "From Existentialism to the Philosophy of Language," Criterion 10 (1971), 14-18, reprinted - cited in: *The Rule of Metaphor*, 315-322, esp. 316, "I had to introduce a hermeneutical dimension within the structure of reflective thought itself."

85 Ricoeur writes of a debt to a "biblical and Greek cultural background that I felt myself obliged to incorporate into reflexive philosophy.... the interpretation of symbols of the stain, of sin, and of guilt." Ricoeur, "Intellectual Autobiography," in: *The Philosophy of Paul Ricoeur*, 16. Also, (Réflexion, 30).

> So I do not hesitate to say that hermeneutics must be grafted onto phenomenology, not only at the level of the theory of meaning expressed in the *Logical Investigations*, but also at the level of the problematic of the cogito as it unfolds from *Ideen I* to the *Cartesian Meditations*. But neither do I hesitate to add that the graft changes the wild stock![86]

Eidetic phenomenology, aiming to get at the essences through bracketing out the empirical, must change if it is going to have anything to say about evil other than the conditions for its potential existence, and the observation of the state of the world. The "direct" (structural) must give way to the "indirect" (expressional). Consequently, hermeneutics becomes an essential element for deciphering humanness.

Ricoeur's simultaneous theological and hermeneutical efforts now intersect with his movement toward biblical hermeneutics. In 1975 he wrote a massive article, published in *Semeia,* on biblical hermeneutics. The article comprises over 100 pages dealing with questions of structural analysis, parables, poetics, narrative, metaphor, and the philosophy of language, notably, the specificity of religious language. This work should be considered Ricoeur's fullest expression to date on the subject of biblical and philosophical hermeneutics. It is significant to recall, that he writes as a philosopher of language, rather than as a theologian or exegete.[87] In this article, he aims to apply something of his hermeneutical theory, reflection on language, and study of symbol and metaphor to the biblical text. He spends a good deal of time in dialogue with structuralism and what he considers its infinite downplaying of the referential dimension of language. Concerning this point, Ricoeur writes:

> A new step was taken when some French structuralists combined the *structural method* with a *structuralist ideology.* By this latter term

---

[86] Ricoeur, "Existence et herméneutique," in: H. Kuhn, H. Kahlefeld, K. Forster, eds., *Interpretation der Welt, Festschrift für R. Guardini zum achtzigsten Geburtstag,* Würzburg: Echter-Verlag, 1965, 32-51, reprinted in: *Le conflit,* 7-28, esp. 20-21, (*Italics* his). ("Existence and Hermeneutics," reprinted in: *The Conflict,* 3-26, esp.17).

[87] Ricoeur, "Biblical Hermeneutics," 29.

> I mean a general conception concerning the philosophical status of discourse as "text."

> For them, the autonomy of the text is not only a factor of distanciation in human communication, but it has the meaning of completely abolishing the *referential* dimension of language.[88]

What happens in narratives for the structuralist, Ricoeur argues, is precisely nothing.[89] We simply have an adventure in language, communication about communication, a dogmatic preference for code over message. Ricoeur, while not against a structuralist method per se, argues against a structuralist ideology. His basis for this is the view of literary genres as modes of production, rather than as merely classifications of discourse. He contends that narratives are messages, not just codes, and as such, they have referents that transcend the text.[90]

Ricoeur's next major contribution to our subject was published in 1980 as a series of essays entitled, *Essays on Biblical Interpretation*. Ricoeur addresses himself to the hermeneutic problem in Christianity, which exists, in his eyes, because Christianity proceeds from proclamation to text. Ricoeur states:

> We must return, in fact, to the witness character of the Gospel. The kerygma is not first of all the interpretation of a text; it is the announcement of a person. In this sense, the word of God is not the Bible, but Jesus Christ. But a problem arises continually from the fact that this kerygma is itself expressed in a witness, in the stories, and soon after in the texts that contain the very first confession of faith of the community.[91]

---

88 Ibid., 51 (*Italics* his).
89 Ibid., 51.
90 Ibid., 63.
91 Ricoeur, *Essays on Biblical Interpretation*, 54.

Since kerygma (proclamation) has become, in Ricoeur's words, "Testament," a new Scripture, interpreters must engage themselves with this text. Hence, the New Testament text must be interpreted, not only with regard to the Old Testament (an ancient hermeneutical problem) or for life and reality as a whole (a modern hermeneutical problem), but as a valid *textual witness* in its own right.[92]

Such textual interpretation, Ricoeur underlines, will always take place at a distance. But this *distance* is not merely a modern problem since the initial written production of the text itself is already distanced from the original events it proclaims.[93] In one sense then, according to Ricoeur, we cannot avoid the hermeneutical problem of distance. In regards to the Scripture, this functioning distance for us as readers today is temporally greater rather than lesser, simply because we are further away from the time in which it was written. Some past forms of hermeneutics, which have concealed rather than illumined this problem, have been surpassed by more recent hermeneutical efforts, which have only begun to discover what was radical in the Christian context from the beginning – a recognized distance between the stories recounted and their readers.[94] Distanciation, however, should not be understood as disabling the authored text's capacity to communicate or the reader's ability to receive this communication.

> To decipher Scripture is to decipher the witness of the apostolic community. We are related to the object of its faith through the confession of its faith. Hence, by understanding its witness, I receive equally, in its witness, what is summons, kerygma, "the good news."[95]

---

92 Ibid., 55.

93 Ibid., 55-57.

94 Ibid., 56, Ricoeur refers to this distance as "constitutive of primitive faith itself."

95 Ibid., 56.

Ricoeur, in this collection, also ventures into the problematic of a hermeneutic of revelation. Revelation, in his view, is not bound to the notion of a Scripture dictated in a literal fashion. Rather, he sees revelation as derivative of and expressed in a *plurality* of discourses: prophetic, narrative, prescriptive, wisdom, and hymnic. What is of further interest, for our purposes, is what Ricoeur writes about narrative. The specific character of biblical narrative is that it testifies to God's "trace" in events.

> What is essential in the case of narrative discourse is the emphasis on the founding event or events as the imprint, mark or trace of God's act. Confession takes place through narration and the problematic of inspiration is in no way the primary consideration. God's mark is in history before being in speech. It is only secondarily in speech inasmuch as this history itself is brought to language in the speech-act of narration.[96]

Ricoeur argues that such speech-acts do not constitute event, but only occur in response to it. The author who speaks and the narrator who tells cannot be absorbed into a constricted theology of the Word, which is exclusively concerned with word events in and of themselves. Ricoeur clearly distances himself from what he calls the "idealism" of the word event, asseverating instead the " 'realism' of the event of history."[97]

In the years of 1983-1985, another of Ricoeur's major contributions to biblical hermeneutics appeared as the three volume *Temps et récit*[98] (*Time and Narrative*, ET).[99] He sees this effort as referring back to, among other writings, *Histoire et vérité* (*History and Truth*), *La Sym-*

---

[96] Ibid., 79.

[97] Ibid., 80.

[98] Ricoeur again points out the importance of his culture biblique in relation to his interest in narrative. "Intellectual Autobiography," in: *The Philosophy of Paul Ricoeur*, 41. "I would like to underscore another source that contributed to my longstanding interest in the question of narrative. It has to do with my intermittent incursions into the field of biblical exegesis." (*Réflexion*, 65).

[99] The relevance of *Time and Narrative* cannot be fully discussed at this point.

bolique du mal (*The Symbolism of Evil*), and the famous debate between, "explanation and understanding," while also forming a pair with *La métaphore vive* (*The Rule of Metaphor*).[100] *Time and Narrative*'s close relationship with *The Rule of Metaphor* is expressed in, what Ricoeur calls, their "meaning-effects." It is Ricoeur's contention, in his ongoing debate with structuralism, that discourse (the event where someone is saying something to somebody) is the common plane on which semantic innovation, be it with regard to narrative or metaphor, takes place.

Ricoeur delves into *narrative* in these volumes, as well as engaging the problematic of two perspectives of *time*: cosmological (Aristotle's universal time - concordant discordance) and phenomenological (Augustine's perceived time - discordant concordance).[101] He proposes a *narrative poetics*, in creating and discovering a "third time," as a partial resolution to the aporias of these two perspectives.[102] Ricoeur, in avoiding any all encompassing solution to the problematic of time argues that the interweaving of both fictional and historical narrative offers an imperfect, yet mediatory vehicle in which both these perspectives (which presuppose each other) can be taken into account.[103] In this relation, and in association with the problematic of explanation and understanding,[104] Ricoeur develops a theory of the text, action, and history, in which narrative is understood as the intersection of all three:

---

100 Ricoeur, *Temps et récit* I, 11, (*Time and Narrative* I, ix). *Réflexion*, 70-71.

101 Ricoeur, *Réflexion*, 69. *Temps et récit* III, 19-35, (*Time and Narrative* III, 12-22).

102 Ricoeur, *Time and Narrative* III, 99-100. This is referred to as "historical time."

103 Ricoeur, *Time and Narrative* I, 77-82; III, 101-102. Ricoeur's intention is not to abolish any distinction between historical and fictional narrative. His aim is to show that one mode of narrative is not mutually exclusive of the other, in that each one "borrows" from the other (history, the narrative imagination; fiction, attempts to reconstruct the actual past), and each one has similar readerly "effects" in the power to "refigure" time.

104 Ricoeur, "Intellectual Autobiography," in: *The Philosophy of Paul Ricoeur*, 45-46. In speaking of his unwillingness to succumb to historical explanation as merely a narrative construction, as if history were just a species of story, he argues: "The case of historical explanation on the contrary provided me with the opportunity to refine the dialectic between explanation and understanding, which I had considered in a more rudimentary form under the heading of the notion of text, or in the framework of the theory of action. If it seemed to me legitimate to see in narrative intelligence, considered the understanding of plots, the matrix for historical explanation, it also seemed to me necessary to take into account the features by which historical explanation, through an epistemological break, distinguished itself from simple narrativity."

Time and Narrative also revived another famous debate, that between explanation and understanding. This turn of events was not unexpected to the extent that the debate, stated in its most general terms, had provided the demonstration of "some remarkable connections between the theory of the text, the theory of action, and the theory of history" (1977). The narrative constituted in this respect a crossroads between the three categories just mentioned: narrative composition operates on the textual level, human action is imitated by the narrative; and, finally, history is what the narrative recounts. It is therefore not surprising that lengthy developments are devoted to the explanation – understanding dialectic, first in the second part of *Time and Narrative I,* devoted to historiography, and then in *Time and Narrative II,* entirely devoted to literary theory on the level of the narrative of fiction.[105]

This focus on narrative is complemented by the discovery of an epistemology of historic knowledge, which had woven together historical explanation and a narrative structure. In response to the impoverishment of French structuralism, Ricoeur employs the English language analytic philosophy of story (récit). This furnishes him with a formal analysis of narrative and a variant to French structuralism, the latter of which he addresses in two ways:

> [...] on the one hand, English-language authors placed the structure of the narrative primarily in relation to the structure of historical knowledge, while French structuralism more readily directed the interest of researchers and readers toward literary criticism; on the other hand, by its semantic twist, analytic philosophy invited an inquiry into the truth value of historical statements, while French structuralism remained deeply marked by its Saussurean origins, retaining a systematic distrust with respect to any extralinguistic ex-

---

105 Ibid., 45. *Réflexion*, 70-71. (*Italics* his).

cursion and consequently dissuading any interrogation of the reality of past events.[106]

Ricoeur's philosophical theme of time is interlaced, in this work, with his literary interest in the problematic of the function and effects of both historical and fictional narrative on the temporality of human beingness. Or, to say it another way, what is the relation between time and narrative?[107] In regard to this nexus, Ricoeur's notion of emplotment and a threefold mimesis (creative imitation) of prefiguration, configuration, and refiguration is insightful for biblical hermeneutics, as well as for his critique of structuralism. The creative imitation involved in narrative, Ricoeur argues, has the ability to prefigure, configure, and refigure human action. Specifically, historical/fictional narrative *prefigures* by portraying personal action semantically, symbolically, and temporally; it *configures* by innovatively arranging a succession of events into a textual whole; and finally it *refigures* by creating a meeting point between the world, the text, and the reader.[108]

> For a semiotic theory, the only operative concept is that of the literary text. Hermeneutics, however, is concerned with reconstructing the entire arc of operations by which practical experience provides itself with works, authors, and readers [...]. What is at stake, therefore, is the concrete process by which the textual configuration mediates between the prefiguration of the practical field and its refiguration through the reception of the work.[109]

One of the most outstanding benefits of Ricoeur's threefold mimesis, in regard to biblical hermeneutics, is its affirmation of an important

---

106 Ibid., 40. 64-65.
107 Ricoeur, *Temps et récit* I, 87, (*Time and Narrative* I, 53).
108 Ricoeur, *Temps et récit* I, 85-128, (*Time and Narrative* I, 52-87).
109 Ricoeur, *Temps et récit* I, 86, (*Time and Narrative* I, 53).

distance between mimesis II and mimesis III. In other words, for refiguration to be a hermeneutical possibility, it cannot merely be a mirror of configuration. Just as there is no confusion between prefiguration and configuration, there is also no confusion between configuration and refiguration. Preserving the distinctness of each phase of mimesis is what enables them to relate dynamically to one another. With this threefold mimesis, texts and readers connect to each other through both time and narrative, but there is no loss of the various levels of their distinctness. In this sense, we again see that distanciation is a crucial component in the operation of a living hermeneutics. Specifically, it is an interpretive approach that opposes a reductionistic emphasis on texts alone (structuralists), or on readers alone (reader response theories). Only in recognizing the inability of either text or reader centered methods to engender human action on their own, will a living hermeneutics begin to take shape.

Ricoeur next published *Soi-même comme un autre* (*Oneself as Another*, ET), in 1990.[110] According to Ricoeur, these essays deal with three major philosophical intentions: reflection as primary over an immediate self-positing; self and self-identity; self and the other.[111] In this context there is an ongoing discussion of a philosophy of language and action, the question of personal identity as a narrative identity, and the ethics of action.

In this work, Ricoeur continues his passionate quest towards a hermeneutics of the self. We clearly see his unwillingness, whether in regard to the self (or for that matter, biblical hermeneutics), to either embrace an *ultimate* self-founding or a *complete* deconstruction of the subject. In this regard, he affirms the validity of his developing indirect philosophy of the subject, over against both Descartes' subject, as ultimate foundation, and Nietzsche's subject, as vast illusion.

---

110 This series of essays was originally given as the Gifford lectures in 1986.

111 Ricoeur, *Oneself as Another*, 1-3. *Soi-même*, 11-15.

> I hold here as paradigmatic of the philosophies of the subject that the subject is formulated in the first person – *ego cogito* – whether the "I" is defined as an empirical or a transcendental ego, whether the "I" is posited absolutely (that is, with no reference to an other) or relatively (egology requiring the intrinsic complement of intersubjectivity). In all of these instances, the subject is "I." That is why I am considering here the expression "philosophies of the subject" as equivalent to "philosophies of the cogito." This is also why the quarrel over the cogito, in which the "I" is by turns in a position of strength and of weakness, seems to me the best way to bring out the problematic of the self, under the condition that my subsequent investigations confirm the claim that I formulate here, namely that the hermeneutics of the self is placed at an equal distance from the apology of the cogito and from its overthrow. [112]

While Ricoeur explicitly leaves out his theological dimension in this publication,[113] we would argue that it is, at least, implicitly integrated in regards to his motivations and interest. Ricoeur writes:

> The ten studies that make up this work assume the bracketing, conscious and resolute, of the convictions that bind me to biblical faith. I do not claim that at the deep level of motivations these convictions remain without any effect on the interest I take in this or that problem, even in the overall problematic of the self. [114]

The *theological* dimension indeed becomes rather more explicit if we take into account the two essays on biblical hermeneutics that were

---

112 Ibid., 4. *Soi-même*, 14-15. (Italics his).

113 Ibid., 24. "If I defend my philosophical writings against the accusation of cryptotheology, I also refrain, with equal vigilance, from assigning to biblical faith a cryptophilosophical function." Ricoeur's ever-present concern is to guard against either a philosophy or a biblical faith being regarded as "ultimate foundation" in his work. In this book, he left out two essays on biblical hermeneutics, bracketing (to what degree this is possible remains an open question) the convictions of his biblical faith, in the pursuit of an autonomous philosophical discourse.

114 Ibid., 24. *Soi-même* 36. (*Italics* his).

originally a part of these lectures,[115] but left out of the book.[116] The question of selfhood in Ricoeur's writings is not without its theological component, and as such, in our opinion, it is ultimately interwoven with the question of biblical hermeneutics, just as the question of biblical hermeneutics is interwoven with that of selfhood.

In 1998 Ricoeur published, in association with A. LaCocque, the volume *Penser la Bible* (*Thinking Biblically*). This effort more clearly expresses his theological orientation as a philosopher and his post *Time and Narrative* and *Oneself as Another* thought on biblical hermeneutics.

We have aimed to show, in this section and through this succession of works, roughly sketched as it is, that Ricoeur's writings exhibit a theological sensitivity, that his hermeneutics explicitly developed in and through his work on symbol, and that these two interests (theological sensitivity and hermeneutics) are intercalated through his writings related to biblical hermeneutics.

It is our contention, however, that this examination of Ricoeur's life and work already offers us several insights and directions towards a contribution to biblical hermeneutics and a denouncing of modernist-postmodernist archetypal extremism. Ricoeur always argues for the "text" in light of sense *and* reference, explanation *and* understanding, history *and* fiction, and faith *and* hope. The context for this *both and* approach is the reality of human limitedness regarding our hermeneutical efforts. Within the sphere of a "living hermeneutics," perhaps it is fair to consider this stage of our investigation as a sort of prefiguring, awaiting the further stages of configuring and refiguring, which are to follow.

---

115 Ibid., 23-25. Ricoeur mentions these two essays, "Le soi dans le miroir des Écritures," and "Le soi mandaté," (now published as "The Summoned Subject in the School of the Narratives of the Prophetic Vocation," in: *Figuring*).

116 This may have something to do with the suspicion that Ricoeur was subjected to in France concerning some of his work. O. Mongin, *Paul Ricoeur*, 20, writes with reference to the response that some of Ricoeur's writings received, "Cet ouvrage consacré à Freud a été violemment accueilli par l'entourage de Lacan ou d'Althusser et ignoré par le premier, avec lequel Ricoeur avait cependant noué des relations. Ricoeur ne cherchera plus guère à relancer la discussion dans l'espace intellectuel français." (This work, focused on Freud, was badly received by the followers of Lacan or Althusser and ignored by the former, who Ricoeur previously had contact with. Ricoeur no longer attempted to re-start the discussion in the French intellectual environment). (My translation).

CONFIGURATION

3. The Text, Interpretation Theory, Biblical Hermeneutics, and Narrative

This section of our research will be fundamental for a configuring of Ricoeur's work. Our contention is that this configuring will demonstrate both the applicability of Ricoeur's contribution to biblical hermeneutics and a way to over-come the modernist-post-modernist polarization of complete sense versus non-sense. We shall begin with the text, move through a detour, and then return to it.

3.1 Why the "text?"

In our examination of the language, literary, and hermeneutical dimensions of Ricoeur's work it is essential to analyze his notion of the text as it relates to his view of language, general hermeneutics, and biblical hermeneutics. Why, in Ricoeur's developing hermeneutics, has he placed such a great emphasis on the text? What problematic is he responding to and why does the "text" provide, in Ricoeur's opinion, a way forward? While much of what is argued for in this section has a somewhat general character, in our appraisal, it can be transferred through the general, to a regional application in reference to the biblical text. It is important to keep this in mind, as we draw out aspects of Ricoeur's interpretation theory, and aim to show the relevance of his developing position, in contrast to that of his interlocutors.

We intend to focus on three aspects of Ricoeur's textual turn in its relation to interpretation theory.[1] First, the central problematic of explanation and understanding,[2] second, the importance of the linguistics of discourse as opposed to the linguistics of language, which includes the movement from speaking to writing, what Ricoeur calls from dialogue to text,[3] and third, the concept of the text as autonomous, and the bearer of a world.[4]

3.1.1. Explanation and Understanding

Regarding the question of *explanation* and *understanding* in relation to written language, it will be helpful to follow Ricoeur's brief historical survey. Ricoeur is apt to critique the "generalizing" tendencies of a hermeneutical over-ontologizing. In other words, he wants to say there is more to understanding than the subject of being. He counters the general in its reductionistic form and suggests a "re-regionalizing" of hermeneutics that reclaims the validity of the text and what it says, as necessary operatives in the hermeneutical enterprise.

The Romantic, psychologizing, historicizing, hermeneutical tendencies of Friedrich Schleiermacher (1768-1834) and Wilhelm Dilthey (1833-1911), faces a strong critique from Ricoeur. He argues that both thinkers go too far in transforming a general understanding into the understanding of a subject, an author, and the life expressions "behind"

---

1   For a fuller discussion of this turn: P. L. Bourgeois, "From Hermeneutics of Symbols to the Interpretation of Texts," 84-95, and Pellauer, "The Significance of the Text in Paul Ricoeur's Hermeneutical Theory," in: *Studies in the Philosophy of Paul Ricoeur*, C. E. Reagan, ed., Athens (Ohio), Ohio University Press, 1979, 97-114.

2   This problematic is a recurring theme in Ricoeur, as evidenced in *The Conflict; From Text to Action;* and *The Philosophy of Paul Ricoeur*, Hahn, ed., esp. 30-31.

3   Ricoeur, *Interpretation Theory*, 34-35.

4   Ibid., 29-31.

the text.⁵ This aggrandizing of the hermeneutical endeavor from its more "narrow" and regional character of the exegesis of texts, raises for the first time, the problem of interpretation as a general problem. For Ricoeur, such generalizing inclinations split the necessary dialectic of understanding and explanation (ontology and epistemology), focusing too restrictively on interpretation as understanding.

> The dichotomy between understanding and explanation in Romanticist hermeneutics is both epistemological and ontological. It opposes two methodologies and two spheres of reality, nature and mind. Interpretation is not a third term, nor, [...] the name of the dialectic between explanation and understanding. Interpretation is a particular case of understanding. It is understanding applied to the written expressions of life. In a theory of signs that de-emphasizes the difference between speaking and writing, and above all that does not stress the dialectic of event and meaning, it can be expected that interpretation only appears as one province within the empire of comprehension or understanding.⁶

Ricoeur argues that the Romantic Movement is characterized by its move away from *philology* and the *exegesis* of texts, to an understanding of the process of understanding itself. With psychology having become the ultimate justification for hermeneutics (not what a text says, but who says it), and the individual historized and situated in the sea of universal history, the problematics of exegesis and philology are subsumed to the problematic of psychology or universal history. Hence, Ricoeur identifies this as the direction of "de-regionalization," which attempts to construct a general hermeneutics at the expense of

---

5   Ricoeur, "The Task of Hermeneutics," 112-128, reprinted - cited in: *From Text to Action*, 53-74, esp. 57, ("La tâche de l'herméneutique," reprinted in: *Du texte à l'action*, 76-100, esp. 80, FT). The hermeneutical task envisioned here is to reach beyond language (text) to the one who speaks. The speaker (writer) is then divided from the text and its language, which become superfluous. We certainly concur with Ricoeur's critique of Romanticism, however, we may question whether the "behind" the text is as completely inconsequential as Ricoeur claims. For example, knowing something about the person of Paul Ricoeur may help us better understand what he has written.

6   Ricoeur, *Interpretation Theory*, 73.

a regional one.[7] Such de-regionalization, whether focused on universal subjectivity (Schleiermacher), or universal history (Dilthey), remains a psychologically and epistemologically centered hermeneutics.[8] At the same time, this generalizing emphasis, according to Ricoeur, blurs the line between epistemology and ontology.[9]

Martin Heidegger (1899-1976), Ricoeur suggests, seeks to eliminate epistemology, or a more refined scientific methodology, and fully ontologize understanding. Heidegger replaces the question of "how we know" with the question of "what does it mean to be a being who understands."[10] Ricoeur calls this the "short route" of grounding hermeneutics in meaning.

> I call such an ontology of understanding the "short route" because, breaking with any discussion of *method,* it carries itself directly to the level of an ontology of finite being in order there to recover *understanding,* no longer as a mode of knowledge, but rather as a mode of being.[11]

Heidegger displaces the hermeneutical discussion from texts (information fixed by writing) to solely the subject of understanding itself. Ricoeur does not dispute the value of such a move, in that it always engages us in a movement back to our situatedness in being, yet he questions its exclusivity. Heidegger's work can be understood as contributing to the critique of the totalizing subject through his de-centering and rooting of the "I am" in being. For Heidegger, ontology supremely reigns over any epistemological notions.[12] In this sense, understanding is not just related to what human beings do, but it constitutes who they

---

7 Ricoeur, "The Task," *From Text to Action,* 55-56, (*Du texte,* 77-78).
8 Ibid., 62.
9 Ibid., 58.
10 Ricoeur, "Existence et herméneutique," *Le conflit,* 10, (*The Conflict,* 6).
11 Ricoeur, *The Conflict,* 6. "Existence et herméneutique," 10. (*Italics his*).
12 M. Heidegger, *Being and Time,* New York: Harper and Row, 182-188.

are.[13] This implies circularity on Heidegger's part – a circularity that, he stresses, is our only access to meaning.[14] Ricoeur argues, however, that such an ontology of understanding does not necessarily have to efface either *epistemology* or *method*. Hence, Ricoeur proposes another route toward being, which he refers to as the "long route."[15]

> The long route which I propose also aspires to carry reflection to the level of an ontology, but it will do so by degrees, following successive investigations into semantics ([...]) and reflection ([...]). The doubt I express [...] is concerned only with the possibility of the making of a direct ontology, free at the outset from any methodological requirements and consequently outside of the circle of interpretation whose theory this ontology formulates.[16]

> [...] substituting, for the short route of the analytic of Dasein, the long route which begins by analyses of language. In this way we will continue to keep in contact with the disciplines which seek to practice interpretation in a methodical manner, and we will resist the temptation to separate *truth,* characteristic of understanding, from the *method* put into operation by disciplines which have sprung from exegesis.[17]

One of Ricoeur's major hesitations concerning Heidegger's direct ontology of understanding is its breaking off of any dialogue with the human sciences, ultimately resulting in an ontology that is limited to only addressing itself. This ontology of understanding, for Ricoeur, lacks the capacity of foundation and critique, both of which are essen-

---

13 In Heidegger's view a hermeneutical ontology is not just concerned with being in the world, but also with the topic of a self-understanding that relates to self-constitution.

14 Heidegger, *Being and Time*, 191-194.

15 Ricoeur, *The Conflict*, 6. (*Le conflit*, 3-26).

16 Ibid., 6.

17 Ibid., 11. (*Italics his*).

tial to the problematic of being.[18] Heidegger's *being* executes the potentiality of the dialectic of explanation and understanding.[19] According to Ricoeur, this dialectic of explanation and understanding (in which neither effaces the other),[20] can remain intact, not through seeking to understand another subject, nor primarily or exclusively oneself, but through a turning to the *text* and what it says.[21]

From a Ricoeurian perspective, Hans-Georg Gadamer (1900-2002), one of the foremost hermeneutician's of the twentieth century, can be described as initiating the movement of hermeneutics back in the direction of the human sciences.[22] This can be perceived, for example, in *Truth and Method* with Gadamer's analysis of a division of the hermeneutical experience into three domains: the aesthetic, the historical, and the domain language.[23]

The title of Gadamer's masterful work, *Truth and Method*, suggests a confrontation with Heidegger and his concept of *truth,* as well as with Dilthey and his perception of *method*. However, one of Ricoeur's questions concerning Gadamer's work is: to what degree does it carry out the promise of Truth *and* Method? And, correspondingly, might a better title have been, Truth *or* Method? In other words, what Ricoeur questions is whether or not Gadamer's vision of historico-traditional ontological truth leaves any room for a critical appropriation of method consistent with the objectivity of the human sciences.[24]

A central feature of Gadamer's work, according to Ricoeur, and that

---

18 Ricoeur, "The Task," *From Text to Action*, 69, (94-95, FT).

19 Ricoeur, *Interpretation Theory*, 74-75.

20 Ricoeur, "Expliquer et comprendre," *Revue philosophique de Louvain*, 75 (1977), 126-147, reprinted in: *Du texte à l'action*, 161-182, ("Explanation and Understanding," reprinted in: *From Text to Action*, 125-143).

21 Ricoeur, "Qu'est-ce qu'un texte? Expliquer et comprendre," in: R. Bubner, ed., *Hermeneutik und Dialektik*, Tübingen: Mohr, 1970, 181-200, reprinted in: *Du texte à l'action*, 137-159, ("What is a Text? Explanation and Understanding," reprinted in: *From Text to Action*, 105-125).

22 Ricoeur, "The Task," *From Text to Action*, 71, (97 FT). Ricoeur writes, "Gadamer's work marks, in relation to Heidegger, the beginnings of the movement of return from ontology toward epistemological problems."

23 Gadamer, *Wahrheit und Methode, (Truth and Method)*, ET.

24 Ricoeur, "The Hermeneutical Function of Distanciation," *Philosophy Today* 17 (1973), Summer, 129-141, reprinted in: *From Text to Action*, 75-88, ("La fonction herméneutique de la distanciation," reprinted in: *Exegesis. Problèmes de méthode et exercices de lecture*, 201-215, reprinted in: *Du texte à l'action*, 101-117, FT).

from which hermeneutics raises its asseveration to universality, is the problematic of belonging to history and the distanciation prescribed by the human sciences as an alienating of such a historical belonging. Ricoeur writes:

> The core experience around which the whole of Gadamer's work is organized, and from which hermeneutics raises its claim to universality, is the scandal constituted, at the level of modern consciousness, by the *alienating distanciation (Verfremdung)* that seems to him to be the presupposition of these sciences. The methodology of these sciences ineluctably implies, in Gadamer's eyes, a distancing, which in turn expresses the destruction of the primordial relation of *belonging (Zugehörigkeit)* without which there would be no relation to the historical as such.[25]

For Gadamer, being a historical being effaces any potential of also being a critical being, as such criticism results in a destructive *alienation* from history and tradition. Tradition and history envelop the human sciences to such a degree that historical being can no longer call historical judgment knowledge, but merely a case of the preservation of tradition.

Writing within this envelop becomes a primary form of alienation in which hermeneutics finds itself facing the task of both over-coming and re-appropriating tradition, (in other words, a "letting say" again of the tradition), which has been textually alienated. Understanding, in this context, is only deemed possible because both text and interpreter are part of the reign of the historical continuum. Thus, in expressly rejecting any *distanciation*, this finally leaves little place for method, a critical-epistemological-explanatory movement within the heart of understanding, potentially leading to new understanding.[26]

---

25 Ricoeur, "The Task," *From Text to Action*, 70, (*Italics his*). (96 FT).

26 Ricoeur, "Herméneutique et critique des ideologies," in: *Démythisation et Idéologie*, E. Castelli, éd., Paris: Aubier, 1973, 25-61, esp. 51-56, ("Hermeneutics and the Critique of Ideology," reprinted in: *Hermeneutics and the Human Sciences*, Thompson, ed., Cambridge: Cambridge University Press, 1981, 63-100, esp. 89-94).

Ricoeur's thought, however, concerning the importance of explanation and understanding in relation to a dialectic of belonging-distanciation must not be overlooked. In arguing for a "dialectic" that pertains to these two dimensions of existence, Ricoeur both accesses and bypasses Gadamer's polarity of negative alienating "distanciation" versus positive "belonging." A methodological distancing, as for example in the human sciences, from Gadamer's standpoint, is destructive in the light of the subject's identity as a being that already belongs to history.

For Ricoeur, distanciation is as much a part of existence as belonging, and it therefore deserves to be perceived as a *productive condition*, not merely an alienation to be overcome. In this sense, distanciation as already there is to be embraced, as opposed to simply being conquered, as with the assumption of its ulterior status to the whole hermeneutical process in the first instance. Distanciation is the precursor of hermeneutics. Without it, hermeneutics would be rendered dormant and unnecessary.

Distance, therefore, in Ricoeur's opinion, is not genesised by the written. Rather, it already occurs, for example, in speaking. That is, the "event" of what's being spoken is distanced from the "meaning" of the said.[27] This distance, however, is ultimately fortified by writing, which exemplifies, in its writteness, the reality of such distanciation.[28] The written then, in Ricoeur's view, is not an act of alienation (contra Plato) in which the lost paradise of knowledge and wisdom is ideally a mere remembrance.

> The inscription in external marks and the encoding of discourse according to the rules of specific literary genres constitute rather the necessary distanciation thanks to which linguistic communication is raised to the level of the written traditions on which our cultural existence relies.[29]

---

27 See below, Discourse and the Dialectic, for a fuller treatment of this subject.

28 Ricoeur, "Biblical Hermeneutics," 66-67.

29 Ricoeur, "The Conflict of Interpretations: Debate with Hans-Georg Gadamer," in: *Phenomenology: Dialogues and Bridges*, R. Bruzina and B. Wilshire, eds., Albany: State University of New York Press, 1982, 299-320, reprinted - cited in: *A Ricoeur Reader*, M. J. Valdés, ed., Toronto: University of Toronto Press, 1991, 225.

The hermeneutical import of this, in regard to the semantic autonomy of the text, is that distanciation is not to be understood as merely related to method, as if it were simply attached to the text. Rather, distanciation is to be perceived as cardinal to the appearance of the text as written, to the limits and conditions of its interpretation, and to a signification of a "being" who writes and reads.[30]

Ricoeur's aim, in contrast to the generalizing orientations of Schleiermacher, Dilthey, Heidegger, and even Gadamer, is to "re-regionalize" hermeneutics through a valuing of the particularities of the text.[31] For Ricoeur, the text affords a moment of *objectivity* in which explanation and epistemology play crucial roles on the road from understanding, as it moves toward new understanding. But how does Ricoeur envision this movement?

We have already pointed out Ricoeur's opposition to interpretation being viewed as solely understanding. He does not dispute, however, that this is where interpretation begins and ends. In the first case, understanding is a rough sketch of the meaning of the text as a whole. Ricoeur refers to this as a "guess," while in the second case, it is a new understanding, enriched and supported by explanation.[32]

"Guess," in the first instance is necessary because the author is no longer present and the text is semantically autonomous, much like one's first impression of another person.[33] This means there's a greater element of risk involved, rendering textual interpretation more hazardous than speech interpretation, because multiple interpretations are invited and misunderstandings are likely. However, through an interpretative approach to the text interested in its analytic structure and objectified meaning, explanation becomes mediatorially, methodologically, and

---

30   Ricoeur, "The Hermeneutical Function," *From Text to Action*, 83-84, (111-112, FT).

31   Ricoeur, "The Task," *From Text to Action*, 54, (76-77, FT).

32   Ricoeur, *Interpretation Theory*, 74-75.

33   For Ricoeur's view of the semantic autonomy of the text see section 3.1.2. below.

scientifically possible and fruitful.³⁴ Possible, because the text is another, bearing a dimension of objective meaning and fruitful because the process culminates in a new, hopefully more informed understanding. Without this epistemological-explanatory component, with its focus on the text and what it says, we are left with "guess" understanding as opposed to "critical" understanding. The result is a greater rather than lesser risk of misconception. Ricoeur remarks:

> An interpretation must not only be probable, but more probable than another interpretation. If it is true that there is always more than one way of construing a text, it is not true that all interpretations are equal. The text presents a limited field of possible constructions. The logic of validation allows us to move between the two limits of dogmatism and scepticism.³⁵

Thus, new understanding, in order to decrease the danger of misconception, must neither be solely based on another subject's intent, nor for that matter on the reader's own. Instead, the emphasis ought to be on the meaning of the text, and its ability to disclose a *world* that constitutes its reference.

3.1.2. Discourse, and the Dialectic of Event and Meaning

Ricoeur's articulation of language as *discourse* opposes what he refers to as the "marginalization" of discourse.³⁶ This has taken place, Ricoeur argues, through a recent over-emphasis on words, as opposed to sentences.³⁷ Such an over-emphasis leads to an inability to decipher truth

---

34   Ricoeur, *Interpretation Theory*, 78, argues that validation concerns procedures for testing our guesses. Such procedures are related to the logic of probability similar to validation as an "argumentative discipline comparable to the juridical procedures used in legal interpretation."

35   Ibid., 79, (parenthesis mine).

36   Ibid., 2.

37   Ricoeur acknowledges his immense semantic debt to Emile Benveniste, especially, *Problèmes de linguistique générale*, Paris: Gallimard, 1966, in: "Philosophie et langage," *Revue philosophique de la France et de l'Etranger* 103 (1978), 455.

or error since isolated words in and of themselves do not have the capacity either to assert or to deny.[38]

Generally speaking, developments in the field of linguistics have led to an opposition between *langue* and *parole*, and message and code.[39] Messages, for example, are diachronic, discretionary, and accidental, while codes are synchronic, stable, and systematic. Langue, as such, is to be the object of scientific investigation, but parole is, in being much more diverse and unwieldy, a less reliable candidate for rigorous examination.

These evolutions in language are most fully expressed, according to Ricoeur, in the structuralist model of interpreting texts.[40] Such structuralist models of texts, developed from Saussurean linguistics have become comprehensive theories of language and interpretation. Ricoeur writes:

> Language no longer appears as a mediation between minds and things. It constitutes a world of its own, within which each item only refers to other items of the same system, thanks to the interplay of oppositions and differences constitutive of the system. In a word, language is no longer treated as a "form of life," as Wittgenstein would call it, but as a self-sufficient system of inner relationships.[41]

Ricoeur's way forward towards a re-constituting of discourse, in contrast to the reign of "system," is to propose an alternative route comprising both *semiotics* (signs/symbols as communication) and *semantics* (meaning formulated in sentences). There are then two distinctive "sciences" necessary for decoding and deciphering language. This *distinc-*

---

38 Ricoeur, *Interpretation Theory*, 1-2. Ricoeur follows Plato and Aristotle.

39 F. de Saussure, *Cours de linguistique générale*, Paris: Payot, 1971.

40 Ricoeur, *Interpretation Theory*, 4. He describes this as a linguistic extension into texts which "eclipses discourse." Also in "Structure et herméneutique," *Esprit*, novembre 1963, 596-627, reprinted in: *Le conflit*, 31-63, esp. 48-53, ("Structure and Hermeneutics," reprinted in: *The Conflict*, 27-61). In referring to the text of the Old Testament and its core meaning, Ricoeur argues that structuralism's sur-accentuation on synchrony is in danger of excluding any possibility of historical action, for example, in the case of the biblical text, on the part of Yahweh, as being the genesis of a tradition which leads to the writing of the text. Actions by Yahweh in history, not classification systems, are the foundation of the meaning of the Old Testament text. Ricoeur argues that structural semiotics is, "anti-historical by nature." Also see, "Biblical Hermeneutics," 29.

41 Ricoeur, *Interpretation Theory*, 6.

tion is important[42] in that it provides Ricoeur with the possibility of enlarging the sphere of language to include both signs and sentences, thereby enabling him to critique structuralist tendencies to reduce language to a codified intra-linguistic series of signs.[43] Such a distinction, however, is not to be thought of as one of equivalence, but rather, in this case, as one of hierarchy, where the sentence both incorporates, and goes beyond the sign.

> The object of semiotics - the sign - is merely virtual. Only the sentence is actual as the very event of speaking. This is why there is no way of passing from the word as a lexical sign to the sentence by mere extension of the same methodology to a more complex entity. The sentence is not a larger more complex word; it is a new entity. It may be decomposed into words, but the words are something other than short sentences. A sentence is a whole irreducible to its parts. It is made up of words, but it is not a derivative function of its words. A sentence is made up of signs, but is not itself a sign.[44]

According to Ricoeur, this methodological decision (the distinction between semiotics and semantics) is the ground for his further development of a linguistics of discourse—referencing meaning, as opposed to a linguistics of language—only referring to itself.[45] This opposition is will now be concretized in a three-fold argument intended to substantiate the differentiating of semiotics and semantics. We shall briefly examine the dialectic of event and meaning in its relationship to the linguistics of the sentence, the phenomenology of meaning, and Anglo-American linguistic analysis.

---

42   Ibid., 8. Ricoeur refers to this distinction as, "the key to the whole problem of language."

43   Ricoeur, "Biblical Hermeneutics," 65. In Ricoeur's opinion, structuralist ideology is, "a dead end the very moment when it treats any 'message' as the mere 'quotation' of its underlying 'code.' " "Such ideology tends to 'kill' the text as message in reducing it to a "pure epiphenomenon of the 'codes'."

44   Ricoeur, *Interpretation Theory*, 7.

45   Ibid., 8.

It is the ontological priority of discourse, Ricoeur argues, that gives event a reign over system. In Ricoeur's opinion, without this priority, system banishes event and relegates it to the status of irrelevance. With this *reversal* of the reign of system over event, Ricoeur argues for an "actuality" of discourse over the "virtuality" of system. Thus, discourse as act or event is not banished, but has propositional content. A something is happening when someone speaks, and this something invokes questions as to "the what" and "how" of the said. But if discourse is somebody saying something in sentences to someone, what does Ricoeur mean by "event" and why is it essential to his position? Several statements shed specific light on the significance of event in relation to discourse.

First, *discourse as event* is to be understood inside of time, in contrast to system which stands outside of time; second, it refers back to its speaker as the *someone* who speaks, whereas language as abstract code has no speaking subject; third, it is always about *something*, a world for example, as opposed to language which merely refers to itself in a self-contained manner; finally, discourse is the realm in which "message" is translocated from speaker to hearer, from addressor to addressee, in short, from someone to the other, while language can only exist as the precursor to this event.[46]

The essential character of the "event" pole of the dialectic of event and meaning, for Ricoeur's project, is that it maintains the "actuality" of discourse as uttered by a speaking subject. Hence, discourse as event refutes the structuralist claim to the reign of the "virtuality" of system and code over subject and message.[47] Note Ricoeur's further insistence that the speaking subject's event of speaking results in something being said. This something said does not begin and end with the psychological intention of the speaker, but goes beyond it, both because of the wealth preceding and contributing to the speaker's content and because of its

---

46   Ricoeur, "The Hermeneutical Function," *From Text to Action*, 75-88, esp. 77-78, (*Du texte à l'action*, 101-117).

47   Ricoeur, *Interpretation Theory*, 13. "Languages do not speak, people do."

outward address to an other. This spoken content, then, falls within the category of the semantic-propositional or the actuality of the said. In this way, the speaking subject's event of speaking is ultimately found only in a linguistics affirming the meaning of discourse—the sentence communicating the said.

The second dimension of Ricoeur's dialectic to be explored is *meaning*. All discourse is meaningful because it is actualized as an event and understood as meaning. Ricoeur writes:

> [...] if all discourse is realized as an event, all discourse is understood as meaning. What we wish to understand is not the fleeting event but rather the meaning that endures. This point demands the greatest clarification, for it may seem we are reverting from the linguistics of discourse to the linguistics of language. But this is not so; it is in the linguistics of discourse that event and meaning are articulated. This articulation is the core of the whole hermeneutical problem. Just as language, by being actualized in discourse, surpasses itself as system and realizes itself as event, so too discourse, by entering the process of understanding, surpasses itself as event and becomes meaning. The surpassing of the event by the meaning is characteristic of discourse as such.[48]

This "meaning that endures" provokes hermeneutics, not only to consider linguistics, but also to develop a theory of speech acts. Such a theory, as represented by the *analytic philosophy of language* of J. L. Austin and J. R. Searle,[49] makes a case for a hierarchical theory of speech acts in three levels.[50] Level one is the act of saying (locution), level two is what we do in saying (illocution), and level three is what we do by the fact that we speak (perlocution). An example of this can be explained in the following way. If I tell you to open the window, I do three things.

---

48 Ricoeur, "Hermeneutical Function," *From Text to Action*, 78.

49 J. L. Austin, *How To Do Things With Words*, J. O. Urmson and M. Sbisa, eds., Oxford: Clarendon Press, 1962; J. R. Searle, *Speech Acts: An Essay in the Philosophy of Language*, Cambridge: Cambridge University Press, 1969.

50 Austin, *Words*, 94-120; Searle, *Acts*, 25-52.

First, the action predicate *open* is related both to the person addressed (you) and to the window. Second, this act of saying is given as an order—it has force. Third, the act of saying, said as an order, and said in a particular way, has the capacity to bring about results. Thus, language as discourse, as it is intentionally exteriorized in speech acts by the speaking subject, moves from event to meaning, objectifying itself into that which is said.

3.1.2.1. Sense and Reference

Under the pole of meaning, in the dialectic of event and meaning, there must be added another dialectic that is indispensable to Ricoeur's interpretation theory. Ricoeur clearly distances himself from a post-modernist non-sense, or structuralist sign system referring only to itself. He does this by arguing that within the discourse of meaning there is a dialectic of sense and reference. The speaker and the sentence both mean and refer. It is only at the sentence level, on the basis of the semiotic - semantic distinction between signs and sentences, that the "what" (sense) and an "about what" (reference) of discourse can be deciphered.[51]

According to Ricoeur, the sense - reference dialectic is so original that it could be considered the *reigning archetype* for language. "Language is not a world of its own. It is not even a world."[52] Ricoeur argues that language is *dependent* on a speaking subject's being in the world and that only the dialectic of sense and reference articulates this relationship. How does this work out and why is it relevant?

As speaking subjects we find ourselves in a world of situations, which results in us of having something to say. We are experiencers who bring our experience of these various situations to expression in language. There is not only sense in our speaking, but also reference.

---

[51] Ricoeur, *Interpretation Theory*, 19-22. Ricoeur follows Gottlob Frege in his essay, "On Sense and Reference," See Translations from the *Philosophical Writings of Gottlob Frege*, P. Geach and M. Black, eds., Oxford: Blackwell, 1970, 56-78.

[52] Ibid., 20.

This intention to speak is related to both our existence and our experience, culminating in our capacity to refer, to having something to say.

> It is because there is first something to say, because we have an experience to bring to language, that conversely, language is not only directed to ideal meanings but also refers to what is.[53]

From Ricoeur's point of view language must be referential if it is to be meaningful. The relevance of this is that the speaking subject is always included in, rather than excluded from language. Language is not merely a system of inter-connected signs or codes, but is discourse as expressed both semiotically and then semantically in sentences, through the event and meaning of speaking, which carries sense and the double reference of discourse, back to the speaker and at the same time to the world.

3.1.2.2. From Speaking to Writing

In Ricoeur's opinion, as we have noted, a theory of speech acts related to intentional exteriorization in which event is surpassed by meaning, articulates the normative versus alienating distance of the act of human communication. This phenomena then ultimately renders the *objectivizing* of the said of speaking equal to that of the said of writing.[54] We shall now turn to investigate this orientation, which will ultimately lead us back to the text and its world.

It is crucial, at this point, that we remind ourselves of the previous dialectic of *event* and *meaning* in discourse. This same dialectic is in operation, and in fact even more transparent, in regard to a written text. It is important to note that Ricoeur's dialectic critiques a modernist immediacy of meaning, while not succumbing, as a result of this, to a post-modernist meaninglessness. The dialectical composition of discourse, Ricoeur argues, stands over against two theories that aim to

---

53   Ibid., 21.
54   Ibid., 28.

fundamentally relate or divide speech and writing. Romanticist hermeneutics over-plays the relationship between spoken and written discourse seeing no distinction, while Jacques Derrida, for example, under-plays the relationship in radically prioritizing the written over the spoken.[55] Such theories, and their over-emphasis of one or the other form of discourse, run the risk of losing both their similarity and their difference.

Let's examine three ways in which Ricoeur's dialectical composition of discourse critiques and goes past both the Romanticist and Derridian extremes, and as such points to a way forward between an interpretative immediacy of sense or a deconstructive non-sense. First, a text "fixes" discourse, objectifying what is said and guarding its meaning, even though the event pole of the dialectic is slipping away.

> What in effect does writing fix? Not the event of speaking, but the "said" of speaking, where we understand by the "said" of speaking that intentional exteriorization constitutive of the aim of discourse thanks to which the *sagen,* the saying, wants to become *Aus-sage,* the enunciation, the enunciated.[56]

Discourse is grounded in speech and objectivized in what is said. But in the written, discourse procures a new type of objectivity which speech does not embody on its own. The written endures, can be preserved and de-temporalized in transcending cultural parameters. In the end, the act of inscribing meaning turns out to be a better shelter for the "said" than speech. Writing then not only "fixes" discourse, but also contributes to a range of social, political, historical, economic, and legal dimensions of human discourse. Ricoeur argues that such a culture of the written enriches and contributes to our humanness, which in turn produces culture.[57]

---

55   J. Derrida, *La voix et le phénomène,* Paris: Presses Universitaires de France, 1967; L'écriture et la différence, Paris: Seuil, 1967; *De la grammatologie,* Paris: Les Editions de minuit, 1967.

56   Ricoeur, "The Model of the Text: Meaningful Action Considered as a Text," *Social Research* 38/3 (1971), 529-562, reprinted in: *From Text to Action,* 144-167, esp. 146, ("Le modèle du texte: l'action sensée considérée comme un texte," reprinted in: *Du texte à l'action,* 183-211, esp. 185).

57   Ricoeur, *Interpretation Theory,* 40-43.

Through this "culture of the written" for example, Ricoeur critiques the concept in Plato's *Phaedrus* of the written as merely a feeble representation or a scant shadow of the real. For Ricoeur, writing, as with painting, has the capacity to *re-describe* reality, making it more *real* than it was previously. Writing then, is not a shadow of the real, but is in fact an expansion of the horizons of it.

Second, Ricoeur points out that through writing the dialogical situation between speaking and hearing is detonated. This should not be thought of however, as severing any relation between the two on the level of the dialectic of event and meaning. In Ricoeur's critique of the *pychologizing* and *deconstructive* interpretative grids, the relation yet distinction, between event and meaning remains operative. He states:

> What happens in writing is the full manifestation of something that is in a virtual state, something nascent and inchoate, in living speech, namely the detachment of meaning from the event. But this detachment is not such as to cancel the fundamental structure of discourse (discussed above). The semantic autonomy of the text which now appears is still governed by the dialectic of event and meaning.58

Writing and reading are not the same as speaking and hearing, but they are related through the dialectic of event and meaning. As such, it cannot be said that an author's intent is to be found outside the text, in merely a psychological translocution of meaning (Romanticists), nor can it be affirmed that the sense of the spoken could not have preceded the written (Derrida).[59]

Ricoeur argues that with written discourse the intent of the author and the meaning of the text resist synchronization. The result of this however, is neither the execution of the author, nor the absolutizing of

---

58   Ibid. 25. (Parenthesis mine).

59   Ricoeur, "Qu'est-ce qu'un texte?" *Du texte à l'action*, 138.

the text.[60] In Ricoeur's opinion, the text remains authored as a discourse (someone saying something to somebody), while at the same time it procures a semantic autonomy that transcends the intent of the author.

Third, Ricoeur affirms that a written text is addressed to anyone who can read. Writing, therefore, has a potentially universal audience since it is not limited by the immediate (event) situation of speaker and hearer.[61] Thus, while the dialogical speaker - hearer ostensive reference is abolished, the reference of the written remains intact and is able to trans-locate its world to anyone who can read. Ricoeur suggests:

> The letters of Paul are no less addressed to me than to the Romans, the Galatians, the Corinthians, and the Ephesians. Only the dialogue has a "thou" whose identification precedes discourse. The meaning of a text is open to anyone who can read. The omnitemporality of the meaning is what opens it to unknown readers.[62]

As such, the written is capable of giving human beings a reference that goes beyond and is liberated from the psychological and situational limits of the spoken. This referential power goes beyond the spoken in referring to a world, which is the composite of the written. Further, this points to ways of being in the world of its projection, which though it cannot be directly described, can be "said" through metaphor or symbol. In reading the "said," the reader, who is challenged to trans-locate their present situation, participates in the world unfolded in *front* of the text.[63] In other words, for Ricoeur, the written mediately opens a world that the narrow immediate situational context of speaking and hearing cannot.

---

60 Ricoeur, *Interpretation Theory*, 30.

61 Ibid., 32, Ricoeur states, "Hermeneutics begins where dialogue ends."

62 Ibid., 93.

63 Ricoeur, "The Hermeneutical Function," in: *From Text to Action*, 86, (*Du texte à l'action*, 114).

3.1.3. The Text

After examining several aspects of Ricoeur's interpretation theory related to the text (explanation and understanding, event and meaning, and speaking and writing, etc.), we are in a better position to evaluate his view of the text as discourse. We must now, more explicitly in this section, explore the rubrics of the text itself. Our intention is to examine three rubrics of Ricoeur's notion of the text, concluding with his vision of the text as autonomous and the bearer of a world.

First, in Ricoeur's opinion, a text is not just an "anything" written, but a text is a *work*. Ricoeur writes:

> The text is a complex entity of discourse whose characteristics do not reduce to those of the unit of discourse, or the sentence. By text I do not mean only or even mainly something written [...] I mean principally the production of discourse as a work.[64]

What Ricoeur wants to emphasize here is the process of creating a body of words, a process understood as the composition of a text. Thus, a text is a work composed as a whole, produced in a series of structured sentences, which is irreducible to its parts.[65] Ricoeur argues that this truth can be demonstrated by the fact that any modification of the succession in a text results in a mutation of its meaning.

Second, in understanding the notion of the text as a work, incorporating labor and production, Ricoeur refers to literary genres as *codes of composition*. Genre is not to be thought of as a mere classificatory system, but rather, parable, narrative and poem are means of production, instruments as it were of working out meaningful discourse.[66] Such production becomes significant to the particular forms of discourse.

---

[64] Ricoeur, *The Rule of Metaphor*, 219, (*La métaphore vive*, 277).

[65] Ricoeur, "Philosophy and Religious Language," 71-85. Ricoeur follows Aristotle's concept of taxis – "composition" - in speaking of a text as an internally organized whole always more than the summation of its partial meanings.

[66] Ibid., 74 and Ricoeur, *Interpretation Theory*, 33.

These particularities characterize the text, and are related to both understanding and interpretation.

> [....] it is the task of hermeneutics to identify the individual discourse (the "message") through the modes of discourse (the "codes") which generate it as a work of discourse. In other words, it is the task of hermeneutics to use the dialectics of discourse and work, or performance and competence, as a mediation at the service not of code, but of the message.[67]

For Ricoeur, over against structuralism in its exclusive emphasis on code, and various other concepts of literary criticism, which understand genre as mere taxonomic classification; literary genres are to be understood as a codification in the production of discourse as message, a sort of "generative poetics," having "tremendous importance for exegesis." Genre, modes of discourse such as, narrative, parable, and proverb, are to be seen as encoding processes, rather than classificatory devices.[68]

The third and ultimately most important aspect of text production is *style*. Ricoeur emphasizes style because it is what makes a poem or novel; *this* poem and *this* novel. In other words, style shapes the work into the singular, particular, individual thing that it is.[69] Style re-enforces the author's presence in the work, not as a psychologically intentional resident, but as a voice with an identity. Thus, the style signifies the singularities of a voice embodying a work structured in a meaningful way.[70]

These three rubrics of the text as a work clearly show Ricoeur's "text" to be related, but not equivalent to a structural or literary critical approach. Structuralism and literary criticism have value in helping one

---

67   Ricoeur, "Biblical Hermeneutics," 70.

68   Ibid., 68-71.

69   Ricoeur, *The Rule of Metaphor*, 219-220, (*La métaphore vive*, 277-279).

70   Ricoeur, "The Hermeneutical Function," 81-82. (*Du texte à l'action*, 108-109).

to identify "codes" and "forms" within literature. What distinguishes Ricoeur's view, however, is that the decoding of codes is only a step, albeit an important one, on the way to the interpretation of message. Literary forms, therefore, are not to be seen as classification systems, but as generative modes of discourse in the production of stories and messages infused with meaning.

In the last part of this section, we now turn back to examine Ricoeur's perspective of the text as semantically autonomous and the bearer of a world. These two *pillars* of Ricoeur's thought, in reference to the text, must be understood as central to his hermeneutics. On the one hand, his arguments against the reader's direct engagement with the intent of the author and meaning of the text, frees his hermeneutics from the modernist tendency of seeking to ground all meaning in a subject. The modernist presupposition that the subject (reader) possesses an ability to immediately comprehend with complete and absolute precision such authorial intent is decidedly dismissed. On the other hand, Ricoeur strongly critiques a post-modernist de-emphasis of the text's capacity to mean and refer to anything outside itself, liberating his hermeneutics from a post-modernist tendency to victimize the text, executing its meaning and the world that it represents.[71]

We have already pointed out that Ricoeur argues that the intent of the author and the meaning of the text desist synchronization.[72] As a result, textual interpretation is always mediate, indirect, a task of seeking sense as opposed to an immediate or direct given of complete sense. The text, as semantically autonomous, goes beyond and is freed from, the psychological constraints of its author. Ricoeur writes:

> With written discourse, the author's intention and the meaning of the text cease to coincide. The dissociation of the verbal meaning of the text and the mental intention is what is really at stake in the inscription of

---

[71] M. C. Taylor, "Text as Victim," in: *Deconstruction and Theology*, T. Altizer, ed., New York: Crossroad, 1982, 65.

[72] Ricoeur, *Interpretation Theory*, 30 as noted above.

discourse. Not that we can conceive of a text without an author; the tie between the speaker and the discourse is not abolished but distended and complicated. The dissociation of the meaning and the intention is still an adventure of the reference of discourse to the speaking subject. But the text's career escapes the finite horizon lived by its author. What the text says now matters more than what the author meant to say, and every exegesis unfolds its procedures within the circumference of a meaning that has broken its moorings to the psychology of its author.[73]

It is because the text has an emerging autonomy that it can transcend its author's intention, its reception by an original audience, and the socio-cultural contexts of its creation.[74] A veritable distance exists between author, text, and reader that is crucial for a dynamic hermeneutical movement from text to reader.[75] In addition to this, the text as a work, a production, a labor, has a form or encoding that renders it explainable. The structures of this code enable the articulation of a *critical* and *epistemological* moment within the hermeneutical process, since certain "rules" do apply. As such, Ricoeur asserts that an understanding of the text is not an aim to understand hidden subjectivities "behind" the text. Rather, the pursuit of understanding ought to aim at engaging the world that the text has opened up in "front" of itself.[76] In other words, Ricoeur emphasizes the movement from the internal structure of the text toward its external reference, in order to prevent a *short-circuiting* of the interpretative effort before it completes its motion. Text, as discourse, intends things (means) and expresses a world (refers) that is potentially relevant for self-understanding, modes of being-in-the-world, and new comprehensions of reality.

---

73   Ricoeur, "The Model of the Text: Meaningful Action Considered as a Text," in: *From Text to Action*, 148, ("Le modèle du texte: l'action sensée considérée comme texte," *Du texte à l'action*, 187).

74   Ricoeur, "The Hermeneutical Function," 83. (*Du texte à l'action*, 111).

75   It is essential to recall, at this juncture, the distinction between configuration and refiguration. There can be no real refiguration of human action, unless there is a distanciation between configuration and refiguration. See above, Life and Work, under *Time and Narrative* (*Temps et récit*).

76   Ricoeur, "Biblical Hermeneutics," 82.

One of the major advantages of this perspective, in addition to a Romantico-structuralist critique, is that it dismisses the reign of subjectivity in either its Cartesian or Fichtean, and to some degree Husserlian forms, denying either self (author or reader) primacy.[77] As the text is freed from the *tyranny* of subjectivities, it becomes recognizable as a structured work with the power to refer outside itself and to confront and transform understanding. Accordingly, interpretation cannot simply be grounded in another subject, nor can it appeal solely to structure for the sake of structure or code. Rather, interpretation must turn to the text and to its message, and engage in the movement from understanding to explanation and from explanation to new understanding.

In regards to this theory of interpretation, it is important to underscore the essential and indivisible relationship of the interlacing without effacing, of explanation and understanding (also crucial for biblical hermeneutics). As expressed by this post-Heideggerian re-situating of the epistemological-critical-analytic moment in interpretation, which full of potential, leads from *being* not merely back to *being*, but moves through the "something said" of the text to the possibility of *new being*. Ricoeur writes:

> [...] on the epistemological level, I shall say that there are not two methods, the explanatory method and the comprehensive method. Strictly speaking, explanation alone is methodical. Understanding is instead the nonmethodical moment that, in the sciences of interpretation, combines with the methodical moment of explanation. This moment precedes, accompanies, concludes, and thus *envelops* explanation. Explanation, in turn, *develops* understanding analytically.[78]

---

77 Ricoeur, "On Interpretation," in: *Philosophy in France Today*, A. Montefiore, ed., New York: Cambridge University Press, 1983, 175-197, reprinted in: *From Text to Action*, 1-20, esp. 17-18, ("De l'interprétation," reprinted in: *Du texte à l'action*, 11-35 esp. 30-31, FT).

78 Ricoeur, "Explanation and Understanding," in : *From Text to Action*, 142, "Expliquer et comprendre," (*Du texte à l'action*, 181). (*Italics his*.)

Our general hermeneutics invites us to say that the necessary stage between structural explanation and self-understanding is the unfolding of the world of the text; it is the latter that finally forms and transforms the reader's being-a-self in accordance with his or her intention. The theological implication of this is considerable: the primary task of a hermeneutics is not to bring about a decision in the reader but first to allow the world of being that is the "thing" of the biblical text to unfold. In this way, above feelings, dispositions, belief, or unbelief is placed the proposal of a world, which, in the language of the Bible, is called a new world, a new covenant, the kingdom of God, a new birth. These are realities that unfold before the text, unfolding to be sure for us, but based upon the text. This is what can be called the "objectivity" of the new being projected by the text.[79]

Our research up to this point has shown that Ricoeur's hermeneutics are to be understood as *ontological* and *textual*. An emphasis on the text, in his estimation, allows for a "re-regionaling" of the hermeneutical discussion, focalizing on the text and its world, and moving through the dialectics of explanation and understanding, event and meaning, and sense and reference. In the previous sections, we have also articulated Ricoeur's unique ability to dynamically mediate between opposing interpretation theories, thereby creating a viable theory of the text and a hermeneutical trajectory that merits consideration and further discussion as it applies to more specifically to biblical hermeneutics.

3.2. Consequences for Biblical Hermeneutics

In building on our previous sections, let us now examine the pertinence of Ricoeur's general interpretation theory for biblical hermeneutics. Ricoeur has argued that a text is an object in the world, and as

---

79 Ricoeur, "Philosophical and Biblical Hermeneutics," reprinted in: *From Text to Action*, 89-101, esp. 95-96, ("Herméneutique philosophique et herméneutique biblique," in: *Exegesis. Problèmes de méthode et exercices de lecture*, 216-228, esp. 222, reprinted in: *Du texte à l'action*, 119-133).

such, it has a sense and reference. The text, it could be said, is full of meaning and therefore creates the need for, and merit of, interpretation. We have already pointed out that this perspective of the text is founded on an understanding of language as discourse, comprising the two components of semantics and semiotics.[80] Discourse, as Ricoeur sees it, following Benveniste, is always someone saying something to somebody, the meaning of which, in transcending the dialogical situation, is ultimately preserved via an inscription in the text, and concretized as the "said," in spite of the passing event of saying it.[81]

The biblical text is a fitting one for applying and working out Ricoeur's theory of interpretation, since he has written a number of books and papers on the topic.[82] In reference to Ricoeur's work on the biblical text, we shall investigate three contours of his thought, which in our opinion may make a significant contribution to biblical hermeneutics: first, the relationship between philosophical hermeneutics and biblical hermeneutics; second, the concerns and limits of methodology; and third, a brief explanation and application of methodology in relation to the biblical text.

3.2.1. Philosophical Hermeneutics and Biblical Hermeneutics

This elucidation is essential in order to locate Ricoeur in the hermeneutical discussion. The problematic here may be stated in the following way: it is argued that Ricoeur's *philosophical* hermeneutics reigns over his *biblical* hermeneutics, thereby resulting in a compromising of the language and world of the Bible, with and through extra-biblical categories of philosophy.[83] In the paragraphs that follow, we undertake an investigation into whether or not this is the case.

---

80 See Discourse and the Dialectic of Event and Meaning.

81 E. Benveniste, *Problèmes de linguistique générale*.

82 Including, Ricoeur, "Herméneutique philosophique et herméneutique biblique," *Du texte à l'action*, 124, ("Philosophical and Biblical Hermeneutics," *From Text to Action*, 94). Also, Ricoeur, "Philosophy and Religious Language," 71.

83 G. Lindbeck, *The Nature of Doctrine*, Philadelphia: Westminster, 1984, 136.

For Ricoeur, in opposition to hermeneutical singularity, there is in fact an inter-relationship between philosophical and biblical hermeneutics.[84] Does this inter-relationship necessarily prioritize a philosophical hermeneutics? In response to the question of whether 'biblical hermeneutics' is merely one of many potential applications of a broader philosophical hermeneutical approach to texts in general, Ricoeur writes:

> [...] it seems to me that there is a complex relation of mutual inclusion between the two hermeneutics. To be sure, the initial movement proceeds from the philosophical to the biblical pole. The same categories of work, writing, world of the text, distanciation, and appropriation govern interpretation in one as well as in the other. In this sense, biblical hermeneutics is a *regional* hermeneutics in relation to philosophical hermeneutics, considered a *general* hermeneutics. It may then appear that we are acknowledging the subordination of biblical hermeneutics to philosophical hermeneutics by treating it as an applied hermeneutics.
>
> However, it is precisely by treating theological hermeneutics as a hermeneutics applied to a type of text – biblical texts – that we cause an inverse relation between the two hermeneutics to appear. Theological hermeneutics presents features that are so original that the relation is gradually inverted, and theological hermeneutics finally subordinates philosophical hermeneutics to itself as its own *organon*.[85]

On the one hand, Ricoeur affirms a hermeneutical movement from the philosophical to the biblical, while on the other side of the same hand

---

84 What we have in mind here, by the use of this terminology, are those who argue for a single hermeneutical strategy, in other words, those who eschew any vital relation between philosophical and biblical hermeneutics. The so called, "Yale school," which sees little relation between the two hermeneutics, would be an example of this. See Frei, "The 'Literal Reading' of Biblical Narrative," 36-77, esp. 45, 50, 56, for a critique of Ricoeur's hermeneutical enterprise. But see Wallace, *The Second Naiveté: Barth, Ricoeur, and the New Yale Theology*, Macon: Mercer University Press, 1990, 96-100, for a cogent defence of Ricoeur.

85 Ricoeur, "Philosophical and Biblical Hermeneutics," *From Text to Action*, 89-90, ("Herméneutique philosophique et herméneutique biblique," (*Du texte à l'action*, 119,) (*Italics his*).

so to speak, philosophical hermeneutics gradually functions within the sphere of a text related biblical hermeneutics. Before examining the relationship between philosophical and biblical hermeneutics any further, let's turn to a clarification. Ricoeur's argumentation shows, in dialogue with the biblical text, that a general (philosophical) hermeneutics is eventually surmounted by a regional (biblical) hermeneutics.[86] It is true that a general hermeneutics, expressing a concern for the structure (explanation), work, and world of any text as text, is both valid and highly valuable. It is also true, however, that the movement from this general hermeneutics to the regional one is reversed through the confrontation with the specific world of the biblical text. In a counter movement to its former direction (philosophical to biblical), there is now the subsequent transformation of the previously referred to general hermeneutics into a regional hermeneutics, thereby affirming the Ricoeurian perspective of the inversing character of our two hermeneutics (biblical over philosophical). The question is how, specifically, does Ricoeur envision this *inversion* taking place?

A brief exploration of two examples of inversing moments in Ricoeur's hermeneutical position will suffice to make the point. The first regards forms of biblical discourse, and the second references "the world of the text" in general, and its connection to the world of the biblical text specifically. The biblical text, according to Ricoeur, uniquely presents its world as a particular world, which no other text articulates in this "subject matter" fashion.[87]

In the first example, Ricoeur views the "confession of faith" articulated in the biblical text, as interwoven with its forms of discourse.[88] As a result of this vision, it can be said that the biblical text has a structure,

---

[86] Ibid., 91, (121, F). Ricoeur points out the double axis of the biblical text, "which possesses at once a historical significance and a kerygmatic dimension," ("qui a à la fois une portée historique *et* une dimension kérygmatique.") (*Italics his*).

[87] Ibid., 126-129, (95-98, ET)."

[88] Ricoeur, "Philosophy and Religious Language," 76. In connection with this relationship, between the discourse form and theological content, it should be pointed out that Ricoeur frequently refers to being indebted to Gerhard von Rad's, *Theologie des Alten Testaments*, 2 vols., Munich: Kaiser, 1957 - 1960, for his understanding of this linkage.

such as narrative, gospel, prophetic, etc. At the same time, however, the text in all its genre richness remains a declaration of faith.[89] For Ricoeur, it is precisely this declaration of the biblical message that challenges philosophical hermeneutics. The result, according to Ricoeur, is that biblical hermeneutics eventually surpasses, though does not efface philosophical hermeneutics. On the ability of narrative to comprise the confession of faith, and the hermeneutic reversal this initiates, Ricoeur writes:

> [...] the relation between the two hermeneutics begins its inversion when one considers the other side of narration, namely, the profession of faith. This other dimension, however, remains inseparable from the structure of the narrative; not just any theology could be tied to the narrative form but only a theology that announces Yahweh as the great actant in a history of deliverance. The greatest contrast between the God of Israel and that of Greek philosophy perhaps resides here. The theology of traditions knows nothing of the concepts of cause, of ground, of essence; instead it speaks of God in agreement with the historical drama instituted by the acts of deliverance reported by the narrative. This way of speaking about God is no less meaningful that that of the Greeks; it is a theology that is homogeneous with narrative structure itself, a theology in the form of a *Heilsgeschichte*.[90]

In Ricoeur's argument, the inversion, and eventual subordination of philosophical hermeneutics to biblical hermeneutics, occurs as the message or content of the biblical text is expressed through its many diverse forms of discourse. Form and content, in one sense synchronize,

---

89 Ibid., 84-85. Ricoeur remarks that faith, "is the limit of all hermeneutics and the nonhermeneutical origin of all interpretation." He refers to faith as "ultimate concern," "a feeling of absolute dependence," or "unconditional trust" attached to a *movement* of hope according to the logic of superabundance. In all the previous, "the thematic of faith escapes from hermeneutics and testifies to the fact that the latter is neither the first nor the last word." However, hermeneutics recalls for us, "that biblical faith cannot be separated from the *movement* of interpretation which elevates it to language." Hope, for example, "would be empty if it did not rely on a constantly renewed interpretation of the sign-events reported by the writings, such as the Exodus in the Old Testament and the Resurrection in the New Testament." (*Italics mine*).

90 Ricoeur, "Philosophical and Biblical Hermeneutics," 91-92, ("Herméneutique philosophique et herméneutique biblique," 122). (*Italics his*).

yet this synchronization does not produce an effacing of either one or the other. The *tensional* relationship between form and content is as follows: the content of the biblical text can be identified by its form (narrative), but that content (God the great actor of deliverance) is not be reduced to merely the form through which it is communicated.

Regarding the second example of inversion, we turn now to "the world of the text," and apply it to the world of the biblical text. Ricoeur calls this "thing" of the text, the "object" of hermeneutics.[91] The Ricoeurian aim of hermeneutics, we can recall, is neither primarily to bring about a decision in the reader (existentialism), nor to better understand the author (romanticism). Hermeneutics, in the first instance, aims at explaining the text and the world of the text by viewing it as a proposed world of possibility, and of possible habitation. Many texts, it can be said, present a particular world, but the specificity of biblical discourse, Ricoeur affirms, lies in its proposal of a new world, new birth, and new covenant.[92]

We shall now expand on the specificness of the biblical text for the purpose of clarifying the second inversing moment, which we are calling "the world of the text." In addition to what has been said above, one of the *emblematic* characteristics of the biblical text differentiating it from other texts is its referent: God. Ricoeur spells this out in the following way:

> One of the features that constitutes the specificity of biblical discourse is, as we know, the central place held by the referent "God." [...] the signification of this referent of biblical discourse is implied, [...], in the various significations related to the literary forms of narration, prophesy, hymn, wisdom, and so on [...] The referent "God" is at once the coordinator of these diverse discourses and the vanishing point, the index of incompletion, of these partial discourses.[93]

---

91 Ibid., 126, (95, ET).

92 Ricoeur points out that these realities are "for us" realities, which however, it must be said, do not originate with the self, but begin with, and are unfolded before the text. "Philosophy and Religious Language," 81.

93 Ricoeur, "Philosophical and Biblical Hermeneutics," 97, ("Herméneutique philosophique et herméneutique biblique," 128-129).

Ricoeur argues that the function of this word (God) in the biblical text resists being converted into a Heideggerian, Medieval, or even theological meta-language concept of being.[94] It is precisely here that we can better perceive Ricoeur's reticence to allow the reign of philosophical-general hermeneutics over biblical-regional hermeneutics.

Another factor characterizing the response of the biblical text is that the word "God" cannot be reduced to being, because according to Ricoeur, it says more than this.[95] He appeals to this word as presupposing a total context under and towards which, the whole diversity of biblical discourses gravitate. Understanding this word involves a supervening of the arrow of sense, an action orchestrated by the word itself. For Ricoeur, this "arrow of sense" avidly affirms a twofold force: first, the image connotes a re-assembling of the entire signification generated by the biblical discourses (incomplete though they may be); second, the image opens up a vista that eludes the closure of discourse.[96]

It is intriguing, at this juncture, to explore the ramifications of this resistance factor for biblical hermeneutics, (still within the context of the second inversion). Ricoeur, ever careful to not go too far, is at the same time arguing for a textual sense. While he desists from saying too much, Ricoeur also argues that there is something to be said, because it has been said. The *sense* spoken of, always partial, mediated, and somewhat open-ended, is nevertheless a sense with an "arrow" that can be followed—one that signifies, and opens up a direction. Although biblical discourses, for Ricoeur, cannot close or complete the word "God" in any *exhaustive* manner, they can and do have the capacity to *refer* outward with a sense that is perceptible, rather than total. Ricoeur then takes what we might term the "radical middle," seeking to avoid the two extremes of complete sense (modern) or utter non-sense (post-modern).

We shall risk taking this even a step further and specify that

---

94   Ibid., 129, (98, ET).

95   Ibid., 98. Ricoeur states, "It is the function of the teaching of the Cross and of the Resurrection to give the word *God* a *density* that the word *being* does not contain." (Ibid., 129).

96   Ibid., 128-129, (97-98, ET).

Ricoeur's position is that biblical hermeneutics subordinates philosophical hermeneutics. Such a claim comes with this second inversing moment, as the *world* of the text speaks. Our emphasis, along with Ricoeur, is to show that it is the world of the biblical text that "organizes" philosophical-general hermeneutics.

It is our viewpoint, that these thoughts not only relate to the "Name" God, but also can have a Ricoeurian double referent that pertains to both self and God. The self, before this disclosure of the biblical text, cannot have complete sense, but it can have a mediated sense. Such a sense flows from the diversity of biblical discourses, the text, and its world, infusing the self with meaning, but only as a self who is dependent on the Other, for itself. This shows then, at the same time, that there is a limiting of the self who is not and cannot be the Self.[97]

Thus, we contend that a co-relationship exists between a self that is limited by the biblical text, and one that is itself limited on the level of its own philosophical discourse. Since this self and the biblical text are each limited, they can be said to become *dependent* on a referent outside of, or beyond themselves. Nevertheless, with this configuration, both biblical discourse and self retain their meaning, albeit without closure.[98]

This double limit, however, can be construed as positive, both for the name "God," as well as for the self. The aggregate meaning of the "Name" goes beyond the biblical text, but it can be partially found within it. This "found in" meaning, in spite of its partiality, has the capacity to confront the self, shattering any illusions of an exclusively philosophically oriented self-authenticated self. The critique the text offers confronts this false self for presuming to have direct access to itself, through itself.[99] In other words, it is the *world* of the biblical text

---

[97] A philosophical-general hermeneutics appeal to "any text" is not extensive or comprehensive enough to give the self a true self-meaning. According to Ricoeur, this is only to be finally found in a dependence on the Other.

[98] Ricoeur, "Biblical Hermeneutics," 34, 107-109, 126-127.

[99] Ricoeur, "Philosophy and Religious Language," 84. Ricoeur connects self-understanding or a grounding of self to the concept of faith in dialogue with the biblical text. "For my part I should link the concept of faith to that of *self-understanding* in the face of the text. Faith is the attitude of one who accepts being interpreted at the same time that he interprets the world of the text. Such is the hermeneutical constitution of the biblical faith."

that goes beyond self. And while the two are related, they also radically distinct, since God and self are not the same thing.

Ricoeur's thoughts then, are applicable in the above ways, both of which attest to the reign of biblical hermeneutics over philosophical-general hermeneutics. Concerning either the "Name" God or the self, and their meanings, there can be no exhaustive comprehension.[100] That is, the sum total of all the discourses in the biblical text referring to God will never give us closure about God, nor will they give us closure about the self. All of the partial discourses referring to God intersect in their naming of God. But they also open up a creative vista, pointing beyond themselves in a manner that defies closure.[101]

We would argue the discussion of these two points, in addition to its usefulness for the understanding of the second inversing moment, is readily applicable to the wider problematic of a modernist totalizing perspective, characterized as closure or complete sense. Whether founded on reason or on the biblical text, the modernist tendency to totalize with its explanations is challenged.[102] Further, a post-modernist perspective of complete non-sense (or at most, what could be defined as merely a self-created sense) is effectively called into question.[103]

Ricoeur is again nuanced on both sides. He argues for a non-closure (whether rational or biblical), maintaining there is no complete sense, but at the same time, this does not prevent him from affirming a sufficient textual meaning that places the "Name" God within and beyond the biblical discourses. At the same time, this places the self in a

---

100 Ricoeur, "Biblical Hermeneutics," 34. Ricoeur refers to these theologically as "limit expressions" and humanly as "limit experiences."

101 Ricoeur, "Herméneutique philosophique et herméneutique biblique," 128-129, ("Philosophical and Biblical Hermeneutics," 98).

102 If human beings are perceived as omniscient and capable of attaining universal knowledge, complete sense then becomes within the reach of the autonomous efforts of human reason. Kant, for example, in: *What is Enlightenment?* New York: Liberal Arts Press, 1959, 85, 132, 137, encourages human beings to make use of their understanding without dependence on another. Have courage to use your own reason is the affirmation of enlightenment. Also see C. Hodge, *Systematic Theology, I*, New York: Scribners, 1921, 1-17, who regards the Bible as a storehouse of facts equivalent to those of natural science's physical facts. In this view, the Bible is made up of solid and unimpeachable facts that give us complete sense.

103 See above, footnote 11.

dependent relationship with that which is outside of it, deconstructing any apparent capacity to be a self contained self.[104] With Ricoeur, we have come to a lucid critique of both the modernist and post-modernist tendencies as applied to biblical hermeneutics. A *mediated* textual sense reigns over the archetypal poles of "complete sense" or "non-sense" that are often presented as the only options in the hermeneutical marketplace.

Thus, Ricoeur furthers this discussion with a valid picture of the place of a philosophical-general hermeneutics in its co-relationship to a biblical hermeneutics. This picture is seen for example, more specifically in the world of the text. Biblical hermeneutics never stands alone and must always be recognized as part of a larger hermeneutical enterprise. However, biblical hermeneutics is, in regard to its specific subject matter and world, a unique enough hermeneutics, to bring about, as Ricoeur suggests, and with which we concur, an inversing, which finally subjects a general hermeneutics to a biblical hermeneutics. The specificness of biblical hermeneutics is embedded in the specificity of the "thing" of the text and the world that unfolds in front of it. Ricoeur states it in the following way:

> We now see in what sense this biblical hermeneutics is at once a particular case of the kind of general hermeneutics described above and a unique case. A particular case because the new being of which the Bible speaks is not to be sought anywhere but in the world of the text, which is one text among others. A unique case because all the partial discourses are referred to a Name, which is the point of intersection and the index of the incompletion of all our discourses about God, and because this Name has become inseparable from the *meaning-event,* preached as the Resurrection. However, biblical hermeneutics

---

104 Ricoeur, "Preface to D. Ihde," *Hermeneutic Phenomenology: The Philosophy of Paul Ricoeur,* Evanston: Northwestern University Press, 1971, xv. In speaking of his "permanent mistrust" of the self's capacity to posit itself, Ricoeur states: "Today this mistrust is reinforced by the conviction that the understanding of the self is always indirect and proceeds from the interpretation of signs given outside me in culture and history and from the appropriation of the meaning of these signs. I would now dare to say that, in the coming to understanding of the signs inscribed in texts, the meaning rules and gives me a self. In short, the self of self-understanding is a gift of understanding itself and of the invitation from the meaning inscribed in the text."

can claim to say something unique only if this unique "thing" speaks as the world of the text that addresses us, as the "thing" of the text.[105]

From our standpoint, as an unfortunate result of over-specialization, biblical interpreters often pay little attention to the ways in which philosophical-general hermeneutics *in*-forms or *de*-forms a reading of the biblical text, while philosophers rarely engage themselves with biblical hermeneutics, thereby inadvertently (or perhaps otherwise), risking the loss of a more informed, or less deformed reading of philosophy.

3.2.1.1. Ricoeur and Bultmann: Reading the Biblical Text

As our previous pages have been primarily focused on Ricoeur's contribution to biblical hermeneutics, it is important to now briefly develop this section a step further in order to see how it works out. Specifically, we will take as our example Ricoeur's discussion of Rudolf Bultmann's (1884-1976) reading of the biblical text.[106] According to Ricoeur, there has always been a *hermeneutic problem* in Christianity, and this is related to the larger question of language. Ricoeur writes:

> There has always been a hermeneutic problem in Christianity because Christianity proceeds from a proclamation. It begins with a fundamental preaching that maintains that in Jesus Christ the kingdom has approached us in decisive fashion.[107]

Language is the common meeting ground of Wittgenstein's investigations, the English linguistic philosophy, the phenomenology that stems from Husserl, Heidegger's investigations, the works of Bult-

---

105 Ricoeur, "Philosophical and Biblical Hermeneutics," 98, ("Herméneutique philosophique et herméneutique biblique," 129). (*Italics his*).

106 Ricoeur, "Préface à Rudolf Bultmann," in: *Jésus. Mythologie, et démythologisation*, Paris: Seuil, 1968, 9-28, "Préface à Rudolf Bultmann," reprinted in: *Le conflit*, 373-392, ("Preface to Bultmann," reprinted in: *The Conflict*, 381-401; *Essays on Biblical Interpretation*, 49-72).

107 Ricoeur, *Essays on Biblical Interpretation*, "Preface to Bultmann," 49.

mannian school and of the other schools of New Testament exegesis, the works of comparative history of religion and of anthropology concerning myth, ritual, and belief [...]"[108]

Ricoeur's perspective points out that language has become a multi-disciplinary question connected to both biblical and philosophical hermeneutics. In his opinion, because Christianity proceeds from proclamation, it has always had a hermeneutic problem. This is because biblical texts are the fixed and written versions of this proclamation. Speech becomes concrete in the written, preserving the fading speech-event through its inscripturated meaning, which then locates the hermeneutic problem in a text. Reader responsibility surfaces when questions as to the ancient text's capacity to be a living word for its contemporary reader are asked.[109] In the next paragraphs, we plan to engage with what, according to Ricoeur, is Bultmann's "short cut" solution to this problematic, and then contrast it with Ricoeur's own "long route," with its resultant, yet tentative resolution.[110]

However, let us first develop and situate the context into which this discussion takes place, in order to better understand its relevance for biblical hermeneutics. Ricoeur advances, what can be referred to, as a three-fold moment of the hermeneutic problem that, in his opinion, has always been a difficulty.

First, there is the problematic of the relation between "two Testaments" or "two Covenants." Ricoeur argues that the question of this relationship flows all the way back to those who attempted to interpret the Christ-event in the light of a re-reading of the Old Testament. Orthodox Christianity has resisted movements such as Marcionism

---

108 Ricoeur, *Freud and Philosophy: An Essay on Interpretation*, trans. D. Savage, New Haven: Yale University Press, 1970, 3. (*De l'interprétation, Essai sur Freud*, Paris: Seuil, 1965, 13-14). (parenthesis mine).

109 Ricoeur, "Preface," *The Conflict*, 382, "This relation between writing and the word and between the word and the event and its meaning is the crux of the hermeneutic problem. But this relation itself appears only through a series of interpretations. These interpretations constitute the history of the hermeneutic problem and even the history of Christianity itself, to the degree that Christianity is dependent upon its successive readings of Scripture and on its capacity to reconvert this Scripture into the living word." ("Préface," *Le conflit*, 374).

110 Ricoeur, *Essays on Biblical Interpretation*, "Preface," 70.

or Gnosticism, which have attempted to sever the gospel from its Old Testament hermeneutic ground. But why is a re-reading of the Old Testament necessary?

> Essentially to make the event itself appear, not as an irrational irruption, but as the fulfilment of an antecedent meaning which remained in suspense. The event itself receives a temporal density by being inscribed in a signifying relation of "promise" and "fulfilment." […] This signifying relation attests that the kerygma, by this detour through the reinterpretation of an ancient Scripture, enters into a network of intelligibility.[111]

Second, the question, more recently renewed by Bultmann, but already addressed by Paul, pertains to the interweaving of the interpretation of the Book, and the interpretation of life. Ricoeur suggests that Paul creates this second form of biblical hermeneutics when the listener of this message is invited to *participate* in decoding their own existence from the perspective of the Passion and Resurrection of Christ. The Pauline death of the "old self" and birth of the "new self" find their significance under the sign of the cross and the subsequent victory over death. The partial task of biblical hermeneutics is to amplify a greater understanding of doctrine, but also to enhance the affiliation between the text, human existence, and the whole of reality as far as it can be known.

Third, there is the question of a more contemporary recognition of what was nonetheless a very early problem in Christianity. Ricoeur refers to this as the hermeneutic situation of the faith, in relation to the primitive constitution of the Christian kerygma.[112] It must be recalled at this stage, that Christianity is grounded on its witness, in the sense that its kerygmatic character is not in the first place textual, but rather the proclamation of the person; Jesus Christ. Subsequently, this

---

111 Ricoeur, "Preface," *The Conflict*, 383-384, "Préface," *Le conflit*, 375.

112 *Ibid., 378, (Essays on Biblical Interpretation,* "Preface," 54).

witness becomes a written text, bearing the hermeneutic situation of new Scripture and New Testament, which require interpretation. This New Testament, as it emerges, immediately engenders the hermeneutic problem in the sense that there is always a degree of distance between the text and the event it proclaims. Thus, the distance that modern interpreters have become acutely aware of is really not so different from what was the case closer to when the text was written. But perhaps this disconnect can better be thought of in terms of time, which inculcates a greater rather than a lesser distance. Ricoeur remarks:

> [...] The meaning and function of our modernity is to unveil, by means of the distance which today separates our culture from ancient culture, what has been unique and extraordinary in this hermeneutic situation since the beginning.[113]

In Ricoeur's view, Bultmann's attempt to "demythologize" the biblical text is related to our third problem. Succinctly, demythologization is an effort to *unmask* the kerygma of the biblical text from its ancient mythical disguise rendering that kerygma comprehensible to a modern person in the twentieth century.[114] Such an attempt, according to Bultmann, would be to connect with the non-mythological "God who acts."[115] In one sense, Ricoeur views this as a *positive* enterprise, if its intention is to discover the meaning-event character of the biblical text. In another sense however, it is *less positive* in aiming to dissolve, or even bypass the majority of the ancient formulations and strands of language comprising the biblical text.

---

113 Ibid., 380, (56-57, ET).

114 R. Bultmann, *Kerygma and Myth*, H. W. Bartsch, ed., New York: Harper, 1961, 3. After giving numerous examples of what is to be considered the New Testament's proclamation in mythological language (Christ's incarnation, dying the death of a sinner, being raised and coming in judgement, etc.) 2, Bultmann states, "All this is the language of mythology, and the origin of the various themes can be easily traced in the contemporary mythology of Jewish Apocalyptic and in the redemption myths of Gnosticism. To this extent *the kerygma is incredible to modern man, for he is convinced that the mythical view of the world is obsolete*. Does the New Testament embody a truth which is quite independent of its mythical setting? If it does, theology must undertake the task of stripping the Kerygma from its mythical framework, of 'demythologizing' it." (*Italics his*).

115 Ricoeur, "Préface," *Le conflit*, 386, (*Essays on Biblical Interpretation*, "Preface," 64).

This "positive - less positive" can be clarified in the following manner. It is crucial to recognize that any connection with the God who acts, for Ricoeur, must come through the sense of the biblical text in its ancient formulations and language. This posture accepts textual sense as the force driving towards significance, while acknowledging the rightful place of the biblical text in the motion of hermeneutics. The only way of bridging the distance between the reader and the biblical text is through the text itself.

Let's refer to it this way. One side of Bultmann, in a non-Diltheyian sense, is not interested in understanding the text as an expression of life, but as that in which the essence of meaning finds its articulation. Meaning, as expressed in the text, is prior to, and reigns over understanding. This understanding is one that is nurtured through the labor of exegesis and its methodological concerns.

> [...] Bultmann has perfectly understood that this primacy of the object, this primacy of meaning over understanding, is performed only through the understanding, through the exegetical work itself. [...] Only in the understanding of the text do I in fact know the object.[116]

However, on Bultmann's other side, what we shall call, following Ricoeur, his hermeneutical as opposed to his exegetical side, Bultmann can be shown to have a *deficient* hermeneutical sub-strata from which to work out his exegetical results. Ricoeur argues Bultmann's exegetical work, whatever one's conclusions about it may be, is non-Diltheyian.[117] This means his exegetical aims are not, via Schleiermacher and Dilthey, to understand authors better than they understood themselves, but rather to submit to the "said" of the text, in both its intent and meaning.[118]

Hermeneutically speaking, however, Ricoeur finds Bultmann to

---

116 Ibid., 382, (59, ET).

117 Ibid., 388-389, (67, ET).

118 Ibid., 389, (67, ET). Ricoeur refers to Bultmann's, *Théologie du Nouveau Testament* et *Commentaire de l'Evangile de Jean*, as examples of this orientation.

be closer to Dilthey, in the sense that for him textual meaning is only realized in personal appropriation. Ricoeur affirms the necessity of personal appropriation is correct, but only as a final moment, after the *long detour* from one context to another, via the meaning of the text. According to Ricoeur, the text does not make a *direct* person to person meaning appropriation possible. Why is this the case? Such immediate appropriation is not possible because of the nature of the text as distanced from the event it recounts. Event, as it were, in textual terms, cannot be considered the same as event per se.

This in turn demonstrates for us the importance of recognizing the reality of distance between *event* and *meaning*, which already exists, even prior to an interpretation of the text. The text both affirms this distance, and offers a way through it to sense, as inscribed sense. Thus, meaning is a text mediated phenomena, finally appropriated from the text, not the author. Ricoeur reproaches Bultmann in the following way:

> Two thresholds of understanding then must be distinguished, the threshold of "meaning," [...] and that of "signification," which is the moment when the reader grasps the meaning, the moment when the meaning is actualized in existence. [...] A theory of interpretation which at the outset runs straight to the moment of the decision moves too fast. It leaps over the moment of meaning, which is the objective stage, in the nonworldly sense of "objective." There is no exegesis without a "bearer of meaning," which belongs to the text and not to the author of the text.[119]

Ricoeur critiques Bultmann for moving too fast and thereby hermeneutically short - circuiting the exegetical moment. This moment, in the interpretative process is not to be envisioned as "existential decision," but as exegetically focusing on the meaning of the text.

In Ricoeur's understanding of biblical hermeneutics, Bultmann's

---

119 Ibid., 389, (68, ET).

division of the "objective" and the "existential," (as also occurs when there is a narrowly restrictive embracing of the opposition between myth and kerygma), militates against the biblical text which links these two moments, connecting them intimately together. Ricoeur points this out clearly:

> It is the objectivity of the text, understood as content – bearer of meaning and demand for meaning – that begins the existential movement of appropriation. Without such a conception of meaning, of its objectivity and even of its ideality, no textual criticism is possible. Therefore, the semantic moment, the moment of objective meaning, must precede the existential moment, the moment of personal decision, in a hermeneutics concerned with doing justice to both the objectivity of meaning and the historicity of personal decision.[120]

Bultmann's "short cutting" of the hermeneutical enterprise evades the following central interpretive question: How does the language of the biblical text, in its diversity of discourses, which in Ricoeur's perspective hold form and content together, transmit a content, sense, and referent to which an interpreter responds?[121] Reductionism from a fullness of language to a naked kerygmatizing of the biblical text risks being so over pre-occupied with a *demythologizing* of biblical language that it is in grave danger of ignoring the potential *abundance* of meaning embedded in this language itself.

In relation to his own view of the hermeneutical task, Ricoeur can affirm Bultmann's emphasis on (in Ricoeur's terms) the text and its meaning. Such an emphasis relates to a methodologically informed submission to and appropriation of the text's subject matter, rejecting a psychological approach to biblical hermeneutics. In one sense then,

---

120 Ibid., 389-390, (68, ET).

121 Ricoeur, "Philosophy and Religious Language," 75. "It is not enough to say that religious language is meaningful, that it is not senseless, that it makes sense, that it has a meaning of its own, and so forth. We have to say that its meanings are ruled and guided by the modes of articulation specific to each mode of discourse."

Ricoeur does not find Bultmann's emphasis problematic; however, in another sense, he does have a number of reservations. In addition to those already mentioned, there are two further points.[122]

First, Ricoeur questions Bultmann's presupposition that as moderns we must demythologize the biblical text to get at its non-mythological core. Perhaps it is us, on the contrary, who need to consider being demythologized, in the sense that our modern world is axed on a scientific and technological paradigm that often excludes myth as the bearer of a possible world—one which defies a techno-scientific reductionism.[123]

Ricoeur argues that *myth* should be understood by something other than a scientific demythologizing (myth should not necessarily be thought of in opposition to science) on the one hand, or by a merely pre-scientific mythological context on the other.[124] If myth is understood and re-defined as an avenue of expressing another world in the language of this world, or in other words, as a human being's attempt to understand the self in relation to the ground and boundary of their existence, its epistemological relevance begins to emerge. Inevitably, this view of myth requires an exegetical-explanatory movement within the interpretative procedure of understanding. This is because our understanding of myth pertains to its objective intention. Thus, in contrasting Ricoeur's biblical hermeneutics with Bultmann's, this point tenaciously holds on to the necessary relationship between understanding, explanation, and new understanding, which allows for a scientific - critical moment (an acceptance of and need for distance), while not being trapped within its constraints.

---

122 Against Frei, "The 'Literal Reading' of Biblical Narrative," 36-77; Vanhoozer, *Biblical Narrative*, 148-150, who argues that Ricoeur one sidedly follows Bultmann, thereby imposing a philosophical-general hermeneutics on biblical hermeneutics.

123 Ricoeur, "Le langage de la foi," *Bulletin du Centre Protestant d'Etudes* 16 (1964), 17-31, ("The Language of Faith," reprinted in: *Union Seminary Quarterly Review* 28 (1973), 203-212, "The Language of Faith," reprinted - cited in: *The Philosophy of Paul Ricoeur: An Anthology of His Work*, C. E. Reagan and D. Stewart, eds., Boston: Beacon Press, 1978, 227).

124 Ricoeur, "Préface," *Le conflit des interprétations*, 383, (*Essays*, 60, ET).

Second, Ricoeur finds Bultmann's references to, "God has acted," "word of God," and "future of God" to be inconsistent in the following manner. Ricoeur, quite rightly in our opinion, argues that Bultmann has merely exchanged the *critique* of what he designates the language of myth, for the *non-critique* of what becomes the language of faith. Such statements, for Bultmann, are neither historically, nor hermeneutically open to inquiry, in that they rest upon faith, engendering their full meaning from our act of compliance. Ricoeur, in his refusal to accept uncritically such a language of faith or its production of a fullness of meaning from our self-decision states:

> I do not say that this act of God, this word of God, find their sufficient condition in the objectivity of meaning; but they find their necessary condition there. The act of God has its first transcendence in the objectivity of meaning which it announces for us. The idea itself of announcement, of proclamation, of kerygma, presupposes, if I may say so, an initiative on the part of meaning, a coming to us of meaning, which makes speech a partner or correlate of existential decision. If the meaning of the text does not already confront the reader, how shall the act it announces not be reduced to a simple symbol of inner conversion [...]?[125]

Ricoeur refers to Bultmann's biblical hermeneutics as being a case in which the "object of faith" and "its foundation," are synthesized into the same thing, jeopardizing the very question of the meaningfulness that such biblical language and expression may have in their capacity as the "said" of the text. Faith, in this sense, loses the potential of being signified and thought, the latter two, as it were, being ultimately sacrificed on the same altar as much ancient biblical language.

In conclusion, it is our opinion that Bultmann's unwillingness to re-think biblical language is clearly a detriment to his exegesis and hermeneutics. Bultmann fails to take seriously enough the potential

---

125 Ibid., 390, (69, ET).

power of biblical language (in both its form and content), to have the genius to communicate meaningfully, be it to the pre-modern, modern, or subsequently even the post-modern person. Ricoeur's more finetuned approach creates a place for an operative philosophical-general hermeneutics as well as a biblical hermeneutics. This weighs heavily on the centrality of the biblical text in terms of its meaning, its world, the relevance of thinking through one's hermeneutics, and the importance of the fullness of biblical language. Thus, Ricoeur offers a more global, yet integrated biblical hermeneutics.

We then concur with Ricoeur's veritable exigency that all "short cuts" in biblical hermeneutics be avoided. His emphasis on the "long detour," is necessary, even essential, if we are to achieve a valid, while not yet final, understanding of the biblical text, as text. As we have seen, the justification of this long detour is to be found in the fact that the text itself, as the bearer of sense, must be accorded a rightful place in the hermeneutical endeavor. A *living hermeneutics* is required, even obligated, to move through the text. When the language or world of the biblical text is hermeneutically bypassed, it results in something other than biblical hermeneutics, as in the case of Bultmann, who it can be said, is more existentialist than biblical hermeneutist.

Lastly, throughout the course of this examination concerning philosophical hermeneutics and biblical hermeneutics, we have shown that Ricoeur, while not ignoring a philosophical-general hermeneutics and its pertinent application to biblical hermeneutics, remains consistent with his position that biblical hermeneutics finally culminates in subordinating philosophical-general hermeneutics to itself, as its own organon. Thus, as first demonstrated through the two inversing moments, and then second in his discussion with Bultmann, Ricoeur is disinclined to let a philosophical-general hermeneutics reign over a biblical hermeneutics.[126]

---

126 In arguing against Frei, "The 'Literal Reading' of Biblical Narrative," and Vanhoozer, *Biblical Narrative*, this is exactly what we have shown, Ricoeur is unwilling to do. In our viewpoint, Ricoeur's philosophical-general hermeneutics (contra Bultmann's as mentioned above), overlaps and synthesizes with biblical hermeneutics, while such an overlap or synthesis, neither de-prioritizes the biblical, nor need it be understood as dissolving the philosophical-general.

3.2.2. Methodology: its concerns and limits

We now turn to our second area of investigation in reference to Ricoeur's contribution to biblical hermeneutics: the question of methodology, with its concerns and limits. Ricoeur considers biblical exegesis, as the place of deliberation and confrontation, while the object of such exegesis is the literature of the biblical text.[127] His perspective aims to avoid the extremes of either the purist, who insists that there is the only one legitimate method, or the interweaver, who mixes and matches a number of methods irrespective of their potential incoherence. Ricoeur has suggested three methods for analysis: the historical-critical, the structuralist, and the hermeneutical.[128]

3.2.2.1. Historical Criticism

The historical-critical method, which Ricoeur considers a designation encompassing a diverse grouping of historical research, has been the method most frequently employed by biblical exegetes.[129] An important question for Ricoeur, while not by any means intending to devalue this method, is the relationship of the historical-critical method to philosophical historicism. Philosophical historicism, it can be argued, had its origin in what Ricoeur terms the failure of the Hegelian attempt to totalize history, resulting in absolute knowledge.

With Hegel's project in ruin, historicism understood history as a relativized history. This meant that history now needed a thorough investigation in order to measure the meaning and validity of an ancient text. Historians-interpreters exclusively questioned the historicity of texts and "exclusified history" became the only well-founded field of inquiry. If we may be allowed to say it so simply, Hegel aimed to put it

---

[127] Ricoeur, "Du conflit à la convergence des méthodes en exégèse biblique," in: *Exégèse et herméneutique*, X. Léon-Dufour, éd., Paris: Seuil, 1971, 35-53, esp. 35.

[128] Ibid., 35-53.

[129] Ibid., 36. Ricoeur mentions several examples: "histoire de la langue, du sens des mots, de leur emploi, - histoire des institutions sociales, des modes de vie, des milieux rédactionnels, histoire des sources, histoire critique des formes." (the history of language, the sense of words and their use – history of social institutions, lifestyles, the editorial environment, source history, history of critical forms). (My translation).

all together, while historicism intended to pull it all apart. Yet, for both "history" is the means to the end. Generally speaking, the effects of philosophical historicism and the historical-critical method in biblical hermeneutics can be considered as both *positive* and *negative*.

First, on the *negative* side, they frequently entrenched and focused biblical hermeneutics exclusively in and on the historical, in other words, on what is, in Ricoeurian terminology, "behind the text." The key factor in referring to this side as the negative side is connected to the "exclusive," single-mindedness, often attached to this method. In our opinion, with such an exclusive emphasis on, and over-reading of history, the interpreter of the ancient text became entangled in the enticing web of infiltrating historical realities. Often, the detrimental result was an inconsiderable emphasis on, and under-reading of the text itself (not all biblical texts present themselves generically as exclusively historically focused texts), along with any present day concerns. Textness and present-ness were unfortunately enveloped in and with a one-dimensional interest in historical affairs, bringing about an irreconcilable rupture between the then and the now.

Permit us a slight digression in order to consider the broader problematic of modernism and post-modernism, before moving on to the positive side. On the one hand, the exclusive concern for the historical mode of investigation as the only legitimate manner of validating the meaning of an ancient text is a modernist orientation. Post-modernism, on the other hand, has radically questioned the necessity of, and even desire to investigate history, affirming the present and its concerns as the sole and exclusive domain of useful inquiry.[130] The validity and meaning of ancient texts is not to be sought in their historicity, but rather in their relation to present interpreters and their interests. We would argue that both interpretative movements, in their exclusivity, fail to reckon with the weighty resistance of the biblical text, in its refusal to be *captured* by one extreme or the other.

---

130 See 1.1. for a fuller view of modern and post-modern perspectives.

Second, on the *positive* side, we agree with Ricoeur's assessment that the usefulness of the historical-critical method cannot be replaced. Ricoeur judiciously argues that many of the biblical texts we read are witnesses to historical events (he appeals to 1 Cor 15:3-8, Christ died, was buried [...] was raised [....] and appeared [...]) and that these events gave rise to the text in the first place.[131] Thus, we are not only interested in texts, but also in the historical character of the events that the texts articulate. This, in our point of view, is entirely justifiable, for example, in regard to the gospel texts, which do not exist for themselves, but testify to occasions of narrative activity (announcements, controversies, and sufferings), resulting in the formation of a narrative plot.[132] Ricoeur states, in reference to the validity of the historical-critical method:

> Why can't it be replaced? Essentially, because the texts that we read in the last instance are not texts about texts but testimonies that themselves are connected to events. This is the target of the text.

> Pourquoi ne peut-elle être remplacée? Essentiellement parce que les textes que nous lisons ne sont pas en dernier ressort des textes sur des textes mais sur des témoignages portant eux-mêmes sur des événements. C'est là la visée du texte.

> One can summarize in the following terms the fundamental motive of the historical-critical method: exegesis is not a reflection on the codes that govern the text, but through the text itself a manner of returning to testimonies that are the origin of the texts. The relation event-testimony is the referent of the text.

> On pourrait résumer dans les termes suivants le motif fondamental de la méthode historico-critique: l'exégèse n'est pas une réflexion sur

---

131 Ricoeur, "From Proclamation to Narrative," 501-512, esp. 501-502.
132 Ibid., 501-504.

les codes qui président au texte, mais, par le moyen des textes, une manière de revenir aux témoignages qui sont à l'origine des textes. La relation événement-témoignage est le référent du texte.[133]

Furthermore, Ricoeur welcomes historical criticism from a perspective that recognizes both biblical text and reader as being historically situated. This recognition is not only a condition of continuity, but also of objectivity and distance, that makes a historical-critical analysis viable, even essential.[134]

We conclude that the ongoing value of the historical-critical method is found in its legitimate concern for history recounted in relationship to the biblical text, based on witness and event.[135] In our opinion, the penetrating and pain-staking analysis of historical research has produced numerous benefits for a better understanding of the biblical text. Interpreters now know more than they did previously about the historico-cultural context and environment from which the biblical texts were composed. Form criticism, redaction criticism, narrative criticism, and others, have all made significant contributions to our understanding of both Testaments. The amount of literature, based in the historical-critical method, and referring to the biblical texts is next to none. In spite of so many contemporary hermeneutical tendencies and options, the historical-critical method remains an important link in the hermeneutical movement of interpreting the biblical text.

In concisely analyzing the general merits and defects of the historical-critical method, we have seen something of the potential values and hazards of such a method for biblical hermeneutics. In the light of this value - hazard ratio, Ricoeur argues for the *irreplacibility* of the method, but also points out this does not preclude its need for *rectifica-*

---

133 Ricoeur, "Esquisse de conclusion," in: *Exégèse et herméneutique*, 291. Also, "Événement et sens," in: *Révélation et histoire. La théologie de l'histoire*, E. Castelli, éd., Paris: Aubier, 1971, 15-34. (My translation).

134 Ricoeur, "Esquisse de conclusion," 291-292.

135 Ricoeur, "L'enchevêtrement de la voix et de l'écrit," in: *Religion, Parole, Ecriture*, Milan: Biblioteca dell'Archivio di Filosofia, 1992, 233-247, reprinted - cited in: *Lectures III*, Paris: Seuil, 1994, 314-315.

tion. He envisions this rectification developing in three directions, and each is related to his interpretation theory. These are: source, author, and audience.[136]

Ricoeur's position regarding the source of the text goes no further back than the text itself. In other words, the diachronic dimension of the text is to be found within the text, which is what articulates and makes understood its own sources. Ricoeur states:

> It is not the source that makes the text understandable, but the text that chooses and articulates its sources.
>
> Ce n'est pas la source qui fait comprendre le texte, mais le texte qui choisit et articule ses sources.
>
> [...] the origin of the text itself is a function of the text, of this text; understanding is always a back and forth from the text to its source and its sources to the text; in this bi-directional voyage the diachronic dimension remains a dimension of the text.
>
> [...] l'origine d'un texte est elle-même une fonction du texte, de ce texte; la compréhension se fait donc toujours dans l'aller et retour du texte à ses sources et de ses sources au texte; sur ce double trajet la dimension diachronique reste une dimension du texte.[137]

Ricoeur questions interpretive attempts to go "behind the text," seeking to reach or reconstruct its source in some historical or psychological fashion independent of the text. For Ricoeur, a better explanation and understanding of the biblical text can only come about by an interpretive orientation that moves through the text. In this sense, the critic's ability to understand the source cannot be founded on the source itself (as sources

---

136 For a fuller presentation of Ricoeur's interpretation theory see 3.1. - 3.1.3. .
137 Ricoeur, "Esquisse de conclusion," 292. (My translation).

are simply no longer available to us). This, in Ricoeur's opinion, is the first "illusion" of the historical-critical method that must be amended.

Ricoeur's second rectification of the historical-critical method aims to develop a different view of the author, and of authorial intent. Again, in relation to his interpretation theory, Ricoeur is not against the author or the authored intent of the text per se. We must recall that texts, in his opinion, are never merely a series of inter-connected codes. Rather, they are structurally authored messages. What Ricoeur challenges is the interpretative tendency, which supposes that the intent of the author is to be discovered in an attempt to uncover the psychological or experiential portrait of that author. Ricoeur points out:

> The author is precisely the one that denounces or announces the text, by a self-reference as the one who writes; the author is the author of this text. In a certain sense the author is a function of the text; this does not signify renouncing a recovery of the author's intent; [...] but that what is important to discover is that the notion of authorship is not a psychological notion, but rather a hermeneutical augmentation, a function of the text itself.

> L'auteur est précisément celui que dénonce ou annonce le texte, par rétro-référence à celui qui l'a écrit; l'auteur c'est l'auteur *du* texte. Lui aussi est d'une certaine façon une fonction du texte; cela ne signifie pas qu'il faille renoncer à retrouver l'intention d'un auteur; [....] mais ce qu'il importe de découvrir, c'est que la notion d'auteur n'est pas une notion psychologique, mais précisément une grandeur herméneutique, une fonction du texte lui-même.[138]

For Ricoeur, the author's intent is only found in the text. The recovery and restitution of an author's life experience, however, is not the goal of hermeneutics. From Ricoeur's standpoint, there are no hermeneuti-

---

138 Ibid., 292. (*Italics his.*) (My translation).

cal grounds for inaugurating, or setting in motion a search for hidden subjectivities "behind the text" that will supposedly result in a better understanding and explanation of the sense and reference of that text. This, in a Ricoeurian perspective, is the second "illusion" of the historical-critical method that must be modified.

Ricoeur targets the audience as a third sphere of the historical-critical method needing revision. In regards to the original or contemporary audience, Ricoeur calls for the most vehement anti-psychologism yet.

> This, perhaps, is where psychologism must be tracked dowm with more vigor. The sense is not what an original audience understood; but neither is it what the present, modern, reader projects back onto the text. All psychologism or all sociology of the reader or author must also be combatted.
>
> C'est peut-être ici que le psychologisme doit être pourchassé avec le plus de vigueur. Le sens n'est pas ce qu'a compris un prétendu destinataire originaire; mais il n'est pas non plus ce que le lecteur actuel, moderne, projette en arrière de lui sur le texte. Tout psychologisme ou tout sociologisme de << lecteur >> doit être aussi combattu que le psychologisme ou le sociologisme de << l'auteur >>.[139]

Once again, in line with his interpretation theory, Ricoeur counters the idea that the sense of the text is carried through the psychological intentions of the author, resulting in an immediate psychological reception by the audience. Meaning, in this view, is pictured as transferred from one psyche to another. Such immediacy, however, for Ricoeur, does not exist. Rather, he argues, the sense of the text is mediated by and through the text itself. In other words, such textual sense is neither finally dependent on a discovery of authorial intention, nor on an original audience and its reception. The focus must be on the text as a

---

139 Ibid., 293.

semantically autonomous text that creates its own audience, comprising virtually anyone who can read. This, in Ricoeur's assessment, is the third "illusion" of the historical-critical method that must be altered.

In conclusion, we shall now elucidate the consequence of these three rectifications for biblical hermeneutics. In his critique of the historical-critical method, Ricoeur aims to re-direct biblical hermeneutics to the biblical text, its sense, and its world. A major liability of the historical-critical method is its one-sided preoccupation with history, often resulting in a potential under-reading of the text itself. As a "written" discourse, the biblical text achieves, in Ricoeur's hermeneutics, a semantic autonomy, severing it from its original situation.[140] This severing is not negative, however, since it focuses the interpretative effort on the objectivity of the text, rather than on a subject-to-subject transfer of meaning via an author or an audience.[141] A robust understanding of the biblical text has less to do with an original source, author, or audience, and more to do with the text, which in a sense, incorporates and disseminates all three.

Ricoeur's biblical hermeneutics, though mindful of the historical-critical method and its benefits, is in no way synonymous with it. In our estimation, his three rectifications begin to move him closer to a structuralist methodology, with its emphasis on the priority of the text as an object, while he nevertheless does not abandon history.[142] This *objective* turn provides Ricoeur with a critique of *subjectivist* tendencies that often result in a psycho-romanticist hermeneutics. In addition, such a prioritizing of the text restricts interpreters, through the passage of distance and objectification, from doing anything they desire with texts.

A Ricoeurian biblical hermeneutics is an attempt to allow the text to unfold its proposal of a *world*, letting speak what has been "said" within biblical discourse. The "said" has been inscribed in a diversity of

---

140 For a discussion of Ricoeur's view of the semantic autonomy of the text see 3.1.2.

141 Ricoeur, "The Model of the Text: Meaningful Action Considered as a Text," 46-150, *From Text to Action*, ("Le modèle du texte: l'action sensée considérée comme un texte," *Du texte à l'action*, 188-190, FT).

142 For a fuller discussion of a structuralist methodology see 3.2.2.2.

forms (structures) directly related to their contents (sense and referent), which in the biblical text, among other things, is called a new world, new covenant, and the kingdom of God.[143]

We find much to agree with in Ricoeur's rectifications of the excesses or "illusions" of the historical-critical method, such as his anti-psychologizing efforts, and text-centered emphasis, for example. Nevertheless, we question the pertinence of an attempt to seal off the biblical text from its situational context. In other words, in our opinion, the historical-critical method remains valuable, not only with regard to the text, as Ricoeur rightly argues, but also in relation to extra-textual research which may shed light on its valid interpretation. In our opinion, all such efforts to investigate the "behind the text," are not necessarily doomed to re-enforce the Romantico-psychologism that Ricoeur so adamantly rejects. Such extra-textual prospects could relate to a dialogical context where information is communicated from speaker to hearer, illuminating the time and environment in and from which a text originates. In addition to this, is it not legitimate to assume that certain references in a text would be more comprehensible if we knew more about the author (and their situation), than was included in the text? While it is true that we must be concerned with the rights of the text, is it not also relevant to discover as much as possible about an author by means of extra-textual information if available, in order to better understand and respect the rights of the author's text as well?[144]

---

143 Ricoeur, "Herméneutique philosophique et herméneutique biblique," *Du texte à l'action*, 126, ("Philosophical and Biblical Hermeneutics," 95-96, *From Text to Action*).

144 J. V. D. Hengel, *The Home of Meaning: The Hermeneutics of the Subject of Paul Ricoeur*, Washington: University Press of America, 1982, 39, who argues that the auditory references in James Joyce's *Finnegan's Wake* become more understandable on the basis of the extra-textual information that such references to a heightened sense of hearing, were due to the fact that when Joyce wrote he was almost completely blind. Also Ricoeur, *The Philosophy of Paul Ricoeur*, Hahn, ed., 494-497, who himself indicates that his writing of certain texts can be better understood by a knowledge of situational contexts that may not appear in the text itself.

3.2.2.2. Structuralism

We shall now turn to an examination of the method of structuralism.[145] Ricoeur, in his writings, has devoted a greater amount of space to this method in comparison to the historical - critical method. Unfortunately, we cannot begin to do justice to all he has written on the subject. Our aim, after a brief introduction to structuralism, will again be to concisely analyze and evaluate, from Ricoeur's standpoint, the potential merits and failings of a structural methodology in reference to biblical hermeneutics.

Structuralism, at the very least, is a *science of linguistics*, often applied to texts, rendering language an object for empirical investigation.[146] Generally speaking, structuralism is what initiated the movement that brought about a reversal of philosophical historicism. In other words, this method is not interested in history per se, but prefers system to history.[147] Ferdinand de Saussure and his distinction between "langue" and "parole," set the movement in motion.[148] Language can be defined as the social conventions or rules allowing for its own use and exercise. Speech is to be understood as the actual activity of speaking persons. The greater, even exclusive, focus of structuralism becomes language as a system of signs, a focus relegating speech and speaking subjects to a non-scientific status without importance. This effacing of "la parole" and an embracing of "la langue," results in semiotic closure. It prioritizes the *synchronic* (present time), which in turn re-enforces a restricted interest in signs. [149] Ricoeur states:

---

145 See also 3.1.2..

146 This is related to the distinction between "la langue" and "la parole" with "la langue" being the objective - scientific and "la parole" the subjective - non-scientific. Structuralism, however, also relates to a wide range of disciplines including anthropology, politics, etc.

147 Ricoeur, "Structure et herméneutique," *Le conflit*, 31-63, esp. 35, ("Structure and Hermeneutics," 27-61, esp. 31, *The Conflict*).

148 F. de Saussure, *Cours de linguistique générale*.

149 Ricoeur, "Biblical Hermeneutics," 49-50. A structuralist perspective often argues for such a synchronic application to, for example, narratives. The system and its relations is said to function synchronically, thereby abolishing any diachronical element. Ricoeur disputes this, arguing, "the structural analysis replaces the syntagmatic sequence by a paradigmatic order." Such a replacing is unjustified. The linear, temporal, or diachronic unfolding of events in narratives remains essential to the narrative in the following way. Ricoeur proposes a corrective, following Greimas, of the possibility that

This separation means much more than just sharing skills as required by the division of labor it involves; it implies, philosophically, the priority of the synchronic over the diachronic; and this priority is a priority in the order of intelligibility; what one understands first, are the arrangements of signs in a slice of the present, in a layer of simultaneity in a state langue.[150]

Inherent in the reign of a synchronic system of signs is the de-absolutizing and de-signifying of words, which, in and of themselves, have no substance, only a form. This results in a closed relationship of words in relation to one another, as well as an antagonism toward words being able to bear meaning beyond their intersignification. Along these lines, langue is to be understood as a closed system of signs - terms, self-contained within itself, with no reference to a world.[151] A structuralist method, in this sense, as applied to texts, leaves the interpreter "inside" the text; a text that is viewed merely as a series of signs related to and in opposition with other signs.

Thus, the structural point of view as a linguistic science excludes a number of things: first, the speaking subject and the act of speaking, second, history, third, the capacity and intention of language, in a speaker-hearer context, for example, to say something (sense) about something (reference) that corresponds to reality and is expressed as such.

Structuralism as a method applied to texts can be considered to have both a *positive* and *negative* impact on biblical hermeneutics. First, on the *negative* side, Ricoeur distinguishes between the validity of a struc-

---

synchronic structure, in fact, "makes more prominent the diachronical residue of the analysis." This opening toward the diachronic provides the possibility of a twofold (non-reductionistic) interpretation of narrative, one emphasizing the structure, the other the diachronic element, with the narrative itself as the mediator of both. Also, "Du conflit," 35-53, esp. 43.

150 Ricoeur, "Du conflit," 35-53, esp. 37. (My translation).

151 Ricoeur, "Biblical Hermeneutics," 51. Ricoeur points out that Roland Barthes is an important example of this. See Barthes, "Introduction à l'analyse structurale des récits," *Communications* 8 (1966), 1-27, esp. 27. Ricoeur argues that from Barthes perspective the autonomy of the text, "has the meaning of completely abolishing the referential dimension of language." From the referential viewpoint language is a celebration and adventure of language alone.

turalist *analysis* and a structuralist *ideology* or *philosophy*.[152] He affirms the former with certain limitations, but eschews the latter without reservation. We shall first examine Ricoeur's negation of structuralism as ideology and other drawbacks of this approach, before moving on to the affirmative.

In Ricoeur's opinion, when the analysis of structuralism propagates itself as an *ideology* it has obliterated its raison d'être, sacrificed a critical awareness of the object (language) of its investigation, and uncritically affirmed as absolute what is merely an event.

> That language is an object goes without saying, so long as we maintain the critical awareness that this object is entirely defined by the procedures, methods, presuppositions, and finally the structure of the theory which governs its constitution. But if we lose sight of this subordination of object to method and to theory, we take for an absolute what is only a phenomenon.[153]

It is precisely, at this stage, that structuralism can begin to move from analysis to tyranny,[154] setting itself up as an "absolute formalism," or in other words, a "transcendentalism without a subject," or a "global mode of thought," which often then results in an all-encompassing ideology.[155] Such an ideology seeks an exclusive reign not only over language, but also over human being itself. In place of the discourse-speaking subject who says something about something to somebody, structuralism installs an anonymous system of codes that functions according to its own rules. What inevitably becomes the exclusive interest of analysis is

---

152 Ricoeur, "Structure et herméneutique," 54, ("Structure and Hermeneutics," 51).

153 Ricoeur, "La structure, le mot, l'événement," ("Structuralisme. Idéologie et méthode"), *Esprit*, mai 1967, 801-821, reprinted in: *Le conflit*, 80-97, esp. 85, ("Structure, Word, Event," reprinted in: *Philosophy Today* 12 (1968), Summer, 114-129, reprinted and cited in: *The Conflict*, 79-96, esp. 84).

154 Ricoeur uses the words "intimidation" and "terrorism." ("Structure, Word, Event," *The Conflict*, 85). *Le conflit*, 86.

155 Ricoeur, "Structure et herméneutique," 55-56, ("Structure and Hermeneutics," 52-53). Also, *Interpretation Theory*, 6.

the code, which functions in the structure of the text as the message of the text. In other words, the code is the message, results in the code is the message, which culminates in only the code is the message.[156]

It is our contention that structuralism's claims, in their *ideological rhetoric*, do a disservice to hermeneutics. This ideology is enclosed within itself, no longer functioning as an analytical tool, but rather as an absolute system. The result is a structuralist bias, which attempts to force a compliance with the system - "inside" the text. But this inside leaves the interpreter ensnared within the consequences of a never-ending communication about communication, with no potential way, theoretically, referentially, or textually, out. This bias, in its exclusivity, is in danger of bringing both the text and its message to its death—a death with no resurrection. Ricoeur, insightfully states:

> Structuralist ideology starts with the reversal of code and message, marking the code as essential and the message as unessential. And it is because this step is taken that the text is killed as message [....] .
>
> Only the way back from code to message may both do justice to the message as such and pave the way to move from structure to process.[157]

We would argue, in its "ultra-structuralist" sense, structuralism as applied to texts, embeds biblical hermeneutics in a text without a subject, a code without a context, a language without a referent, and a synchrony without a diachrony. The excesses of a structuralist ideology render biblical hermeneutics a dead end, leaving text and interpreter in the solitude of a universe of signs that speak only of and to themselves.[158]

Once again, if, as in the case of the historical-critical approach discussed previously, a form of analysis unalterably re-creates itself as a

---

156 Ricoeur, "Biblical Hermeneutics," 56-57. Ricoeur refers to Louis Marin's approach to biblical hermeneutics as "ultra-structuralist."

157 Ricoeur, "Biblical Hermeneutics," 65. (*Italics his*).

158 Ibid., 65.

universal, exclusive, or sole agenda for textual interpretation, the inevitable and detrimental result is a paradigmatic reductionism. In our opinion, the implied fullness and totalizing statements of such perspectives are often a telling mark against them and their claims to exclusivity. It is ironic, how in today's looming battles between analytical approaches (but also a battle for being or non-being, among other things), the ones which become ideologies claiming absolute comprehension of the world are frequently incurably reductionistic.

From the standpoint of the previous paragraph, we would also argue that both modernism and post-modernism are examples of ideologies that are finally *reductionistic* in this broader sense. Paradigmatically, both attempt to function as an exclusive worldview. For example, both the historical-critical and the structural - deconstruction-reading strategies are two outworking of modernist and post-modernist trajectories. Further evidence of the failure of such reductionistic tendencies is to be found in the inability of either ideology to be entirely sufficient within itself, whether as entire worldviews, or in reference to biblical hermeneutics in particular. Exclusivism, as it were, is not what it appears to be. Unmasked for their reductionism, these ideologies desperately need to borrow from what does not belong to them.

The negative aspects of structuralism as ideology mentioned in the last few paragraphs now gives way to a discussion of additional drawbacks of the structuralist perspective. A use of linguistic sciences or structural analysis in biblical hermeneutics, when exclusively focalized on "la langue," entrenches a study of the biblical text in, what we would argue is, a "sens unique," or a "uni-directional" movement from which there is no return. Linguistic sciences, for example have a place, but only a place within the hermeneutical process. In our opinion, linguistics, or system ratiocination (structural analysis), cannot be the sole aim of biblical hermeneutics. We contend that such an over-emphasis on linguistic-code-system as applied to texts categorically results in a negation of the message, or the "said" of the biblical text for the following reasons.

Any absolute restriction or reduction of texts to codes effectively executes speakers and enthrones structure, leaving texts caught in a *web of signs* that structurally cannot, in and of themselves, communicate anything other than a communication about communication. Furthermore, from a structuralist viewpoint the biblical text is autonomous, bracketing out the subject, as well as eradicating the referent, which as we have seen in Roland Barthes opinion, renders the text a celebration of language and language alone.[159] These two aspects of a structuralist textual autonomy are unnecessarily restrictive. With no speaking subject, no external referent, and closed within a universe of signs, the text is now a prisoner, forbidden from saying something about something.[160] This understanding of a text as a web of codes inaugurates a continual intra-linguistic motion that never ends, leaving the text with no way back from its structure to its sentences, from its sentences to its sense, and from its sense to its world.

It is however "la parole" (the author's intention to say) that results in the said (structure and sense), which in turn, extra-linguistically says something about something (reference). In this perspective, "la parole" has the capacity to "discourse-speak" a message, whereas, "la langue" is left virtually "speechless" within a system of signs.[161] In conclusion, structuralism expresses itself through a totalizing ideology that becomes an absolute system saturated with an exclusive interest in code, analytically and linguistically related to a thorough and final opposition between "la langue" and "la parole," which results in the entombing of "la parole," within "la langue."[162]

---

159 Barthes, "Introduction à l'analyse structurale des récits," esp. 27. " 'ce qui arrive,' c'est le langage tout seul, l'aventure du langage, dont la venue ne cesse jamais d'être fêtée." ('what arrives,' is language alone, the adventure of language, and its coming never ceases to be celebrated). (My translation).

160 Ricoeur, "Contribution d'une réflexion sur le langage à une théologie de la parole," in: *Exégèse et herméneutique*, 307. Also, "The Hermeneutical Function," 85 *From Text to Action, (Du texte à l'action*, 113, FT). "Herméneutique philosophique et herméneutique biblique," *Du texte à l'action*, 128, ("Philosophical and Biblical Hermeneutics," 97, *From Text to Action*).

161 Ricoeur, "Esquisse de conclusion," 290, "Une théorie de l'écriture qui serait un simple démarquage d'une théorie de la langue passerait entièrement á côté du problème central du langage: la mise en oeuvre de la langue dans le discours, que celui-ci soit oral ou écrit." (A theory of writing that is solely the marking of a theory of la langue entirely side-steps the central problem of language: the production of la langue in oral or written discourse). (My translation).

162 Ricoeur, "Contribution," 310-311.

Let us now move on to the *positive* side of structural analysis. We agree with Ricoeur's appraisal. In spite of the immoderation of ultra-structuralism, a valid structural analysis of the biblical text is not only helpful, but also essential to the task of biblical hermeneutics.[163] An investigation into text's structure has the potential to disclose new avenues of meaning that the historical critic may not have unveiled. A structural analysis of the biblical text does have a role, but one which does not function as an exclusive or comprehensive system for discovering the meaning of the text. We envision a structural analysis as *a* movement, as opposed to the *only* movement, in what we have chosen to call a "living hermeneutics." There is a necessary movement to the deep structures (la langue) of the text, but also a required movement from these to the surface-structures (la parole). As Ricoeur states:

> I call a dead end not all-structural analysis, but only the one which makes it irrelevant, or useless, or even impossible to return from the deep-structures to the surface-structures.[164]

Since a structural method of textual analysis centers on the deep structures of the text, it has in turn initiated and required a greater degree of concern in exegeting the biblical text. This highlights the necessity of a heightened textual awareness pertaining to the gravity of signification, embedded in and through the text's structure.[165] In exchange for a historical or psychological emphasis, structural analysis focuses on a semiotic accentuation, which is more concerned with how language is saying, than with what it is saying. From Ricoeur's interpretative point of view, focusing on the text's structure elevates the function of the language it employs, as well as its encoding and signification, all of

---

163 Ricoeur, "Biblical Hermeneutics," 64-65, 68-69.

164 Ibid., 65. Also, "Qu'est-ce qu'un texte? Expliquer et comprendre," *Du texte à l'action*, 154-155, ("What is a Text? Explanation and Understanding," 120-121, *From Text to Action*).

165 Ricoeur, "Contribution," 307-310. "Structure et herméneutique," 33, ("Structure and Hermeneutics," 30).

which are legitimate concerns for an informed biblical hermeneutics.[166] Essentially, what this means is that when it comes to interpreting the biblical text there must be a consideration of its structure, expressed through the rigor of a meticulous structural analysis. This will provide some measure of objectification and distance, in an effort to uncover and explain the grammatical base upon which the discourse is constituted.

When these concerns are valued, the analysis is empowered to view the text as an object. Thus, text as object affirms it as a scientifically analyzable, and no longer ultimately dependent on its author, its audience, or its situational context. Such an objectifying of the text is, in Ricoeur's perspective, vital for assigning the text a non-psychologized worth. Hence, this recognition renders the text suitable for critical examination, which therefore makes this moment in Ricoeur's trajectory so crucial to his interpretation theory.[167]

Text as object also engenders a perspective of the text as synchronic. Such an emphasis, from our viewpoint, while problematic for the text as a whole is nevertheless valuable in terms of an understanding of biblical words, as the final text, is of ultimate concern. A synchronic corrective here complements, though many times even effaces a more dubious diachronic analysis. Ricoeur affirms:

> We can no longer mix, as has so often been the case, even in significant works such as Kittel's Theological Dictionary, the synchronic and diachronic points of view; it is not valid to put in the same sequence the different senses of a word from different periods of time. James Barr, in an important work on biblical Semantics, shows that many of the works on biblical semantics do not satisfy certain structural requirements, which are current today in linguistics, notably the distinct synchronic and diachronic points of view.[168]

---

166 Ricoeur, "Biblical Hermeneutics," 68.

167 Ricoeur, "The Hermeneutical Function," 82-84, *From Text to Action*, (*Du texte à l'action*, 109-110).

168 Ricoeur, "Contribution," 308-309. (*Italics his*.) (My translation).

Biblical hermeneutics, because of the work of scholars such as James Barr and the stimulus of a structural analysis, has become increasingly aware of the necessity to analyze the biblical text synchronically and linguistically, according to the rules and conventions of how language actually functions within a given context.[169]

Thus, an outstanding value of the structural method for biblical hermeneutics is its uncompromising emphasis on the text. Such an anti-subjectivist restricting of textual interest to the text alone can lead to more careful attention being paid to the codification of language, its "how" of saying, and the mechanisms through which the text is "said." This in turn, has the capacity to contribute to a more objective explanation of the biblical text with an attesting to and affirming of an interpretative distance that should lead to a better understanding of the text's subject matter. Ricoeur states:

> This is precisely where the benefit, for the idea of truth, passes through the objectivation and distanciation required by structural analysis; the distancing of the text shelters it from subjectivist fantasies. Structural analysis forbids one from doing anything whatever one wants with a text.

> C'est précisément ici le bénéfice, pour l'idée de vérité, du passage par l'objectivation et par la distanciation que requiert l'analyse structurale; cette mise à distance du texte le met à l'abri des fantaisies subjectivistes. L'analyse structurale interdit que l'on fasse n'importe quoi d'un texte.[170]

In our opinion, Ricoeur rightly affirms the utility, even necessity, of the *analytical* as opposed to the *ideological* dimension of structuralism in the following sense. A literary analysis of the structure of the

---

169 J. Barr, *The Semantics of Biblical Language*, Oxford: Oxford University Press, 1961. Also, J. P. Louw and E. A. Nida, Greek - *English Lexicon of the New Testament: Based on Semantic Domains*, New York: United Bible Societies, 1988.

170 Ricoeur, "Esquisse de conclusion," 295. (My translation).

biblical text is arguably an appropriate moment, within the movement of the hermeneutical process; for understanding – explanation – new understanding.[171] This moment thus enables a structuralist analysis to provide biblical hermeneutics with a rigorous focus on the text that calls into question a subjectivist reading and thereby contributes to preventing a hermeneutical shortcut, which attempts to move from understanding to new understanding, without explanation.

Having succinctly considered the general benefits and drawbacks of structuralism as they pertain to the biblical text, we have opened up some of the potential advantages and disadvantages of such an approach. From Ricoeur's perspective, as we have seen, structural analysis is an *indispensable* moment in biblical interpretation. However, in his opinion, this does not suggest that structuralism has no need of critical qualification and revision in its application to the biblical text. Ricoeur envisions a revision-qualification that unfolds in at least three areas, each of which can be linked to his interpretation theory.

First, in opposing any absolutist views concerning structuralism, Ricoeur challenges the exclusive and enveloping character of such an applied method in that it reduces, through extension, the possibilities of language or text. This extension of the structural orientation (the opposition of la langue to la parole) to texts is a daring endeavor. Is not a text more on the side of parole - or speech - than of langue? Is it not a succession of utterances, hence in the last analysis, a succession of sentences? These questions show, at least that the extension of the structural method, borrowed from the level of la langue, and transferred to the level of la parole and of discourse, either spoken or written, does not exhaust the field of possible attitudes in regard to a text. Thus, we must take this extension of the linguistic model to the domain of texts as one of several possible approaches and not the sole approach to the text.[172]

In this sense, the structuralist perspective by ignoring the sentence,

---

171 Ibid., 290.

172 Ricoeur, "Biblical Hermeneutics," 52.

la parole, and discourse, becomes incapable of viewing language or text as anything more than an absolute system. Ricoeur aptly suggests revising this method, arguing that while it (in a non-absolutist sense) remains beneficial for biblical hermeneutics, it must be modified by additional linguistic concerns and other methods, including the historical-critical and the hermeneutical. The inclusion of the latter two makes space for the relevance of history and la parole, within our understanding of language and texts.

Second, in questioning the structuralist perspective of language as absolute code or absolute object, Ricoeur addresses the issue of what actually takes place in the human experience of language.[173] He argues that the experience of language, both for those who speak and those who listen, intervenes to demarcate any absolutist-reductionism of this object. Ricoeur affirms:

> The experience we have of language reveals something of its mode of being which resists this reduction. For us who speak, language is not an object but a mediation. Language is that through which, by means of which, we express ourselves and express things. Speaking is the act by which the speaker overcomes the closure of the universe of signs, in the intention of saying something about something to someone; speaking is the act by which language moves beyond itself as sign toward its reference and towards what it encounters. Language seeks to disappear; it seeks to die as an object.[174]

It is equally our assessment (following Ricoeur), that within such a structuralist reductionism, la langue reigns and la parole is silenced. This not only renders speaking subjects unable to speak, but undermines any potential unificatory moment in which language is under-

---

173 We must recall here, that for Ricoeur, language may be an object, but it is never an object in and of itself. See also Ricoeur, "Esquisse de conclusion," 293, Ricoeur, "La Structure, le mot, l'événement," 85, *Le conflit*, ("Structure, Word, Event," *The Conflict*, 84). Also, "Contribution," 311.

174 Ricoeur, "Structure, Word, Event," *The Conflict*, 84-85. ("La structure, le mot, l'événement," 85, *Le conflit*).

stood as both code and message. Ricoeur's position is preferable in arguing that in fact the inverse more accurately and acutely describes and accounts for the way language is experienced. In his opinion, the intention of language is to say something about something to somebody in a way that takes place through an act of speech. La langue does not speak; it is silent and therefore cannot reign. In this sense, language is de-throned, but not annihilated, as speech, and speech alone, is spoken by a subject who articulates both sense and reference.[175]

As a result of a structuralist reduction of language to la langue and an attempt to absolutize code, there is an *effacing* of message. This in turn results, at the expense of la parole, in what may be referred to as a *semiotic hubris*, culminating in a divestiture of the capacity and destiny of language to speak.[176] A legitimate aim here is to unify language, once again allowing it to speak, without effacing or absolutizing its differences from the act of speech. Ricoeur remarks:

> The task is then [...] to reclaim for the understanding of language what the structural model excluded and what perhaps is language itself as act of speech, as saying. [...]
>
> Our task appears to me to be rather to go all the way with the antinomy, the clear conception of which is precisely the ultimate result of structural understanding. The formulation of this antinomy is today the condition for the return to an integral understanding of language; to *think* language should be to think the unity of that very reality which Saussure has disjoined, the unity of language and speech.[177]

Seeking to modify the structural excess and exclusion of la parole,

---

175 Ricoeur, "Contribution," 311, "A vrai dire, la langue ne dit rien, la langue est muette. Toute parole signifiante comporte ces deux seuils de signifiance: seuil de sens et seuil de référence." (It is true, la langue says nothing, la langue is silent. All intelligible speech carries two levels of significance: the level of sense and the level of reference). (My translation).

176 Ricoeur, "La structure, le mot," 84-85, ("Structure, Word," 84).

177 Ibid., 86 (*Italics his*). (85, ET).

Ricoeur moves la parole, sense, reference, and the speaking subject, in the direction of his phenomenological roots. He does so in order to combat the loss of the speaker. In distinguishing a science of language from a philosophy of language, Ricoeur nevertheless sees the two as complementing one another. In our perspective, the goal of re-uniting what has been severed is essential to Ricoeur's biblical hermeneutics.[178] Without la parole, there is no message, no hermeneutics, no speaking. Ricoeur suggests, on the contrary, the place for a development of what he terms "une théologie de la parole,"[179] and affirms the centrality of both hermeneutics and la parole. Such a movement engenders an unavoidable confrontation with linguistics.

> At the same time, the work of une théologie de la parole is twofold, systematic and critical: the systematic work is to unify all the domains of theology under the concept < process of speech > (the internal constitution of its object); but critical work consisting in the confrontation of this hermeneutic of the process of speech with diverse disciplines that are connected to language.[180]

This confrontation is indispensable for biblical hermeneutics, which is then rightly obligated to dialogue with a diversity of interpretative moments. The goal here is a unifying of language, bringing together the parts of la langue and la parole; thus opening up a possibility for the biblical text to speak.

Third, in order to avoid an insufficient and non-productive sheer opposition of a phenomenology of speech, or une théologie de la parole (which may come too close to "psychologism," and a science of language), Ricoeur chooses another itinerary in his goal to accomplish the task of unifying language and speech. Unsurprisingly, he argues that it

---

[178] See also 3.1.2.2..

[179] Ricoeur, "Contribution," 301-302. Ricoeur's "théologie de la parole," merits much more space than we, at this point, can give it. It remains a question for further investigation in Ricoeur's thought.

[180] Ibid., 302, (parenthesis his). (My translation).

is reflectively, and at the semantic level, within a hierarchy of language levels that we are able to "think correctly" the reversal of language and speech.[181] Semantic, in this sense is not a mere signifying, but is understood as a saying of something; referring sign to thing. This saying takes place at the level of the sentence or utterance, again stressing the "actuality of event," speech, the instance of discourse and la parole, in contrast to the semiotic "virtuality of system."[182]

In conclusion, we elucidate the import of these three modifications for biblical hermeneutics. Ricoeur combats the structuralist methodological excess by pointing out its militant *reductionism*, which excludes other possible methods of textual investigation. While the structuralist model remains useful for biblical hermeneutics, its one-dimensionalism renders it an insufficient vehicle for articulating the complex hermeneutical motion we have described. Again, ours is a movement from the production of textual sense and reference in understanding to new understanding as it pertains to God, history, self, and world, all skillfully embedded in the biblical text. As such, the structuralist method suffices as an explanatory moment, but in its own terms and on its own grounds, it is limited from taking us any further.

In addition to this, the value of Ricoeur's innovative turn to semantics in response to a structuralist semiotic excess is that it anchors and interiorizes an interpretation theory within *language* itself, eschewing the mere positing of one theory versus another. In the aim to unify language by turning to the semantic and the sentence, we strike at the heart of the desire of language to say.[183] Thus, this step toward discourse moves from discourse as speech event, to discourse as meaning, to discourse as referential text.

Clearly, Ricoeur cannot be considered singularly structuralist as

---

181 Ricoeur, "La structure, le mot," 86, ("Structure, Word," 85).

182 See also 3.1.2..

183 Ricoeur, "La structure, le mot," 92, ("Structure, Word," 91).

an interpreter of the biblical text.[184] In our opinion, his three revision-qualifications move him closer to a linguistics of discourse, a philosophy-science of language, a phenomenology of speech, and a unique hermeneutics. The last of these aims to incorporate, albeit on its own grounds, the structuralist method, its view of language and the text, while nevertheless arguing that such a method is limited and in need of revision if it is to be useful for biblical hermeneutics.

Such a hermeneutics, in rejecting reductionism, engenders a sensitivity to history, the necessity of a re-constitution of la parole (based on a phenomenology of speech), a linguistics of semantics (understood as the science of the sentence, related to the concern of sense and referent), and a unifying of language. Together, these orientations allow for and recognize the capacity of the biblical text to discourse its message—a message that is more than merely a communication about communication. In this sense, we endorse Ricoeur's notion of the biblical text as discourse in its diversity of forms, as opposed to a structuralist referent-less intra-linguistic sign system. We affirm the text's capacity to break the chains of such a constriction through a robust biblical hermeneutics, one that acknowledges the *power* of the text to refer to extra-linguistic reality, as for example, to God.[185]

3.2.2.3. Hermeneutical

We shall now investigate what Ricoeur refers to as a hermeneutical method, which in his opinion is by far the most dis-engaged from our previous two methodological examinations.[186] In this section, our goal will again be to concisely analyze and evaluate potential benefits and defaults of the hermeneutical method in reference to biblical hermeneutics.

---

184 Against C. Amerding, "Structural Analysis," *Themelios* 4 (1979), 96-104, esp. 103, who incorrectly identifies Ricoeur as a "structuralist."

185 Ricoeur, "Contribution," 314-318. Also, "Herméneutique philosophique et herméneutique biblique," *Du texte à l'action*, 128-129, ("Philosophical and Biblical Hermeneutics," 97-98, *From Text to Action*). *Interpretation Theory*, 34.

186 Ricoeur, "Du conflit," 47, *Exégèse et herméneutique*.

Generally speaking, modern hermeneutical method, influenced by Schleiermacher and Dilthey, divides *explanation* from *understanding* in the following ways.[187] Explanation and understanding represent different fields of application in the natural and human sciences. Natural sciences, on the one hand, in their co-relation with and mirroring of nature, offer the suitable realm for facts, laws, and verifications, whereby one may say, they "explain" the subject matter at hand. Natural sciences, then, are described as methodical and objective. Human sciences, on the other hand, in their co-relation with human minds, find their scientific interest in the experiences of these other human minds. The human sciences focus on meaning, as humanly expressed in a diversity of forms, including speech and written texts, whereby one may say, they "understand." Thus, human sciences require the major principle of empathy in order for the understanding from one mind to another to occur, or for the possibility of entering another's mental life.[188]

According to Ricoeur, this division between explanation and understanding, for example in someone like Dilthey's hermeneutical orientations, meant that he was pre-disposed to use the same method and epistemology from the natural sciences and then apply this to the human sciences, notably to history. Dilthey aimed to render the human sciences as credible as the natural sciences.[189] For Dilthey, an epistemological notion of how historical knowledge produces understanding and the method by which such knowledge could be realized remains intact. But his emphasis on historical knowledge as understanding, albeit using the presumed reliability of the techniques of the natural sciences, came at the expense of severing historical knowledge from explanation. The task of understanding now belonged to the humanities, whereas explanation still belonged to the realm of nature.

Dilthey sought to methodologically confer upon the human scienc-

---

187 See also 3.1.1..

188 Ricoeur, *Interpretation Theory*, 71-75.

189 Ricoeur, "The Task," 58-60, *From Text to Action*, (82-85, FT). "Qu'est-ce qu'un texte?," *Du texte à l'action*, 137, ("What is a Text? Explanation and Understanding," *From Text to Action*, 105).

es the ideal of an objective scientific status, comparable to and analogous with the epistemology and method of the natural sciences.[190] History was thought to offer this objective environment; that is, one with a definitive, certain, and universally valid status for the understanding of human beings. Furthermore, Dilthey equated historical study with human being study, proposing the *ultimate* goal of self-knowledge. Thus, hermeneutics became an inquiry into the understanding of another mind, which surfaced through the historical expression of the life of that mind, as seen for example, in written texts.

This in turn, however, had the result of *relegating* the interpretation of written texts to the psychological investigation of another mind. Human beings are not alienated in the same way from each other as they are from a natural object. Human beings express signs of their existence; signs, which then provide an access-ability to understand and be understood by another human being. In reference to the interpretation of texts as an example of such sign expression, the emphasis is not essentially on what a text says, but on who says it. What is now primary is not the question of textual interpretation because the main focus is the value and continuity of the expression of a particular human mind, and how that mind is interconnected with the flow of history.

Hermeneutic method, constructed along these lines and when applied to written texts, has had both *positive* and *negative* impacts on biblical hermeneutics. First, regarding the *negative* impact, the inherent lack of synchronization between explanation and understanding reduces Diltheyian hermeneutics to a psychological enterprise. The result is an idealism (giving preference to the otherness of the writing mind) that inevitably forgoes the very objectivity that a hermeneuticist such as Dilthey so vigorously attempted to establish. Ricoeur writes:

---

190 For a hermeneuticist such as Gadamer, this is Dilthey's major problem. Gadamer argues that Dilthey capitulated to the ideals of the natural sciences, becoming pre-occupied with an Enlightenment - modernist, emphasis on method and objectivity. In Gadamer's opinion, the inherent historicity of all human understanding renders the ideal of objectivity or that of method per se, in the human sciences, essentially unachievable. Gadamer, *Truth and Method*, 5-10.

The question of objectivity thus persists in Dilthey's work as a problem that is both ineluctable and insoluble. It is ineluctable because of the claim to respond to positivism by an authentically scientific conception of understanding. Hence Dilthey continued to revise and perfect his concept of *reproduction*, rendering it always more appropriate to the demands of objectification. But the subordination of the hermeneutical problem to the properly psychological problem of the knowledge of others condemned him to search beyond the field of interpretation for the source of all objectification. [...]

Dilthey's work, even more than Schleiermacher's, brings to light the central aporia of a hermeneutics that subsumes the understanding of texts to the law of understanding another person who expresses himself therein.[191]

With an over-emphasis on the psychological, the biblical text is rendered a mere expression of a mind's life experiences. This underplaying of an interpretative interest in the text itself unavoidably results in a silencing of the biblical text in regard to its capacity to *speak* and present a *world* of its own. In this sense, when interpretation becomes a specific instance of understanding the author's mind alone, de-asservating the difference between speaking and writing, and de-relationalizing the dialectic of event and meaning, the possibility of explaining a text is negligible.[192]

Second, on the *positive* side, Dilthey made an important contribution to hermeneutics with his emphasis on the necessity of a mediation of meaning in order to realize self-knowledge. As such, Dilthey rejects the possibility of any understanding of the other or the self in an immediate sense. In his opinion, the interpreter must always pass through a detour, a detour of objectified signs, as manifested for ex-

---

[191] Ricoeur, "The Task," 61-62, *From Text to Action*, (*Italics his*). (85-86, FT).
[192] Ricoeur, *Interpretation Theory*, 73.

ample, in written texts. Ricoeur argues, that it is at this juncture that Dilthey "glimpsed" an appropriately interpretative manner of "transcending finitude," while at the same time, negating the fallacy of absolute knowledge.[193] For Ricoeur, the biblical text, as text, is then able to go beyond the narrow constriction of self-meaning. But this "going beyond" according to Ricoeur, does not culminate in complete knowledge. Rather, the offer, discovered through this interpretive detour, is of a world like no other world—the unfolding subject matter of the text itself.

Having briefly highlighted several key characteristics of the Diltheyian hermeneutical method, we have identified some general benefits and defaults in relation to the biblical text. As we have seen, the opposing of explanation and understanding, and the interpretative goal of establishing an inter-connection with the psychic life of another, results in the negative equating of a hermeneutical enterprise with a psychological enterprise. The grounding and ultimate justifying of hermeneutics on psychology, rather than on the biblical text and its world, presents significant shortcomings. At the same time, however, Dilthey's orientation towards a necessary detour through objectified signs in order to understand proves to have some traction for biblical hermeneutics.

We turn now to Ricoeur's view of hermeneutical method, which in our perspective, offers a unique contribution to the discussion. To properly understand the hermeneutical pole in Ricoeur's thinking, it is important to envision this method as a theory of interpretation.[194] As such, this theory should be articulated with at least two preliminary clarifications: first, a theory of interpretation is not an exclusive property of exegesis; second, hermeneutics is concerned with the relationship of the understanding and explanation of any text. Ricoeur, in reference to the hermeneutical method, states:

---

193 Ricoeur, "The Task," 63, *From Text to Action*, (87 FT).

194 Also see section 3.1.1..

Hermeneutics, or a theory of interpretation, does not have an exclusive link with exegesis. It should be the theory of what it means to understand in relation with explanation texts in general. If, therefore, hermeneutics can be called the reflective or reflexive part of exegesis, with respect to its theoretical dimension it significantly exceeds even systematic exegesis.

L'herméneutique, ou théorie de l'interprétation, n'a pas de lien exclusif avec l'exégèse. Elle veut être la théorie de ce que c'est que comprendre en relation avec l'explication des textes en général. Si donc l'herméneutique peut être appelée la partie réfléchie ou réflexive de l'exégèse, en tant qu'espace théorique elle déborde largement l'exégèse même systématisée.[195]

According to Ricoeur, in observing the motion of reflection, a hermeneutical method should be considered partially related to exegesis. However, the arc of this *motion* exceeds merely reflective or exegetical interests. With concerns beyond an exclusive posture of either reflection or exegesis, this method nevertheless incorporates the demands of both. Regarding a theory of interpretation, Ricoeur establishes a general theory of sense and a general theory of texts, both of which define and set the parameters for a general hermeneutics.[196] We must recall that essentially, for Ricoeur, a hermeneutical question or problem exists because there are texts—texts understood as the fixation of discourse by writing.[197]

A Ricoeurian hermeneutical method is distinct from a structuralist method, for example, in the sense that Ricoeur's interpretive action occurs on the level of the sentence, which is understood as a unified instance of discourse irreducible to its constituent parts. The structuralist method, however, focuses on a system of inner referential parts

---

195 Ricoeur, "Du conflit," 47, *Exégèse et herméneutique*. (My translation).

196 Ibid., 47.

197 Ibid., 47. Also "Biblical Hermeneutics," 67.

and whole, while Ricoeur's notion of discourse is connected to an *actual* event, related to a subject and a referent addressed to someone.[198] Working from the irreducibility of discourse and an affirmation of the sentence as that which grounds hermeneutics, Ricoeur goes on to argue that the most important distinctions between writing, texts, and speaking can only be articulated on the basis of discourse itself.

Ricoeur develops four key distinctions between the three genres of communication. First, the event of speaking as an instance of discourse is surpassed by a textual inscription and a fixed intentionality of meaning. Second, the written as discourse, is detached from its author who can only be found in the text. Third, the referent (like the author), is no longer ostensive, but radically modified by the orientation of the text. Such a modification, however, does not necessarily efface the dynamic ability of written discourse to reference the referent. Texts refer to worlds and possible ways of being in the world, regardless of whether or not ostensive reference is surpassed. Fourth, the audience of a written discourse is anyone who can read, exceeding the "you" to "me" closure of the immediate dialogical situation. With these four distinctions in place, Ricoeur is now able to affirm what he refers to as the "objectivity" of the text. This objectivity re-enforces his insistence on the place of a critical-explanatory movement in textual interpretation, which is now grounded in the hermeneutic method, as within the interpretive process itself.

> These four traits taken together constitute the "objectivity" of the text. From this "objectivity" derives a possibility of *explaining* which is not derived in any way from another field, that of natural events, but which is congenial to this kind of objectivity. Therefore there is no transfer from one region of reality to another – let us say, from the sphere of facts to the sphere of signs. It is within the same sphere of signs that the process of objectification takes place and gives rise

---

198 See 3.1.2..

to explanatory procedures. And it is within the same sphere of signs that explanation and comprehension are confronted.[199]

In addition to the *centrality* of discourse, there are at least two other components of Ricoeur's hermeneutical method related to the text. First, a concern for *literary genre* sheds light on particular kinds of texts and their distinguishing characteristics. In Ricoeur's approach, a mode of discourse is formed by the style and composition of the text, which in turn invites a structural "treatment" — interested in the communicative code of the speech acts voiced and preserved in such discourse. Thus, literary genres indicate the particular production processes of various works (parable, poem, etc.); processes that should be understood as the generators of message.

Second, an engagement with narrative illustrates the mutuality of code and message. Narratives function as the vehicle for both codes and messages, linking "la parole" and "la langue," which renders them methodologically significant for hermeneutics. Ricoeur agrees with Barthes' estimation that narratives function structurally on three levels: "functions" (the basic units of action), "actions" (as Greimas' actants), and narrative communication (the story).[200] The third level, concerned with the giveness and reception of the narrative as communication, goes beyond a view of narrative as self-contained, and thus opens it to a world. In this sense, methodological considerations are included, such as the significance of both the "giver" and "hearer" of the narrative. In addition to this, Ricoeur argues, for a referential dimension of narrative from the perspective of story telling as an experienced phenomenon. People tell stories to bring, among other things, order to their lives through a narrative "plot," the mimesis of actions and characters.

We shall conclude in the following manner. In Ricoeur's preferred

---

199 Ricoeur, "The Model of the Text: Meaningful Action Considered as a Text," 157, *From Text to Action*, ("Le modèle du texte: l'action sensée considérée comme un texte," *Du texte à l'action*, 199).

200 Barthes, "Introduction," 18, 21.

hermeneutical method, we are indeed far removed both from the Romantico-historicist hermeneutics of Schleiermacher and Dilthey, as well as from Gadamer's under-valuation of method. A Ricoeurian perspective of the text as meaningful, productive, narrated discourse, eschews any traces of anti-methodology, while in addition, incisively refutes the psychologistic movement *behind* the text as the goal of interpretation. This perspective thereby creates a new situation in which a discussion and dialectical integration can occur, without effacing the need for explanation and understanding. The integrative hermeneutical process takes its place in the realm of the human sciences, as expressed in the domain of textual interpretation. Ricoeur clarifies his position in the following way:

> If there is a feature which distinguishes me not only from the hermeneutic philosophy of Schleiemacher and Dilthey, but also from Heidegger and Gadamer (despite my great proximity to the work of the latter), it is indeed my concern to avoid the pitfall of an opposition between an 'understanding' which would be reserved for the 'human sciences' and an 'explanation' which would be common to the latter and the nomological sciences, primarily, the physical sciences.[201]

In Ricoeur's assessment, the valid interpretative *movement* from understanding, to explanation, to new understanding, necessitates an operative hermeneutical method. Such a method, however, must be capable of over-lapping with, but finally incorporating within itself, both a historico-critical (in modified form) and a structural analytical movement (within its limits), in which the motion of each is understood as necessary to and in relation with the other in reference to textual interpretation. Again, no singular method has the capacity to reign on its own. The fecundity of an interlacing of methodologies in tension

---

201 Ricoeur, "A Response by Paul Ricoeur," in: *Hermeneutics and the Human Sciences*, 36.

with one another, avoids a subverting of diversity or divergence between various methods in seeking to interpret the sense and reference of the biblical text.[202]

3.2.3. An Application to Biblical Parables

We intend to engage next a third dimension of Ricoeur's contribution to biblical hermeneutics. In order to move us a step further, we will explore how aspects of Ricoeur's interpretation theory and its methodologically pluralist approach are developed in reference to the biblical text. Specifically, we have chosen to work with biblical parables for several reasons. First, Ricoeur has written a number of essays on this subject, showing that despite the de-valuation of the ancient language, it is possible to listen to the parables of Jesus in a way that we are once again, "astonished, shocked, renewed, and put in motion."[203] Parable, therefore, seems a fitting region in which to explore Ricoeur's reading of the biblical text. How does Ricoeur read parables?

Second, the domain of parable is one of Ricoeur's most important contributions to the discussion of biblical hermeneutics; here he articulates the capacity of such texts to *redescribe* and *reveal* reality.[204] How do the biblical parables, as a mode of discourse, articulate the movement of understanding, explanation, and new understanding that is coherent with Ricoeur's hermeneutical concerns? Why might Ricoeur's perspective offer us a way forward between the restricted options left to us from the ashes of modernism and post-modernism? Parables will be a fruitful literary genre within which to explore a *living* hermeneutics.

Our aim is to proceed by first implementing Ricoeur's text interpretation theory with respect to parables, focusing on the two *pillars* of "sense" and "reference." In so doing, we will demonstrate the pertinence

---

202 Ricoeur, "Du conflit," 51-53, *Exégèse et herméneutique*.

203 Ricoeur, "Listening to the Parables," *Criterion* 13 (1974), 18-22, reprinted - cited in: *The Philosophy of Paul Ricoeur: An Anthology of His Work*, Reagan and Stewart, eds., 1978, 239-245, esp. 239.

204 Ricoeur, "Biblical Hermeneutics," 75. Also "Listening," 240.

of such a theory for a hermeneutics of parables, as well as its salient critique of modernist - post-modernist interpretative strategies, the latter as especially represented by the work of J. D. Crossan. Second, we develop a Ricoeurian analysis of the use of the historical-critical, structural, and hermeneutical methodological strategies concerning parables. Throughout this section, we affirm that Ricoeur does not attempt to give a complete exegesis of parables, but rather writes as philosopher of language seeking to contribute to the discussion of biblical hermeneutics.[205]

3.2.3.1. Parables: Crossan - Ricoeur

We turn now to the question of how Ricoeur's interpretation theory relates to his reading of parables. As we have seen, he is highly concerned with affirming that texts have both "sense" and "reference." How does this pertain to parables? Parabolic sense, Ricoeur argues, is not so much found in the central theme of the *Kingdom of God* and what it is compared to. Rather, the sense is revealed through what *happens* in the story. As readers, we may presume that the hearing audience to which the parables were spoken is historically situated in, and informed by the life-setting of the parable. The situations presented in the parables at first, would have been relevant and recognizable to these listeners. However, the hearer, at the same time, does not seem to fully grasp the sense of the parable at the instance of hearing it. We, therefore, as readers, are awakened to the parabolic relevance of the plot, its dramatic structure, and its denouement, producing a sense for us beyond the original context. The *dissonance* for the hearer at that time is also, what opens up the text for us now as readers. Ricoeur undoubtedly distances himself (developed further below) from the modernist single idea - general principle theory, that emanated from a focus on Aristotle's Rhetoric versus his Poetics (Jülicher),[206] and from post-modernist

---

205 Ricoeur, "Biblical Hermeneutics," 29.

206 A. Jülicher, *Die Gleichnisreden Jesu*, 2 Vols. Tübingen: Mohr, 1910. Jülicher thought that the parables of Jesus made one point.

theories, which argue that parabolic texts in and of themselves lack the capacity to mean or refer extra-linguistically. The latter usually takes one of two forms: parables do not disclose, they solitarily and formally subvert; or parables only have the capacity to mean, what their readers make them mean.[207]

Since there has already been a tremendous amount of attention given to the work of Jülicher and other modern interpreters of parables, we have chosen to concentrate on what has been suggested in this study to be a post-modern viewpoint. A closer look at this orientation will be useful in bringing more sharply into focus the hermeneutical distance between Ricoeur and a post-modernist perspective on biblical parables.[208]

We find, in the work of J. D. Crossan,[209] one of the most significant commentators of biblical parables over the last twenty-five years, an illuminating *literary* and *theological* analysis of Jesus' parables.[210] Crossan focuses on a number of questions and issues related to the interpretation of parables. We shall limit ourselves, however, to one of his particular concerns: why is there such a multiplicity of interpretations of parables, and such differences between those interpretations?[211] We have already briefly referred to the post-modernist (as defined in the Introduction) interpretative tendencies of Crossan.

---

207 See for example Crossan, *The Dark Interval*, 121, and *Raid on the Articulate*, 44, who argues for an entirely negative functioning of metaphor and parable, ultimately rendering language itself, a failure and contradiction. Taylor, "Masking: Domino Effect," *JAAR* 54 (1986), 547-557, esp. 554. Fish, *Is There A Text?* 3. W. Harnisch, *Die Gleichniserzählungen Jesu: Eine hermeneutische Einführung*, UTB 1343, Göttingen: Vandenhoeck und Ruprecht, 1985, esp. 158.

208 Also, see the Introduction and Setting the Scene.

209 Crossan refers, in many of his works (see Introduction and Bibliography), to the influences of writers such as Stevens, Yeats, and Pound, philosophers such as Heidegger and Nietzsche, and critics such as Derrida and Barthes. One example of this is found in Crossan's book, *In Parables: The Challenge of the Historical Jesus*, San Francisco: Harper, 1973, 81-82. "Heidegger says: 'Because it thinks Being, thought thinks Nothing.' It is this nothing that is, this Nothing, this Nothingness, that Nietzsche warned about with such terrifying accuracy: 'rather than want nothing, man even wants nothingness.'" The frightening challenge, for Crossan, is to dwell in the dialectic between Being and Nothingness. Crossan states, "We are frightened by the lonely silences within the parables."

210 See F. B. Brown and E. S. Malbon, "Parabling as a Via Negativa: A Critical Review of the Work of John Dominic Crossan," *Journal of Religion* 64 (1984), 530-538, esp. 530. "Few can claim to have shed as much new light on any genre of biblical literature as Crossan has on parables."

211 Crossan, "A Metamodel for Polyvalent Narration," *Semeia* 9 (1977), 106.

He harkens back to the day when there was the *illusion* of stability, solutions, and a distinction between world - reality and our perception of it.[212] In Crossan's view, interpreters now find themselves in a world with no fixed center, a world that can be described as something of a labyrinth. His proposal is that this labyrinth relates not only to the world, but also to the *play* of text interpretation. Parables, for example, can be played repeatedly and continuously. Since you cannot interpret absolutely, you can interpret forever.

> [.....] we create the labyrinth ourselves, it has no center, it is infinitely expansible, we create it as play for play, and one can no more consider leaving it than one can envisage leaving one's skin.[213]

In the case of text interpretation, Crossan takes up what he refers to as the *metamodel* of play.[214] Play, for Crossan, is characterized as a totality that impinges on all interpretation. This notion is not: *play, as opposed to something more stable or fixed*, as if there was some standard or point of reference. Rather, it is to be understood as that which defines *reality* as a whole. Crossan argues that play is revealed in communication through signs, and that semiosis (his terminology) is a restricted system of signs that endlessly refer to each other.[215] All external referents disappear inside signs. There is no question here of a sign - referent, but always a sign-to-sign system that is enclosed within itself. In this sense, we align Crossan, to some degree, with structuralism. However,

---

212 Ibid., 107. Crossan argues that reality used to limit and prevent "an immediately dangerous and vertiginous possibility of regressus ad infinitum," but those days are lost forever.

213 Ibid., 139, and 112.

214 Ibid., 113.

215 Ibid., 117. Crossan gives his readers two options here. He affirms the latter. "Either semiosis is mimetic or it is ludic, it either reflects a reality without it or it creates a reality within it." However, while not focalizing on these options per se, we would want to challenge Crossan on his attempt to offer an "either – or" option with regards to semiosis in what he has already argued is a metamodel - world of play. Do not either - or's relate to antithesis, rather than to infinite play?

his views, as we have seen, are not merely ideological structuralism.[216]

With regard to parables, Crossan affirms that one necessarily finds parable to be a permanence of paradox. Parable, in this sense is related to Crossan's metamodel of play as its literary counter-part.[217] He states:

> Polyvalent narration, [...] that is, a paradox formed into narrative so that it precludes canonical interpretation and becomes a metaphor for the hermeneutical multiplicity it engenders. I would like to retain the term parable for this most profound and disturbing form of story.
>
> There is a small room in Vienna's Schönbrunn Palace walled with mirrors. Locate yourself in the middle and you will see corridors stretching in all directions as far as the eye can see. [...] the corridors of hermeneutics stretch as far as the imagination can reach.[218]

Those who argue that Jesus' parables are clear - cut moral messages are mistaken. There is nothing *stable* in parables. Crossan disputes any claims of clarity in the parables and prefers to view Jesus as the greatest satirist and subverter, "a master of paradox, and indeed of double paradox. He who finds the meaning loses it and he who loses it finds it."[219] In Crossan's view, the parables of Jesus are not timeless truths or a defense of a previous proclamation; they are what characterize Jesus' historicity and his experience of God, both of which incorporate everything else.[220]

Crossan, in his first book length venture, already views parables in intra-linguistic terms. The historical Jesus is to be understood as the lan-

---

216 See the Introduction above which is also important for a reading of Crossan's views as discussed here. Also Brown and Malbon, "Parabling," 531-533, who argue that Crossan's ideas have undergone a perceptible evolution and one can detect the influence of literary theorists and philosophers who some would classify poststructuralist, deconstructionist, or as in our terminology, post-modernist.

217 Ibid., 106.

218 Ibid., 140.

219 Ibid., 139.

220 Crossan, *In Parables*, 22, 32-33.

guage of Jesus and most importantly the parables themselves.[221] Parables, within this framing, are not potential messages, but merely linguistic processes that have a structure, yet are lacking in content and referent.[222]

Parables aim to *subvert* and *shatter* the known, while leaving little room for reconstruction in the wake of the debris. According to Crossan, the subversiveness of parables moves readers into a dark interval of insecurity in the face of "the dark night of story."[223] As parables subvert, they also disorient, shock, and surprise. Jesus' parables, for Crossan, overturn assumptions and bring about reversals, but they are unable to disclose anything positive about new understanding in regards to the person of Jesus, the world, the Kingdom of God, or the hearer.[224] Crossan writes:

> Parable is an attack on the world, a raid on the articulate.
>
> [...] parable will establish the very principle of irreconciliation and non-mediation. Parable establishes the principle of doubt against all security. Like satire, parable as such has no programmatic content. Its function is negative and its creativity is that of via negativa.[225]

In commenting on the short parable of hidden treasure in Matthew 13:44, Crossan briefly refers to a distinction between rabbinic parables and Jesus' point of view.[226] In rabbinic parables the actions of selling, buying, and finding follow in sequence. All is done, as it should be.

---

221 Ibid., xiii.

222 L. M. Poland, *Literary Criticism and Biblical Hermeneutics: A Critique of Formalist Approaches*, Chico: Scholars, 1985, AAR Academy Series 111, argues that, "Crossan is more interested in describing how parable becomes metaphor than he is in the parable narrative itself. Crossan focuses on the structure and function, at the expense of the content, of the meanings and beliefs embodied in the story. He does not seem to see that the content, as well as the function, of metaphor is also dependent on the concrete situation that the narrative depicts and the auditors recognize."

223 See Crossan's next book, *The Dark Interval*, 57-60.

224 Crossan, *In Parables*, 26-27. *Cliffs of Fall*, 94, where parables are referred to as "metaparables" which results in parable being a perfect mirror, not of the world or the kingdom, but of itself.

225 Crossan, "The Good Samaritan: Towards a Generic Definition of Parable," *Semeia* 2 (1974), 82-107, esp. 98, 105.

226 Crossan, *Finding the First Act: Trouvé Folktales and Jesus' Treasure Parables*, Philadelphia: Fortress, 1979, 104-106.

However, Jesus reverses the succession making the movement of actions suspect from a virtuous perspective. Crossan argues that Jesus' parable suggests a present opportunity, which remains imprecise. The act of purchasing the field alludes to a making room for detection, but the undetectable remains the *substance* of the story. The parable is an affirmation of how language is not disclosive, but subversive and non-referential. Crossan claims:

> I will tell you, it says, what the Kingdom of God is like. Watch carefully how, and as I fail to do so and learn that it cannot be done [...] the more magnificent my failure, the greater my success.[227]

For Crossan, the answer to why there are multiple and differing interpretations of parables is that parables intentionally subvert meaning. His primary focus remains on the negative. In his world, meaning is harder and harder to come by. As such, a lack of total meaning results in no orientation, no normativity, and no predication in the language of Jesus.[228] In the parables of Jesus, Crossan privileges discontinuity over continuity,[229] the negative over the positive, and assumes that parabolic language is arbitrary, plurivalent, with a "void of meaning at its core."[230]

With such a view of language as relativized, deficient of meaning and extra-linguistic reference, Crossan argues that parables are polyvalent. While we agree with him on some points—the polyvalence of parables, and his emphasis on their subversion, shock, and disorienting character—we would nevertheless disagree with his conclusions. In our opinion, he overemphasizes the negative side of meaning, which comes from a facet of post-modernist interpretation theory that is then too

---

227 Ibid., 120.

228 A. N. Wilder, *The Bible and the Literary Critic*, Minneapolis: Fortress, 1991, 122.

229 Ibid., 123. "With respect to Jesus' sayings there must have been some substantial appropriation and continuation of the language of the past and its meaning. I myself see the continuity at the level of denotative symbol and conception which Jesus both exploited and revisioned."

230 Crossan, *Cliffs of Fall*, 9-10.

comprehensively read back into Jesus' parables.²³¹ As a result of this analysis of the text, parables seem to only be able to affirm Crossan's views, rather than to offer any positive resistance to an interpretative paradigm that is imposed upon them.

Crossan argues that a search for parabolic meaning culminates in the acknowledgment that there is none. This is because God has unleashed, through Jesus' parables, an unrelenting attack on the very form and content of human language.²³² In our estimation, Crossan is entirely too pessimistic. The force of his argument is driven by this affirmation: since there is no absolute interpretation, you can interpret forever. While we do not disagree with the former, we would want to question the latter. Crossan can only substantiate this former half of his hermeneutical orientation, but when it comes to the latter, the conclusion is presupposed, rather than argued. He seems to exchange the *failure* of one absolute for the supposed success of another.

Indeed, we question Crossan's view of parables as unable to resist, at some point, an infinite number of interpretations. The indeterminacy or opaqueness of meaning, for Crossan, is paradox and paradox is negative.²³³ This is what parables are about: negation. However, if we follow Ricoeur, the indeterminacy of parables can, to some degree, be seen as situated within the boundaries of the text. We would argue that parabolic texts resist a *total* escape from meaning and extra-linguistic referents. Thus, and here's the point, they *disclose* as well as subvert. In addition, the possibility exists that parabolic opaqueness is also positive. For Ricoeur, the failure to arrive at an absolute interpretation can

---

231 Brown and Malbon, "Parabling," 536, point out, "One experiences a tension between Crossan's expressed concern for interpreting the language of the historical Jesus and his concern for a certain philosophy he is predisposed to ascribe to the 'linguistic' Jesus. To equate reality with language, to locate the metaphoric center of language as a semantic void, to see Jesus' parabling as self-conscious, polyvalent linguistic play that reflects its own limits and thereby displays this void - to reason this way is in effect to come dangerously close to making Jesus out to be a first century structuralist/deconstructionist."

232 Crossan, *Cliffs of Fall*, 20.

233 See Crossan, "Stages in Imagination," in: *The Archaeology of the Imagination*, C. E. Winquist, ed., *JAAR Thematic Studies* 48/2, Chico: AAR, 1981, 56, where he argues that "paradox is the highest and final stage of imaginative development." Paradox is defined purely negatively. Also, Brown and Malbon, "Parabling," 537. "In this (Crossan's) scheme, parable is judged to be of positive value only because it is negative in strategy. He gives priority to subversion." (parenthesis mine)

also be understood as a *surplus* of meaning, rather than a wholesale negation of it.[234] In contrast to leaving their readers completely in the dark, in the concave of the tumultuous uncertainty that Crossan says reigns in language and life, parables as texts have the capacity to *re-figure* reality and to bring about a transformative new understanding of God, the world, and the self. Furthermore, we argue that parabolic polyvalence is not entirely open to a gratuitous free-play. Texts, even parabled ones, have interpretations that can be considered more or less probable, in spite of those interpretations not being absolute.[235]

Another point of difficulty in Crossan's analysis of Jesus' parables is his *restricted* focus on the parables alone. In our estimation, when concentration is placed too narrowly on Jesus' parables, the danger looms of a reductionistic distortion at the expense of the wider context of the stories. Parables, as a genre, arguably militate against Crossan's totalizing perspective. Furthermore, when situated in their wider narrative contexts, it is unlikely that parables so readily support Crossan's extreme hermeneutical assessments concerning language, sense, and referent.

Having critically analyzed Crossan's views concerning the lack of sense and extra-linguistic reference in Jesus' parables, we now turn to further elaborate Ricoeur's position. Ricoeur's *distance* (already touched on above) from a post-modern orientation will now become even more transparent. His affirmation of parabolic sense in the biblical text, points to a refusal to accept any notions of total sense (modernist), total non-sense, or an exclusive readerly sense (post-modernist).

Ricoeur works with several parables, but for our purposes, we shall focus again on the very short parable of Matthew 13:44.[236] He argues that the parable is full of sense. The implication that parabolic sense is found in the emplotted drama suggests three critical movements: 1) finding of the treasure, 2) selling everything, 3) buying the field. In

---

234 Ricoeur, *Interpretation Theory*, 45-46, 55-57.

235 Ibid., 79.

236 Ricoeur, "Listening," 240-241, *The Philosophy of Paul Ricoeur*.

Ricoeur's observation, as this motion percolates through the interpreter's imagination, thoughts, and feelings, there is a discovery that "much more" is meant than the parable's normal situational context delivers. The finding in the story is a finding of something; and importantly for Ricoeur, that something is given as opposed to acquired.[237] This expression evokes a variety of encounters: with people, with death, or with tragedy, all of which affirm and disclose that our lives are not solely an achievement of ourselves. These various findings then point in the direction of time and a way of being in time. In Ricoeur's view, this mode relates to "Event par excellence," that is, something happens and the incident incites an awakening in the hearer who is now primed for the newness of the new.[238]

As we continue through the parable, we will explore further its artful meaning in two critical movements, both of which are linked dialectically to this notion of finding. These movements are selling and buying, which can also be referred to as reversal and decision. In reference to this Ricoeur remarks:

> [....] much has been invested in this word "conversion," which means much more than making a new choice, but which implies a shift in the direction of the look, a reversal in the vision, in the imagination, in the heart, before all kinds of good intentions and all kinds of good decisions and good actions. Doing appears as the conclusive act, engendered by the Event (finding) and by the Reversal. First, encountering the Event, then changing one's heart, then doing accordingly. This succession is full of sense: the Kingdom of God is compared to the chain of these three acts: letting the Event blossom, looking in another direction, and doing with all one's strength in accordance with the new vision.[239]

---

237 This "giveness" is important to note, as Ricoeur, in both his philosophical and biblical writings emphasizes the original giftedness of the "given," in contrast to the acquiring of the "something." "Listening," 241.

238 Ibid., 241.

239 Ibid., 241.

While the work of the finder and the emplotment of reversal and decision are instructive and "sense-full" elements in the parable, we question whether this rendering is able to account for the *theological* component of the Kingdom of God. Ricoeur is convincing in his view of the Event as gift, but is this the limit capacity of the symbol, *Kingdom of God*, as used by Jesus? In a Ricoeurian perspective, the response to this question is to point out that the gospel says nothing about what the Kingdom of God is, only what it is like.[240] Jesus is not to be understood as a theologian, who uses concepts, but as a teacher who taught by images.[241] While we partially affirm Ricoeur's emphasis on images featured in the parables, we also contend that he could legitimately say more, without risking an overstatement, when he refers to Jesus' usage of the Kingdom of God.

We shall explain our position in the following way. The parabolic Kingdom of God seems indeed to be "like" many things; but might this be the case because the Kingdom is first of all *one* symbol that then functions at a *multiplicity* of levels?[242] It is entirely possible, in our opinion, that Jesus is able to use all the images he does, precisely because the "sense" of the phrase is both *conceptual* and *imagical*. Might this multifaceted sense then invoke a complex constellation of thoughts, feelings, observations, and imaginary processes that relate to God as King: God

---

240 Ricoeur, "Le 'Royaume' dans les paraboles de Jesus," 15-19, esp. 16. However, Ricoeur does seem to go beyond this in, "From Proclamation to Narrative," 501-512, esp. 508, footnote 14, where he points out the Kingdom of Heaven is "like," says what God does.

241 In our opinion, Ricoeur is in danger of succumbing to the same reductionistic tendencies he critiques in others. Why not concept and image? Ricoeur's penchant to minimize the significance of concept, in this context, relates to his bias against scientific language as opposed to poetic discourse. However, Ricoeur does, in another context, stress the discourse relevance of the concept and seeking its clarity in aiming to hold understanding and imagination together in the hermeneutical process. See Ricoeur, *La métaphore vive*, 383, (*The Rule of Metaphor*, 303).

242 D. O. Via, Jr., "The Parable of the Unjust Judge: A Metaphor of the Unrealized Self," in: *Semiology and Parables*, D. Patte, ed., Pittsburgh: Pickwick, 1976, 26. Via writes of Jesus' narrative parables, as stories of God's reign. Also, R. T. France, "The Church and the Kingdom of God: Some Hermeneutical Issues," in: Carson, ed., *Biblical Interpretation and the Church*, Nashville: Nelson, 1985, 38. France convincingly points out that the Jewish background of the phrase, along with the variety of associated linguistic forms and areas of reference in Jesus' teaching, shows that the Kingdom of God does not conform to any single subject sphere and therefore functions as a symbol. The point is, the belief that God is King cannot be restricted, exhausted, or entirely expressed by any one referent. "The phrase serves then not so much to define the subject-area of the statement in which it occurs as to establish the conceptual framework within which that statement is to be understood."

is portrayed as active, and his action is to reign.[243] Jesus' proclamations of the good news of God (Mt. 4:23), that the Kingdom of Heaven was near (Mt. 4:17), and that it had arrived already in his person, deeds, and signs, at the very least points to the image-concept that God was King, and that this Kingship was manifesting itself in word, deed, and action (Mt. 12:22-29), all of which were considered treasures.[244]

Despite our challenge that Ricoeur "say more" in regard to how the Kingdom of God is being presented in scripture, we affirm his insistence (in opposition to Crossan) that parables are *full* of sense, perhaps even more full than Ricoeur acknowledges. This fullness shows that parables are not only about subversion, but also are open to disclosure. Since the configured parable is full of sense, it has the capacity to disclose and refigure reality, and to bring about a new understanding of God, the world and the self.

These perspectives lead us into the related dimension of Ricoeur's concern for the status of texts and their capacity to refer outside themselves, something Crossan denies. While Ricoeur has strongly affirmed this dimension of the biblical text, we must go further and ask how it plays out in parables. We have seen that for Crossan the parables are referent-less. But if Ricoeur argues specifically to the contrary, what referent does he have in mind? Ricoeur has argued that *human experience* is the reference for parables. He writes,

> Could we not say that a poetic language, such as that of parables, proverbs, and proclamatory sayings, redescribes human reality according to the "qualification" conveyed by the symbol Kingdom of God? This would indicate that the ultimate referent of parabolic (proverbial, proclamatory) language is human experience centered around the *limit-experiences* which would correspond to the *limit-expressions* of religious discourse.

---

243 This surely would have been conceived of, in some fashion, by a good percentage of Jesus opponents to whom many of the parables are performed and addressed.

244 G. E. Ladd, *The Presence of the Future*, Grand Rapids: Eerdmans, *1974, 227-228*. Also, N. Perrin, *Rediscovering the Teaching of Jesus*, New York: Harper, 1967, 76-77.

> The referent, we could say, of the parable is human experience, conceived as the experience of the whole man and of all men, as it is interpreted in the light of the *mimetic* resources of some realistic *and* extravagant *fictions*, themselves embedded in specific narrative structures.[245]

We agree with Ricoeur's argument that parabolic discourse refers to human experience and is able to *redescribe* human reality. However, the question arises: is human experience the only referent of such a discourse? In other words, are parabolic referents exclusively anthropological, or is it conceivable that they also include a theological element? How shall we read Ricoeur? Is it not possible that Ricoeur's advocacy for the meaningful self engenders a potential reductionism of parabolic reference and religious language in general? Some of Ricoeur's interpreters would argue this is indeed the case.[246] In their conception, Ricoeur reduces parabolic referents and religious language to selfhood, or a way of being in the world. While it is true, perhaps, that a more constricted reading of Ricoeur may produce such a conclusion, in our view, Ricoeur's overarching position resists such a critique in the following way.

Notably, he argues that biblical discourse proposes the referent of a new world, a new birth, the coming of the Kingdom of God, and a new covenant. All of these have their genesis for us, neither in the given self, nor in the autonomous me, but in the biblical text.[247] We suggest that Ricoeur goes even further. Rightly affirming that the referent of the biblical text (in addition to human experience and a world) is God,[248] Ricoeur argues it is because God is the referent that there can be a *given*

---

245 Ricoeur, "Biblical Hermeneutics," 34-35. (*Italics his*). Limit-expressions are understood to be saying what can be said, without that ever reaching completion.

246 Frei, "The 'Literal Reading' of Biblical Narrative," 50; W. C. Placher, "Paul Ricoeur and Postliberal Theology: A Conflict of Interpretations?," *Modern Theology* 4 (1988), 35-52, esp. 43; Vanhoozer, *Biblical Narrative*, 140-141.

247 Ricoeur, "Philosophy and Religious Language," 81.

248 See above, "Philosophical Hermeneutics and Biblical Hermeneutics."

self in opposition to an *autonomous me*.²⁴⁹ If this is the case, as we have previously demonstrated, then it is possible to refute the critique of Ricoeur mentioned above. God, as Ricoeur has already stated, is the *central* referent of biblical discourse.

> One of the features that constitute the specificity of biblical discourse is, as we know, the central place held by the referent "God."²⁵⁰

In Ricoeur's view, the notion that God is the referent for the true signifying capacity of biblical discourse expressed in its multiple literary forms - narrative, hymn, prophecy, parable, etc. - is clearly affirmed. Parables, for example, in the contrast between their realism and extravagance, the extraordinary within the ordinary, move readers through the plot and its point in the direction of the Wholly Other.²⁵¹ Parables name and refer to God through the combination of narrative structure, metaphorical process, and limit expression. This works out in the following ways: the narrative structure recalls the "original rootedness" of the faith-language comprised in the narratives; the metaphorical process "discloses" the poetic character of the language of faith in its genre; and finally, the limit expression supplies the "matrix" for a theological language that brings together analogy and negation (for example: "God is like, and God is not [...]").²⁵²

In drawing from a broader scope of Ricoeur's texts, we are confident in affirming the presence of a triple biblical referent: first, God; second, the proposed world of the text; and third, human experience.²⁵³ Thus, human reality can be robustly *redescribed* in parables

---

249 This is reminiscent of Ricoeur's well known critique of the self-positing subject.

250 Ricoeur, "Herméneutique philosophique et herméneutique biblique," 128, *Du texte à l'action* ("Philosophical and Biblical Hermeneutics," 97, *From Text to Action*).

251 Ricoeur, "Nommer Dieu," *Etudes théologiques et religieuses* 52 (1977), 4, 489-508, reprinted in: *Lectures III*, Paris: Seuil, 1994, 281-305, ("Naming God," reprinted in: *Union Seminary Quarterly Review* 34 (1979), 4, 215-228, Also, reprinted - cited in: "Naming God," *Figuring the Sacred*, 217-235, esp. 229).

252 Ricoeur, "Naming God," *Figuring the Sacred*, 230.

253 In our opinion, Ricoeur's interlocutors focus too narrowly on his *Semeia* 4 article.

because both God and the world of the text are referents that always precede self/me.[254] The correspondence between these referents in no way eliminates their distinction from one another. In fact, the *tension* between their relation to and distinction from one another is, on the one hand, what makes them "limited" in their capacity to give a totalizing perspective of that which is beyond "limit." On the other hand, this same tension is what enables them to go "to the limit" with a surplus of meaning.

To develop this a step further and to elaborate on these referential possibilities, we shall next concentrate on the example of the parable in Matthew 20:1-16. In terms of parabolic reference, Ricoeur argues that the vineyard owner - householder is God.[255] Thus, God is the one who determines how much is to be received, and by whom. God is the character in the story who discloses the criteria for generosity and goodness, and in so doing, he challenges, shocks, and provokes human experience, turning expectations into occasions of revelation.

This parable's challenge to a norm of goodness based solely on equal pay for equal work creates a *shock* in the hearers (both within the story and without) that disorients, before it reorients them. Those who grumble (20:11), who jealously question the distribution of wages are effectively disoriented by this paradox and its apparent perversion of what is good and fair (20:13-15). For them, the enigmatic reorientation comes with the denouement that the last will be first and the first last. Such a sharp *clash* resonates in the mind, heart, experience, and imagination in the wake of a disturbance of the norm. God's generosity transcends and defies such norms, thus breaking any attempt to construct a claim to explanatory totality. The revelation of reality redescribed in the text is incessantly connected to human existence with a directional reorientation towards a new world, new being, and new way of living.

---

254 From our perspective this too stands against those (Frei and others) who argue that Ricoeur's general hermeneutic reigns over his biblical. It is however, not any or every text that refers to God, nor can human experience or reality be redescribed in precisely the same way as the world the biblical text proposes.

255 Ricoeur, "From Proclamation to Narrative," 501-512, esp. 508.

Equally distributed to all, this *grace* is the reason why being first is not the paradigm for life (20:15-16). Ricoeur states it in the following way:

> Nevertheless, these are not ironical or skeptical words of wisdom. In spite of everything, life is granted by this paradoxical path. The challenge to conventional wisdom is at the same time a way of life. We are first disoriented before being reoriented.[256]

Before moving on to our examination of methodology, a brief summary is in order. We have shown that Ricoeur's concern for textual sense and reference in biblical parables engenders a valid critique of both modernist and post-modernist interpretive theories; the latter was expressed more specifically in the work of Crossan. Ricoeur's interpretation theory effectively affirms the existence of parabolic sense and reference, crediting the parable-story with making textual sense as opposed to non-sense. Furthermore, this sense is liberated from the constraints of an intra-linguistic sign system lacking any referent or mimetic power to "redescribe" human existence. Thus, Ricoeur's efforts lead us far beyond the contours of Crossan's relentless negations and defeatist absurdity within the parabolic scenario, and towards a vehement affirmation of a parabolic fullness of sense and its capacity to refer to God, the world, and ourselves.

3.2.3.2. Methodology for Parable Interpretation: Complementarity in Tension.

We shall now move on to methodology in respect to the biblical parables. Our aim, at this point, is to apply the trinity of methodologies previously examined in order to show, along with Ricoeur, their inner-connected value and pertinence to interpreting the parables of Jesus.

---

[256] Ricoeur, "Listening," 244. Ricoeur is commenting on the paradoxical proverb, 243, "Whoever seeks to gain his/her life will lose it, but whoever loses his/her life will preserve it." This point, in our opinion, holds for the present context as well.

3.2.3.2.1. Reading Parables from a Historical-Critical View.

Ricoeur rightly recognizes the value of the historical - critical work of scholars such as C. H. Dodd,[257] J. Jeremias,[258] and N. Perrin,[259] as well as A. Jülicher,[260] and his critique of the allegorical method of interpreting parables, which has its roots at least as far back as Augustine. Dodd, Jeremias and Perrin's efforts to picture the parables within their historical setting motivated their critico-eschatological lens. Specifically, they focused on the situational confrontations and crises that the parables of Jesus address to their hearers, and their significance for that historical context. In presenting these moments of crisis, parables challenge their audience to recognize and respond to the teaching of Jesus, as the one who reveals a new situation with the in-breaking of the Kingdom of God. Hence, interpreters must not neglect, or seek to eliminate the background of the particular circumstances of Jesus' contemporary life and religious context, in their attempt to "read" parables.

The historical-critical method, in its affirmation of the original context of Jesus' parables, maintains that parables often have an argumentative and polemical force. Dodd and Jeremias both point out that the parables of Jesus are often a reply to a questioner who may be overtly antagonistic. For example, the Pharisees and teachers of the law question Jesus for eating with "sinners" and associating with social dregs in Lk. 15, or the slick lawyer of Lk. 10 who inquires about eternal life and the notion of a neighbor, both of which provoke parables from Jesus. As such, Jeremias refers to parables, for the most part, as weapons of warfare aimed at critics and opponents of the gospel.[261]

---

257   C. H. Dodd, *The Parables of the Kingdom*, London: Nisbet, 1935.

258   J. Jeremias, *The Parables of Jesus*, Revised Edition, London: SCM, 1963.

259   Perrin, *Jesus and the Language of the Kingdom*, Philadelphia: Fortress, 1976.

260   Jülicher, *Die Gleichnisreden Jesu, 2 Vols*. While Jülicher has performed biblical interpreters a service in debunking over-allegorical parable interpretation, the implausibility of his case reverberates in a number of ways: first, in a straining out of all allegory; second, through the adoption of Aristotelian categories as the archetype for parable understanding; third, reducing parables to general moral platitudes; fourth, one parable has only one point of correspondence. I am indebted to K. E. Bailey, *Poet and Peasant and Through Peasant's Eyes: A Literary Cultural Approach to the Parables in Luke*, Grand Rapids: Eerdmans, 1983, for these insights.

261   Jeremias, *The Parables of Jesus*, 21.

According to Ricoeur, Jeremias and Perrin offer a judicious critique of Bultmann's negation of the *historical* Jesus. Bultmann describes the endeavor as "useless," in that it is not scientifically modern, and even "dangerous," from the point of view of works that endanger and pervert faith. This astute critique, by the work of Jeremias and Perrin, rests on both historical analysis and the futuristic orientation in Jesus' proclamation, notably discovered and historically reconstructed in parables. Bultmann is right in arguing that it is not possible to entirely separate the historical Jesus from the kerygma. However, it is possible, Ricoeur argues, to historico-critically isolate what he calls the "words and actions of Jesus," distinguishing them from both Judaism and the post-Easter context, which can be understood as "occasions" for the narrative composition of the gospels.[262]

Ricoeur's acceptance of the important function of the historical-critical method, for the eventual re-interpretation of parables is not, however, to be considered a movement "behind" the text. From our standpoint, Ricoeur remains consistent with his methodological provisos, as previously discussed. In his opinion, there is an intersignification within the domain of parables that also applies to other "sayings" and "deeds" of Jesus. Ricoeur is concerned with Jesus' historical, sociological, and cultural context, and for his way of dealing with a variety of people and situations through parables. Ricoeur tenaciously refuses, however, to see this as a return to a biographical interpretation:

> I emphatically deny that this is the case. The "deeds" of Jesus are no less accessible - as *meant by the texts* - than are the parables and other sayings of Jesus. The process of "intersignification" remains itself contained *within* the boundaries of "textuality": it interprets a text *through* another text.[263]

---

262 Ricoeur, "From Proclamation to Narrative," esp. 503-504.

263 Ricoeur, "Biblical Hermeneutics," 102, (Emphasis and *Italics his*).

It is because the parables are *historical* texts, in other words, texts with a history, written in history, and related to other texts, that they can be said to merit the modified historical-critical investigation that Ricoeur has proposed earlier in our study.[264] We shall not, at this point, take the historical-critical method any further. Its indispensability for a reading of parables is not in question, and while Ricoeur clearly affirms this, he offers no additional reflection of its particular significance and application to biblical parables.[265] In our assessment, Ricoeur rightly has no objection to reading parables historico-critically. But even more importantly, he has realized that this methodological approach is merely one part of a massive orchestra; a *living* hermeneutics. Ricoeur is correct to critique the historical-critical method for its exclusive interest in historicity, and in his attempt to expand the exegesis of parables further than a mere recovery of a historical context or situation, in consideration of other approaches to the text.[266]

> While hermeneutics can address meaning that is the *meaning of the text*, open to interpretations located in another present than that of the author and original audience, the exegete as such can oppose to this a final result of non-reception and declare that his work is complete when he establishes an intelligible correlation between a certain type of discourse and a certain historical situation. The same exegete could even declare, with brutality, that all "application," all "actualization" of meaning for the reader concerns the preacher, not the exegete.
>
> I would like to believe that the historical critical exegete has finished his/her work. Is this true of all exegesis?[267]

---

264 We have already questioned, however, the comprehensiveness of Ricoeur's views on this subject. See above, Historical Criticism.

265 The important question, concerning the historicity of the biblical text in Ricoeur's work, will have to, for the moment, be deferred.

266 Also see our discussion, 3.2.2.1..

267 Ricoeur, "Préface," in: A. LaCocque, *Le livre de Daniel*, Commentaire de l'Ancien Testament, Xb, Neuchâtel: Delachaux, 1976, 5-11, esp. 8, (Emphasis and *Italics his*). (My translation).

Thus, exegesis may begin with uncovering contextual information, but it cannot end here. According to Ricoeur, it needs to enlarge its horizons. The parable itself, through its configuration, obligates exegesis to give thorough and detailed attention to the composition, sense, referent, and present impact of the text. A sufficient exegesis of parables must be both enraptured with, and restricted by, the sense and reference of the parable. In light of this tension embedded in the text, we are spurred on to recognize that the potential application of the *tension* has the capacity to refigure human action today.

3.2.3.2.2. An Evaluation of a Structural Rendering of Matthew 13: The Parable of the Sower

The biblical parables have increasingly come under the scrutiny of other methods of interpretation. There has been a movement in the direction of the *synchronic* over the *diachronic* study of language in scripture. This is expressed, for example, in a semiotic analysis of structure that focuses on the final form of the biblical text, rather than on its evolving development. We shall examine this structural methodology, as the second of our trinity of approaches to biblical parables.

Ricoeur argues that in regards to the text, the historical-critical method is far from being intrinsically unrelated to the structural method, but rather, is fortuitously relevant to it as both opposant and condition.[268]

It is equally our opinion, that both the historical critic and the structuralist de-limit the parameters of the text, but each do so in conflicting, yet inevitably complementary ways.

This scenario unfolds in the following manner. The historico-critical interpreter argues that the sole key to interpreting the parables is

---

268 Ricoeur, "Sur l'exégèse de Genèse 1,1 - 2,4a," 72, *Exégèse et herméneutique*. See also, L. Dornisch, "The Book of Job and Ricoeur's Hermeneutics," *Semeia* 19 (1981), 3-21, esp. 10. Dornisch argues, that as Ricoeur sees it, these methods, "do not necessarily contradict each other." In our opinion, however, Ricoeur does not argue for a methodological convergence without conflict. There is convergence, but it is in spite of conflict, that is neither negated, nor dissolved. In other words, the contradiction stands, but this does not preclude a possible complementarity at some level.

a submersion, deeper and deeper back through the text, until we hear the original voice of Jesus,[269] while the structuralist critic resists and eschews any interest in such submersion, focusing solely on a single parable/text and its complex internal relations.[270]

While historical criticism rightly focuses on the layeredness of the text—the trajectory of sense that unfolds from one layer to the other—it requires the corrective emphasis of a structuralist perspective that targets the final text as the goal of interpretation. This is the case, we would argue, because every text must be considered for itself, not merely for its genetic movements. A capacity to discern redactional levels, is dependent on, and presumes a command of the structure of the final text. On the other hand, the structuralist final text arguably requires the remedial accentuation of historical criticism. For example, the phenomenon of parables provokes questions when one notices that they are not the same final text in each synoptic gospel. This argument is valid from the standpoint that the gospels, as we have them, do not always make use of Jesus' parables in precisely the same way, which has some contextual and historical reasons behind it. In this case then, the gospel texts must be analyzed as both synchronically *flat*, and diachronically *textured*.

Ricoeur, as was stated earlier, has done substantially more methodologically with structuralism than with historical criticism. We shall therefore, examine a parable in light of a semiotic analysis. It must be said at the outset that there are various angles and a diversity of ways to read a text, under what might be referred to as the structuralist method. We shall not engage in a detailed ratiocination, but offer both Ricoeur's analysis of an ultra-structuralist approach, and our own reading in order to discover some of the traits of a structuralist position.[271] Specifically, these methods will be applied to the Parable of the Sower,

---

269 Jeremias, *The Parables of Jesus*, 22.

270 L. Marin, "Essai d'analyse structurale d'un récit-parabole: Matthieu 13/1-23," *Etudes théologiques et religieuses* 46 (1971), 35-74.

271 Ricoeur, "Biblical Hermeneutics," 54-74. This combines Barthes, Greimas, and Lévi-Strauss.

examined by Louis Marin.²⁷² We have chosen to work with Marin, as he has often applied a structural analysis to the biblical text and therefore can be considered a valid proponent of such a perspective.

The irrelevance of any *historical* investigation permits Marin an initial interest in the limit of the text. In this case, the text is to be understood as Mt. 13:1-23. There are several reasons for this, but perhaps the structural relationships between the four principal "fragments" (1-3a, 3b-9, 10-17, 18-23) and the operative motifs of coming out/going in, or of open/closed are important to notice.²⁷³ What is referred to as, "l'unité textuelle," is determined by the two narrative elements of Jesus coming out (vs 1) and going in (vs 10).²⁷⁴ This structuralist approach is concerned with the parable itself (3b-9), why Jesus speaks in parables, a quotation of Isaiah (10-17), and an explanation (18-23). In reference to such a de-limiting of the text in this fashion, Marin is faced with the difficulty of not being able to align and compare the parable with others. Unfortunately, this is overlooked due to a *singular* focus on the interplay of retroactive effects within that particular text, which are said to break any linear surface structure. In addition to this, reflection on the "plot" and the "dramatic" composition of the parable are undermined in favor of an emphasis on the laws of transformation at work within 13:3a-23.²⁷⁵

The first fragment consists of vs 1-3a and 10. The model for this text is characterized by four articulations: first and second concern space, third, the word, and fourth, the word and space. Marin argues that

---

272 Marin, "Essai," 35-74.

273 Ibid., 48-52. These oppositions are to be conceived of as a system of movement based on the central opposition - closed/open. According to Marin, such oppositions show an interdependence between three semantic relations in which an inversion occurs: in the collectivities (crowd/disciples), space, (coming out/going in), and the word (hidden/disclosed). The one "semic" category (open/closed) reigns over the three inversions.

274 Ibid., 49-50. This allows for a closure of the text at vs 23. We are required to understand vs 10 (les disciples, s'approchant, lui dirent) as an, "effacement essentiel de la function 'retour à la maison' " as Jesus is now disjoined with the crowds and conjoined with the disciples. See also vs 36.

275 Marin, "Essai," 48-54. Marin refers to these transformations as connected to a de-coding of the double level of Jesus' word, which is both closed and open. This then relates to: two groups (crowds/disciples), two spaces (coming out/going in), which relate to the oppositional forces of open and closed. These operative transformations, the codes, and the structure, are the message of the text.

there is a structural equivalence between the "déplacement" (displacing) of space and language, resulting in the parallel dualisms: leaving/entering and speaking in parables/speaking clearly.[276]

In vs 3b-9, the second fragment, we have the parable itself as a narrative within a narrative, "A sower went out to sow [... .]" Vs 10 brings closure to the parable in the form of a request for information. This information is given to the disciples, but it concerns information that was given to the crowds, creating different levels of discourse that can be correlated with both disjunction and conjunction. From a structuralist perspective, a notable characteristic is the "topography" mentioned (path, rocks, thorns, good soil) in the parable and its correspondence to the information given to the disciples in 18-23. This is transcodage. Transcodage shows that Jesus can now affirm to the disciples that they can listen to the parable in the form and according to the code that is suitable for them as disciples.[277] Furthermore, the "coming out" of the sower and the "act" of sowing are said to relate to the topography, bringing out the oppositions between "opponent" (birds, sun, thorns) and "helper" (good soil). At this juncture, the act of "sowing" is thought to replace that of speaking, and therefore, functionally becomes the operator between space and language.

The third fragment, vs 10-17, is referred to as a metalinguistic discourse—that is, language about language.[278] This fragment is considered central and necessary for the transformations seen in fragments two and four. Marin argues that these verses must be understood as a discourse on vs 3a; it is a teaching discourse, on a certain form of communication. The passage is further characterized by an inner structure of oppositions, such as given/not given and you/they, which command the modality of the communication and create a positive and negative way of hearing and understanding. This is further connected with the

---

276 Ibid. 57-58. This equivalence allows us to discover the central paradigm of the text which is "communication."

277 Ibid., 55.

278 Ibid., 54-56, 66. We shall understand Marin's use of the term "metalinguistic" as basically meaning, language about language.

rule of competence in the utilization of the code (having/receiving and not having/losing and seeing/not perceiving and hearing/not listening), somewhat paradoxally expressed in vs 12-13.

The fourth and final fragment is vs 18-23. Marin views this discourse as transcodage, rather than decodage, for the following reasons: one, it is the first discourse that addresses the code of the parabolic message; two, it appears as a quotation within the story, and Jesus himself refers to it as a parable. In these verses, we have our usual oppositions and retroactive features.[279] Transcodage, versus decodage (direct connection), is in play here as the topographical details are now applied to discipleship.

As a result of the coming out of Jesus, along with that of the sower, Marin argues, the sense begins to make its appearance. Jesus, however, does not reveal the sense of the parable outright (vs 3b-9), rather he "re-tells" it in another way. This re-telling weaves together within the same text the elements of both code and message, creating a hybrid of language and metalanguage. This hybrid between language itself and an accompanying reflection on language reveals a new mode of transformation seen in the fragment: that of a paradigmatic *vertical* relation. Rather than the previous relation between space and language, the relation between code and message is now introduced.

Further, Marin points out that the sower is neither decoded nor transcoded, but rather, his role is merged with that of the seed-word. This assimilation leaves the place of Jesus, the speaker of the parable, vacant. Jesus is considered in this case, to be absent as character, speaker, giver of the rule of competence, and referent for the relation between code and message. In this sense, Jesus, the character (1-3), speaker, (3b-9) and giver of the rule of competence in the metalinguistic discourse (10-17), is designated by absence.[280] For Marin, this results in the *gospel*

---

279 Ibid., 63-64. Oppositions take on the character of exterior (along the path) and interior (good soil) with their correspondent results. Marin also argues for a homogeneity between the coming out of Jesus, the coming out of the sower, and the coming out of truth.

280 Ibid., 65-66.

being a communication about communication. The surface narrative of the text is merely pointing to a deeper narrative, which tells the story of the exceptional moment when the words of code become the things of message.

By now we have seen clearly the direction that Marin's structural analysis takes. There is room for a more detailed analysis of the parable according to his method, but this has not been our aim. Rather, our concern has been to outline the traits of a methodology and how they are applied to a biblical parable.

Following this outline, we shall now evaluate the structuralist methodology as exemplified in the Parable of the Sower. In our opinion, there are at least two problematic areas to discuss: first, the over-emphasis on the deep structure (codes) of the text as the meaning of the narrative; and second, the failure of an ultra-structuralist perspective to view the text multi-dimensionally as having the dual aspects of both sense and reference.[281]

First, Marin's emphasis is on uncovering the codes in the text—the codes for him are the *message*. This primary importance of the code manifests itself as the main sense of the narrative as well, finally rendering the message of the parable itself secondary to this focus on code. We find that this narrow search for a deeper linguistic structure has a tendency to overlook equal concern for the surface structure of the parable, and is therefore in danger of undermining any alternative meaning that may be discovered through the use of a different methodology.[282] Such an over-emphasis on structure results in an exclusive textual interest in codes as message. Necessarily then, narrative is viewed solely as the sum total of its smallest units contained in a codified system of inter-relations. This picture of parables lends them too readily to a certain kind of analysis and reduction, but does not make space for the

---

[281] Ricoeur, "Qu'est-ce qu'un texte?," *Du texte à l'action*, 140-141, ("What is a Text? Explanation and Understanding," *From Text to Action*, 108-109).

[282] Ricoeur, "Biblical Hermeneutics," 61-62, critiques the one-sidedness of such methodological hubris. Structural analysis must return from deep to surface structure.

fullness and meaningful ability to refer profoundly to the world they provoke and describe. The examined portion of the biblical text becomes merely an interconnected sign system, ultimately pointing and re-pointing to itself.[283]

Second, Marin's position leaves the parable univocally stranded inside a text that is said to be a communication about communication; language about language.[284] If it's true that the text has only this one meaning, it can only be to the exclusion of the other aforementioned extra-linguistic referents of God, the world, and the self. This notion of text as a language-word event directly corresponds to the proposed *emptiness* of the parabolic text. The focus is on a code that confounds meaning and bares witness to a message of absence. This referent-less void, Marin argues in his essay, is "a transtextuality, a form of transcendence."[285] However, it is difficult to comprehend, from our perspective, how such a structuralist ideology can affirm anything of the sort. The referent-less, in a subtle fashion, becomes the referent. Thus, Marin's contention is that the parable is to be understood as a communication to its current reader of a circuit of communication of the Other.[286]

In the light of these two problematic areas, it is clear that a structural analysis, while of interpretative value, must face the *consequences* of its inability to "go it alone." Structuralism fails to account for anything outside the text itself. Furthermore, within its own methodological constraints, interpretation reaches an impasse, no longer having the capacity to move from code to message or from message to application. There is no way out of, or beyond the text. It is a view of the text that

---

[283] Another clear example of this can be found in, Marin, "Les femmes au tombeau: Essai d'analyse structurale d'un texte évangélique," in: *Sémiotique narrative: récits bibliques*, C. Chabrol and L. Marin, éds., Paris: Didier/Larousse, 1971, 39-50, ("The Women at the Tomb: A Structural Analysis of a Gospel Text," reprinted in: *The New Testament and Structuralism*, D. Patte, ed., Pittsburgh: Pickwick, 1976, 73-96, ET). Marin argues, in reference to Mt 28:1-8, that "The Lord is risen," is to be understood as a textual event and only a textual event, just as, for example, Jesus speaking in the parable of the Sower. The missing referent signifies a present word.

[284] Marin, "Essai," 62-63, footnote 34.

[285] Marin, "Essai," 72.

[286] Ibid., 74.

circuitously leads back to the text, rather than to a speaker, world, or extra-linguistic reality.[287] Ricoeur states it in the following way:

> Either the Other is *only* a "hole" in the texture of the text, or it is designated as an extra-linguistic being by the *residues* of the system of interplay and interaction and then structural analysis has to open itself to another kind of interpretation, which takes seriously the movement of transcendence of the text beyond itself.[288]

Thus, structural analysis of parables must be complemented by and give access to a broader method of interpretation. A more *holistic* method is necessary. Specifically, a viable approach to the text must incorporate within its own framework, the possibility of an alternate, but not necessarily entirely incompatible view of at least three things: first, language (not just as la langue, but as unity of la langue and la parole); second, the text (not just as code, but as discourse, generic, narrated); and third, reference (not just as an inter-linguistic sign system, but as extra-linguistic reality). Therefore, only if a structural analysis is complemented by other methodological concerns (historical-critical and hermeneutical) can it be understood as a necessary, yet intermediary stage, within a hermeneutics in motion.

A structural analysis of a biblical parable need not necessarily be understood as encumbered with or determined by Marin's conclusions. However, when the discovery of the deep structure of the parable becomes the interpretive end in and of itself, a structural analysis becomes a structuralist ideology, which then results in what Ricoeur rightly refers to as an interpretative "dead end."[289]

---

287 See our discussion above, 3.2.2.2..

288 Ricoeur, "Biblical Hermeneutics," 63, (Emphasis and *Italics his*).

289 Ibid., 65. What Ricoeur means here is that within a structuralist ideology there is no room for a return from code to message, hence, there is a univoicity which forbids any dialectical movement in the narrative. A return to message (la parole), we would argue, in distinction to, but in relation with code (la langue), must be understood as part of the motion from structure to process as required, for example, by an understanding-explanation-new understanding of parables.

3.2.3.2.3. Parables: A Hermeneutic Trajectory

Having examined both the historical-critical and the structuralist method for interpreting biblical parables, we have affirmed their value, as well those ways in which we would critique their status as able to go it on their own. We now direct our investigation towards the hermeneutical method and its application to the parables of Jesus.

This method is concerned with a number of factors. At the outset, it must again be pointed out that Ricoeur wants to develop a hermeneutical theory that is related to exegesis, but not restricted by its concerns. Exegesis, in Ricoeur's perspective, is the preparatory procedure for a "reprise" of the text by a contemporary reader, who through appropriating it, overcomes the cultural/textual distance accentuated by both a historical-critical and a structural analysis.

In this sense, Ricoeur is aiming for a general theory of interpretation that is not a *reductionistic* monologue, but rather a *multi-vocal* discourse with the capacity to incorporate various interpretative methods in an inter-related way. Significantly, this "way" of Ricoeur's is neither totalizing nor complete in that it affirms both the "limit" of the text and the capacity of the text to go "to the limit," with the meaning it presents. In other words, this is a *web* of complementarity and tension, of many sides and a constellation of angles; in short, a shape that resists ultimate closure, even while pushing the boundaries in every possible way.

It is here that Ricoeur relates his hermeneutical method to the text through the necessity of a poetico-narrative lens. At this point, a degree of common ground may be discovered between the methodologies of historical-criticism and structuralism. The *irreducible* character of discourse, Ricoeur argues, founds hermeneutics.[290] While the structuralist exhorts interpreters to discover the signs of the narrator in the parable, the historical critic implores them to uncover the historically organized and interpreted form of the discourse.[291] Coherence between

---

290 Ibid., 48. Also see our discussion above on discourse criteria.

291 Ibid., 46.

these two approaches to the parables is supported by the fact that narrative parabolic discourse is a genre of narratives within a narrative. Their interpretation cannot be merely focused on individual parables (or even on all of them). Rather, in addition to the final text, a thorough interpretation must also include how the final text has reached its present state of existence. In other words, what is the narrative context in which a parable finds its raison d'être, within the narrative as a whole?

In some sense then, it can be said, that a narrative is both closed and open. Many of the parables of Jesus are narratives within a narrative. This same narrative closure (the joining of "la parole" and "la langue"), which intersignifies and intertextualizes the parables with other biblical texts (proverbs and eschatological sayings of Jesus, etc.), is also what arms the parables (in a poetico-narratological fashion) with the capacity to be open to a referent.[292]

For Ricoeur, narrative parables are a form of *poetics*, albeit one rooted in and related to other forms of biblical discourse, such as proverb and proclamation.[293] These three modes of biblical discourse are distinct, and yet they converge in the following way. All three genres can be said to "transgress" more ordinary forms of description: the proverb, through its hyperbolic and paradoxical intensification; the proclamatory, through its freeing of temporal symbols beyond their literal interpretation; and the parabolic, through its extravagance.[294] Apocalyptic discourse, proverbs, and parables, as used by Jesus, all intersignify and point towards the meaning of the Kingdom of God.

Ricoeur is using the phrase, the Kingdom of God, as a "qualifier" which, in his opinion, confers upon these modes of discourse their

---

292 Ricoeur, "Biblical Hermeneutics," 73, insightfully argues here for the mimetic function of both parable and narrative. In other words, both parable and narrative, as parable and narrative, imitate human action and redescribe reality at the level of composition and final text.

293 Ricoeur, "Le 'Royaume' dans les paraboles de Jesus," 15-19. This is important to recognize in a critique of structuralism's interpretation of parables. Ricoeur forcefully, in this sense, shows the relevance of intersignification within the global character of the text, pointing to a divergence and convergence, which cannot reduce parables to one story, or a mere system of codes. Also, "Biblical Hermeneutics," 100-101.

294 Ricoeur uses, among others, the work of Perrin, "The Parables of Jesus as Parables, as Metaphors, and as Aesthetic Objects," *Journal of Religion* 47 (1967), 340-347, and W. A. Beardslee, *Literary Criticism of the New Testament*, Philadelphia: Fortress, 1970, 30-41, to complement his own work on parables.

specific religious use.²⁹⁵ In other words, without the qualifier, a parable could remain poetic, but non-religious, in its application to life. Ricoeur explains qualifier in the following way:

> It is the "index" which *points beyond* the structure, beyond even the metaphorical dimension, and which calls for a corresponding factor of *radicality* in the "redescription" of human reality.²⁹⁶

In Ricoeur's perspective, a "qualifier," such as the Kingdom of God, in parabolic discourse, can be thought of as a symbol that gives rise to thought. As such, symbols are in need of interpretation and contribute as one of several strands of intersecting meaning within the discourse. Each strand then, which is interdependent on the others, gives insight into the sense of the saying—the message of the Kingdom of God.

Ricoeur argues for three cardinal traits within the literary genre of biblical narrative parable: narrative form, metaphorical process, and "qualifier." Since we have already touched on the latter, we shall focus briefly, on narrative form and metaphorical process.²⁹⁷ In terms of narrative, a parable may be re-presented as a story that refers beyond itself to reality.²⁹⁸ However, if this is the case, the problematic of sense and its connection to reference is complicated. Narrative parables, it is often argued, are referent-less intra-linguistic sign systems, that is, stories with their own insular set of rules and sense.²⁹⁹ This immediately reminds us of Ricoeur's ongoing debate with structuralism, with its solitary emphasis on code over message in regards to parables. If narrative, according to a structural analysis, is a "closed" story, how is it possible

---

295 Ricoeur is indebted to I. T. Ramsey, *Religious Language*, New York: Macmillian, 1957, for this terminology.

296 Ricoeur, "Biblical Hermeneutics," 33, (Emphasis and *Italics his*).

297 We are unable, at this juncture, to undertake a more comprehensive examination of Ricoeur's views on narrative, religious language, and metaphor, which will have to be discussed at another stage. We shall, however, deal briefly with metaphor and parable below.

298 Ricoeur, "Biblical Hermeneutics," 30.

299 As we have seen in the examination of Crossan's and Marin's work above.

to speak of parables referring outside their narrative structure?

It is here that Ricoeur turns to the *metaphoric process* principally found in the plot, which allows the parable to detonate a charge of action. This charge sets the narrative in motion, a motion from the inside - closed, to the outside - open, or in other words, from and within the narrative form of the parable, to a refiguration of reality. Ricoeur states it this way:

> Metaphor includes a denotative or referential dimension, the power of redefining reality.[300]

> My suggestion is that the trait that invites us to *transgress* the narrative structure is the same as that which *specifies* the parable as a "religious" kind of "poetic" discourse. This trait is, to my mind, the element of extravagance, which makes the "oddness" of the narrative, by mixing the "extraordinary" with the "ordinary."[301]

This metaphoric process is neither a mere ornament of discourse, nor a scant shift in the meaning of words; rather, it operates at the level of the whole sentence or narrative, creating a *tension* we might call: semantic-narrative- reality impertinence.[302] In this sense, the parabolic discourse is open to realms beyond the parameters of its narrative structure, and this openness is due to the tension between form and process. A form - process narrative tension can be accessed through a poetico-hermeneutical approach. Such a hermeneutical method effectively questions the excess and exclusivity of a structuralist or historical-critical methodology in their attempts to go it on their own, and focuses on the capacity of the para-narrative to produce a sensible story and a message with the power to "refigure" human existence.

---

300 Ibid., 75.

301 Ibid., 99, (Emphasis and *Italics his*).

302 Ibid., 77, 95.

This functioning role of sense and referent, established by the para-narrative, calls normal human existence into question and critically challenges the para-normal with the para-abnormal. The abnormal takes place both on the level of form (a genre characterized by its mixing of the extraordinary with the ordinary), and on that of content (these stories feature a surprise factor that shakes its readers' reality sensibilities). Within the narrative, these two levels create a striking *extravagance* unique to parables. We shall briefly explain this more specifically in the following way.

For the most part, the parables of Jesus are *ordinary* stories about fishing, sowing, receiving, finding, selling, and buying, among other things. There is nothing immediately unusual about these ordinary people and their ordinary situations, until the *extraordinary*, the Kingdom of God, is included in the picture.[303] It is in this realization, that these apparent narratives of normalcy produce a shock, disorientation, and an upheaval, through an announcing that the time has come for a *new* vision of reality and of being in the world. This moment of surprise is provoked by the "drama" of events and by the actions of the characters—that is, through the *plot* of the story. On occasion, parables display an "intrigue" involving a moment of crisis and denouement. Often times this intrigue is tragic, as in the case of Matthew 25:1-13, where upon the bridegroom's arrival, certain virgins have no oil and therefore cannot join the wedding banquet. Other instances of this are happy, as in the case of Luke 15:11-32 when the lost son returns and receives a joyous reception and celebration.[304]

Thus, parables have a *mimetic* power to poetically and narratively enrich our view of the "other" through form and content alike. Vividly, the metaphors employed articulate another view of the world, a world frequently unfolded on the level of suspense.[305] This emplotted world mean-

---

303 Ricoeur, "Listening," 239-240.

304 Ricoeur, "Le 'Royaume' dans les paraboles de Jesus," 16-17.

305 Ricoeur, "Biblical Hermeneutics," 99.

ingfully and referentially, creates, calls for, and coerces a tension between two views of reality, thereby leading to a re-thinking and re-evaluation of the "ordinary" way of perceiving things. Ricoeur points out:

> Poetic language also speaks of reality, but it does so at another level than does scientific language. Poetic language does not say literally what things are, but what they are like. It is in this oblique fashion that it says what they are.[306]

Ricoeur's focus on the qualifier and the form of the narrative plot, which is the conveyer of the metaphoric process, provides the possibility to re-create and open the significant movement from the deep structure of the parable (semiotic) to its surface structure (semantic). This is viewed as hermeneutically essential for the explanation - understanding of the parabolic "crisis" as related to existence and its redescription of "reality."

The interpretation of a narrative parable, according to this hermeneutic methodology, necessarily recognizes the failure of a given "coherent" explanation of reality that no longer makes sense. However, this operative deconstruction, or apparent unmeaning, is transferred meaningfully back onto the narrative in the form of a disturbance that propels a reaction from the characters and a *new* vision of the situation from the reader. Through these semantic metaphorical devices (often in the form of a striking inconsistency about the reality being portrayed), another genre of sense emerges. In other words, these oddities displayed in the narrative provoke the reader to thought, invite a second look at the apparently absurd happenings, and finally prompt a multi-layered sense. This method for making sense, in Ricoeur's view, includes the possibility of a production of *new* meaning, both on the level of the sentence, and the vision of reality.

It is important, at this juncture, in order to evaluate Ricoeur's ap-

---

306 Ibid., 87-88.

plication of his views on metaphor to biblical parables, to turn to one of his interlocutor's. Wolfgang Harnisch, while adopting much of Ricoeur's terminology and insight in regards to the interpretation of biblical parables, nevertheless argues for a modification, within a hermeneutical methodology, of his conclusions.[307]

Harnisch does not focus on the fecundity or lack thereof, of a Ricoeurian methodological complementarity in tension, but rather investigates, among other things, the methodological legitimacy of *transferring* a theory of metaphor to the parables of Jesus, as Ricoeur attempts to do. One question begged by Harnisch that is of interest to us, is whether narratives in the Synoptic tradition are received as parables because they cause a linguistic movement or process, inaugurated by *extravagance*, which Ricoeur argues, is the case concerning metaphor.[308]

There is no question that Harnisch concurs with Ricoeur's perceptive critique of the rhetorical definition of metaphor, which focuses attention entirely on single word, substitution, or comparison.[309] Metaphor, according to this perspective, is similar to linguistic circumlocution, incapable of being either innovative or saying anything new about reality. Thus, the aim of metaphor, in this case, is not to create, but merely to repeat differently what is already known.

Ricoeur and Harnisch both oppose such views, arguing that these assumptions are misleading.[310] Metaphor finds its place, not on the level of words, but rather, in the context of the semantics of the whole sentence. The "tension" then, between sense and non-sense does not function on the level of individual words exchanged; rather, tension manifests itself

---

307 Harnisch, *Die Gleichniserzählungen Jesu*, esp. 125-141 and 151-167.

308 Ricoeur, "Biblical Hermeneutics," 75-89.

309 In respect to the interpretation of parables, A. Jülicher is a good example of an interpreter who embraces the rhetorical tradition in its definition of metaphor. For a poignant critique of this tradition and its influence on parable interpretation see Ricoeur, "Biblical Hermeneutics," 89-92; Harnisch, *Die Gleichniserzählungen Jesu*, 127-128. For a fuller discussion of the rhetorical tradition and metaphor see Ricoeur, *La métaphore vive*, 13-85, (*The Rule of Metaphor*, 9-65).

310 Harnisch, *Die Gleichniserzählungen Jesu*, 125-141. Ricoeur, "Biblical Hermeneutics," 75-106.

with the "odd" word in the context of the whole related sentence, generating a twist in the meaning, which causes the whole sentence to be understood as metaphorical. Metaphor is not to be thought of as based on a theory of *substitution*, but on a theory of *tension*, which has the capacity to recognize metaphorical words, which in turn powerfully engender a modification of the sentence. Ricoeur states:

> [...] an entire statement constitutes the metaphor, yet attention focuses on a particular word, the presence of which constitutes the grounds for considering the statement metaphorical. This balance of meaning between the statement and the word is the condition of its principal feature, the contrast within a single statement between one word that is taken metaphorically and another that is not. In 'The chairman *plowed* through the discussion,' the word *plowed* is taken metaphorically, the others not. We shall say then that metaphor is 'a sentence or another expression in which *some* words are used metaphorically while the remainder are used non-metaphorically.'[311]

In this instance, metaphor is not to be viewed as rhetorically inappropriate to language, but must be perceived as poetically creative in its dissonance, thereby constituting a new possibility of sense. When metaphor is considered in this context, Ricoeur and Harnisch agree. However, when the *transfer* or movement from a theory of metaphor to parable takes place, according to Harnisch, there is an increased necessity of emendation.[312] Ricoeur has proposed that it is in a "tension theory," at the level of the sentence that metaphor can be recognized. Harnisch does not dispute this. Rather, he questions Ricoeur's understanding of such a tension theory as it applies to parables.

Ricoeur himself is aware of the difficulties and with three points, he attentively warns against "too hasty" an interchange between a ten-

---

311 Ricoeur, *The Rule of Metaphor*, 84. (*La métaphore vive*, 110).

312 Harnisch, *Die Gleichniserzählungen Jesu*, 153-157.

sion theory of metaphor and that of parabolic discourse.[313] First, there is a hierarchy of discourse. Ricoeur means here that the tension theory operates at the level of the sentence, while parabolic discourse executes meaning at the level of composition, which is then to be understood as a whole meaningful work. Second, metaphors exist in immediacy. Ricoeur's point is that metaphors do not find their status in a normally established lexical code, but in *semantic* origination. As such, in a tension theory scenario, highly figurative narratives would be dead metaphors. But this is not the case with parables because they function on another genre of tension related to the next point. Third, parables exhibit none of the metaphorical tension between literal and figurative. Ricoeur argues that the tension theory of the sentence, in its identification of the literal and metaphorical, cannot be applied to parabolic discourse. In parables, there cannot be some words that are taken metaphorically and some literally, as the narrative whole is recounted on the level of ordinary life events. For Ricoeur, this means there is no *inner* tension within the parable, or sub-text of meaning going on under the surface. He states:

> The "tension" is entirely on the side of the vision of reality between the insight displayed by the fiction and our ordinary way of looking at things.[314]

Harnisch too argues that there is a parabolic tension, but in his opinion, it is to be found in the *configuration* of the narrative itself. We shall explain this in the following way. It is *intrinsically* the narrative, in its defamiliarization of the familiar that produces the two poles in tension. While it is clear that Ricoeur is careful to not, in a facile way, synthesize metaphor and parable, he *fails* to point out this creative tension that exists on the literary level of the narrative itself. Harnisch affirms

---

313 Ricoeur, "Biblical Hermeneutics," 92-96. Against C. L. Blomberg, *Interpreting the Parables*, Leicester: IVP, 1990, 136, who misses Ricoeur's nuanced exposition here.

314 Ibid., 95-96.

that the para-narrative tension is what creates the metaphorical process. Therefore, the tension must not be understood as existing between the narrative form and a metaphoric process as such. In other words, Ricoeur equates the narrative form with what is already the "ordinary," while the "extraordinary" is to be viewed as correspondent to the metaphoric process, which then in turn creates a parabolic "clash" for the reader. Harnisch, in focusing on the narratological tension *within* the parable, places the "clash" in the narrative and its two presentations of reality, which comprise the parable. For Ricoeur, the tension relationship is actualized *outside* the parable, as it clashes with our own understanding of the familiar. For Harnisch, the parable is metaphor in a story, a story that creates a reality-tension *within* itself.

According to Harnisch, the narrative configuration in and of itself creates a parable, which is to be understood from and by its narrative context. The parabolic movement or motion is from the *inside* towards the *outside*.[315] Thus, the production of sense and reference is related to the parable; and its "insides" are related to the creation of the familiar and accompanying defamiliarization, within the parable. The parable produces an entirely new vision of the world, one in which everyday reality and extravagant reality are woven together, announcing the necessity of new ways of viewing and living in the world. The narrative parables of Jesus, Harnisch argues, in and of themselves, present a possibility that affects reality in so far as it has the power to change it. This possibility does not pre-exist the parabolic formulation, but the parable *engenders* it.

In our estimation, Harnisch has brought a valid and valuable exegetical-methodological insight into the discussion of the interpretation of parables. Ricoeur's perspective, in some ways, *misses* the uniqueness of the parable on the level of its own configuration; a configuration that intrinsically equips the parable, with the capacity to powerfully

---

315 Harnisch, *Die Gleichniserzählungen Jesu*, 312, argues that any form of allegory would stifle the creative power of the parable in assigning it the role of portraying an "outside" reality that pre-exists its own creation of reality.

change reality. Perhaps, in Harnisch's terms, the narrative parables of Jesus are to be thought of as metaphors in motion. The familiar narrative world given to the hearer is rivaled by its own defamiliarization that carries the story beyond the limits it presents, thereby surpassing the familiar world. In the joining together of what does not go together, there is an act of creation, rendering the whole scenario extravagant, even outlandish, as in the father who jovially welcomes the forlorn son (Lk. 15:11ff), or the debtor who is "let off" from paying a colossal debt (Mt. 18:23ff). With the emphasis of Harnisch, we are able to pay closer attention to what is created by, and internally takes place in the narrative parables of Jesus, without assuming or resorting to external considerations that are not in the context of the story.

It is precisely here, however, that the perspective of Harnisch becomes problematic. Having recognized the value of a Harnischian emendation of Ricoeur, we nevertheless perceive the need of further modification. Harnisch aims to interpret parables, as if it is possible, in his disdain for allegory, to ignore any pre-existing "already" outside of the parable, in either its diachronic or synchronic dimension.

Harnisch strongly critiques those who, in his opinion, go *outside* the story and hold that the landowner in the parable is a figure or symbol of God, yet he attempts to argue that this parable expresses, by its impertinence, in a displacement of the conditions of everyday life, "the phenomenon of goodness, which for its part corresponds to the source of love and manifests love. Love is the new possibility of life." The story, in its distance from the everyday, "calls attention to the abundance and richness of love and in doing so comes to express God himself."[316] This may be the case, and in principal, we have no objection to this perspective, but would only want to point out that Harnisch himself seems to start *outside* the story in speaking of the correspondence of goodness and love, a conclusion that is not necessarily engendered in the parable itself.

---

316 Harnisch, "The Metaphorical Process in Matthew 20:1-15," in: *SBL Seminar Papers*, P. J. Achtemeir, ed., Missoula: Scholars Press, 1977, 231-250, esp. 243-244, 246.

Indeed, Harnisch makes a bold effort, but in our opinion, one that is not completely realizable, for the following reasons. First, if it is true that the parables of Jesus emanate from Jesus, the parables point to their speaker, a speaker who performs the speech act of parables.[317] Such a speaker, in our case Jesus, pre-exists the parable and therefore cannot be disregarded in its interpretation. In addition to this, Harnisch himself, as interpreter, as hearer, is outside the parable and therefore is, in some sense, the agent of a pre-existing reading and hearing that cannot be ignored.[318] Second, the parables of Jesus find themselves in the Jewish tradition, as does Jesus. In this sense, they are intersignified with other Jewish texts, which may help in their interpretation. Parables are not forced to stand-alone.[319] They are preceded by a message, a world, a speaker, and a hearer. Harnisch therefore, *overstates* his case, when he argues that there is no pre-existing interpretive aspect outside the parable that is coherent with its parableness.

Keeping these two perspectives in mind, we shall draw the following conclusions. Parables are always producing sense-referents, while at the same time, they are not sense - referent sealing. There is then a *double* tension. In one sense, as Harnisch argues, parabolic *internal* tension exists between two views of reality in the narrative, which creatively produces sense and referent. In another sense, as Ricoeur argues, a parabolic *external* tension exists between the parable and its pre-existing already "ordinary," and the new "extraordinary," which produces sense and reference.

What is "new" in the parable is created in a way that is new, but perhaps, not exclusively or entirely "new." In other words, because of the

---

317 Vanhoozer, "A Lamp in the Labyrinth: The Hermeneutics of 'Aesthetic' Theology," *Trinity Journal*, Spring (1987), 25-56, esp. 54. Also, R. G. Gruenler, *New Approaches to Jesus and the Gospels*, Grand Rapids: Baker, 1982, 44. While it is true, in Ricoeur's opinion, that discourse is written, he also points out that it refers back to a speaker.

318 Harnisch, "The Metaphorical Process," 236. Also, Harnisch, *Die Gleichniserzählungen Jesu*, 154, where Harnisch clearly affirms the importance, following the influence of Ingarden and Iser, of a reader-response perspective in the interpretation of the parables of Jesus. The question to Harnisch, on this level, is: what is the position or status of this reader as a pre-existent to reading the parable?

319 N. T. Wright, *Jesus and the Victory of God*, London: SPCK, 1996, 174-182.

narrative parables networked intersignification with a diversity of biblical texts, the world, a speaker, and a hearer, as Ricoeur's hermeneutical methodology has pointed out, there is what we shall refer to as both *continuity* and *disjunction*. Continuity occurs, for example, at the level of message, if narrative parables truly do tell us something about God, the world, and the necessarily best ways of being in it (as Harnisch would affirm). There is also, however, disjunction, in that this message creatively arrives in a unique and new way that had not before preceded it. Might we say that the partial extravagance of parable is that both Ricoeur and Harnisch are right? The parables of Jesus are not restricted to the mutual exclusivity of either a Ricoeurian or a Harnischian perspective; but this is no way renders either one of them on their own, or the combining of both theories, non-sensical.

We suggest the following application to parables. In our opinion, there is the possibility of viewing the parables of Jesus as a *prism*.[320] Why this metaphor? On the one hand, parables insidedly create light in a motion from the inside to what is outside; but on the other hand, they outsidedly reflect light in a motion from the outside to what is inside. In this perception, we could say, there is a doubling of sense and referent. Methodologically, text and world, as it were, do not cancel each other out, but contribute to each other in a mutual production of sense. Hence, both text and world reflect and create during the course of their interactions with one another, instigating a motion towards new ways of viewing God, the world, and ways of being in it. As life itself always has a surplus of meaning, so too, many of the narrative parables of Jesus cannot be restricted to one, and only one approach or perspective. If this is the case, both life and parables symmetrically require a surplus of methodologies, which complement one another in tension, and lead to the possibility of a better interpretation of both.

---

320 What we have in mind here is a transparent body, as of glass, with three or more sides. The function of a prism is to both refract and disperse light. This means that a prism is both a creator and a reflector of light. As the light strikes the prism from the outside, it creates a new light from the inside. In this sense, it both is, and is not, the same light.

This examination of Ricoeur's work on parables enables us to better evaluate his hermeneutic methodology. Ricoeur's principal contribution is not that of an exegete, nor primarily that of a theologian. His work, however, offers crucial insights into the parables of Jesus as *poetic discourse*. Parables, in a Ricoeurian perspective, have both sense and reference. As such, they have a speaker, a history, a discernible structure, and a world, all of which helps interpreters to understand, explain, and newly understand them. This world of the text is a world that its interpreters may inhabit, a world that can move them to new understanding.

The strength of Ricoeur's hermeneutic method for biblical hermeneutics (applied specifically to parables) is its ability to incorporate both the historical-critical and structuralist methods, without rendering them non-sensical or irrelevant to the hermeneutical task. Ricoeur is careful to give adequate place for the interests of each methodological orientation, while eschewing their hubris. We should not, however, understand Ricoeur to merely be mediating or synthesizing for the sake of mediation or synthesis. In methodological complementarity, a tension remains, which complementarity cannot vanquish. Characteristically, this is Ricoeur's way: always moving first through the *detour* and then to the *goal*—a goal that remains to be thought, but can be thought, a goal that remains to be given, but can be given.

The weakness of Ricoeur's hermeneutical methodology for biblical hermeneutics is a heavy-emphasis on the hermeneutic axis, without incorporating enough exegesis. As Ricoeur rightly points out, a hermeneutic method is concerned with more than exegesis, but we would suggest that such a method is not concerned with less.

In concluding this section, we shall argue, Ricoeur's more broad based hermeneutical methodology, in reference to the narrative parables of Jesus, is complemented and enhanced by the more narrowly based exegetical perspective of Harnisch. In our viewpoint, however, the two focalizations can best be understood in an *interdependent matrix*, bringing forth a less reductionistic and therefore more holistic interpretive trajectory. Although tension remains regarding the best method for approaching the parables of Jesus, as well as interpretations of life lived, there is also a complementarity to be reckoned with.

3.3. Narrative

We proposed that the early part of our study was a pre-figuring of Ricoeur's work, and we then moved into a configuring mode, forging through the questions of text, interpretation theory, and biblical hermeneutics. It is imperative to now continue in this mode of configuration a step further, since, according to some interpreters, narrative has become the "leitmotif" of Ricoeur's recent thought.[321] Narratives are configured agents and therefore vital for our project of a "living hermeneutics." To explore Ricoeur's forays into narrative will be instructive in and of itself, but it will also open up onto the final stage of our trajectory, which Ricoeur posits as refiguration.

This sphere of inquiry has received a fair amount of reflection in Ricoeur's writing and his engagement with these questions and issues is clearly evidenced by a myriad of texts, including the three volume *Temps et récit* (*Time and Narrative*) and *Penser la Bible* (*Thinking Biblically*).[322] Thus, Ricoeur's work is one of the most prominent and thought provoking enterprises to peruse for an investigation into narrative and a contribution to biblical hermeneutics.

3.3.1. Why Narrative?

Why has Ricoeur inaugurated such a thorough study of narrative in his writings? Briefly, we shall now examine how his focus on narrative situates his hermeneutical trajectory, as well as the relevance of this for a further configuration of his work.

---

321 Wallace, "Introduction," in: M. I. Wallace, ed., Ricoeur, *Figuring the Sacred*, 11.

322 Ricoeur, *Temps et récit, I - III* (*Time and Narrative I - III*). P. Ricoeur and A. LaCocque, *Penser la Bible*, Paris: Seuil, 1998 (*Thinking Biblically: Exegetical and Hermeneutical Studies*, trans. Pellauer, Chicago: University of Chicago Press, 1998).

It is argued that the writing and interpretation of narratives is at the very root of Western culture.[323] No doubt, narratives have played a significant role in the telling of our pasts, giving perspectives to the projected future, while at the same time, enlivening the present. But, why has Ricoeur delved into narrative? It is not our intention to touch on all the reasons for Ricoeur's move into an analysis of narrative, but after a few general comments on narrative problematics, we shall delineate several interests and connections that have motivated his orientation.

The study of narrative in recent years has drawn the attention of literary theorists, theologians, philosophers, and historians. Such attention has become the object of intense debate.[324] What is the relation, or lack thereof, between fiction and history, between narrative and the real world? These central aporias continue to plague the various disciplines just mentioned.[325]

It is argued that *modernist* interpretative orientations have been based on the objectivity of the past and the objective character of the investigator, who examines the facts of the real world with the ability to render a true account of what happened.[326] Historical patterns are found rather than made, discovered, not constructed. Within this interpretative paradigm, meta-narratives exist and thrive, since fiction and history are assumed to occupy completely distinct realms of dis-

---

323 Ricoeur, *Temps et récit, I*, 315, (*Time and Narrative, I*, 226) points out that history and fiction are the "great" narrative modes. See also, K. J. Vanhoozer, *Is There A Meaning in This Text? The Bible, The Reader and the Morality of Literary Knowledge*, Grand Rapids: Zondervan, 1998, 38.

324 F. Kermode, *A Sense of Ending: Studies in the Theory of Fiction*: London: Oxford University Press, 1966; S. Chatman, *Story and Discourse: Narrative Structure in Fiction and Film*, Ithaca: Cornell University Press, 1978; Ricoeur, *Temps et récit I - III*, (*Time and Narrative I - III*); D. Carr, *Time, Narrative, and History*, Bloomington: Indiana University Press, 1986; W. J. T. Mitchell, ed., *On Narrative*, Chicago: University of Chicago Press, 1981; P. Bühler and J. F. Habermacher, éds., *La narration. Quand le récit devient communication*, Lieux théologiques 12, Genève: Labor et Fides, 1988; W. R. Stenger, *Narrative Theology in Early Jewish Christianity*, Louisville: Westminster, 1989; S. S. Lanser, *The Narrative Act: Point of View in Prose Fiction*, Princeton: Princeton University Press, 1981; and M. Ellingsen, *The Integrity of Biblical Narrative: Story in Theology and Proclamation*, Minneapolis: Fortress, 1990, offer a variety of different perspectives and orientations.

325 D. Carr, "Life and the Narrator's Art," in: H. J. Silverman and D. Ihde, eds., *Hermeneutics and Deconstruction*, New York: State University Press of New York, 1985, 108-121, esp. 119, points out, "Perhaps the central problem is that of the narrative voice, which seems to be hoarse and cracking or to have fallen silent altogether."

326 Something of such a perspective goes back, at least as far as, Lucian of Samosata who wrote the pamphlet, "How to Write History" somewhere around 166-168 A. D. See also, K. Jenkins, "Introduction," in: K. Jenkins, ed., *The Postmodern History Reader*, London: Routledge, 1997, 1-25, and the illuminating essay of C. S. Evans, "Critical Historical Judgement and Biblical Faith," in: R. A. Wells, ed., *History and the Christian Historian*, Cambridge: Eerdmans, 1998.

course. However, compelling critiques of modernism have questioned this paradigm, forcing it to face a radical change.[327] As a result of this, some argue that we find ourselves in a so-called crisis of narratives.[328] The illustrious designs of the meta-narratives of modernism and the goals of neutral objectivity are argued to be in disarray, beyond the point of collapse.[329]

From a *post-modernist* perspective, the interpreter is pictured as wading through an opacity in which the outmoded attempt to narrate a past - present object or subject can never be secured.[330] Some say narratives can only end in a failure to offer any sense or referent, as the screech of perpetual deferral careens and rebounds off the walls of intra-textual closure.[331] Thus, what sorts of narratives, if any, are meaning-full, as opposed to meaning-less? With meta-narratives under fire in many circles, the suggestion is that we are left only with local narratives, opinion narratives, little narratives, or merely erring narratives.[332] Do interpreters face the constraint of having to choose between these two orientations? Shall it be either the "sharp boundaries" of modernism or the "radical indeterminacy" of post-modernism? Several other questions concerning narrative require consideration. What is the relationship (or lack thereof) between time and narrative? Do narratives create time, history, art, and life or do they mirror them? How do narratives and the events they portray relate to each other, and can they do so? Is it possible to speak of human action as fiction, or of history as narrative? These questions and others have made the narrative quest

---

[327] B. Southgate, *History: What & Why?, Ancient, Modern and Postmodern Perspectives*, London: Routledge, 1996, 9.

[328] Lyotard, *The Postmodern Condition*, xxiii.

[329] Ibid., xxiv.

[330] G. Himmelfarb, "Telling it as you like it: postmodernist history and the flight from fact," in: Jenkins, ed., *The Postmodern History Reader*, 158-174, esp. 170. Himmelfarb argues that the postmodernist tendency is more prevalent in literary criticism, but that such a perspective has also had an impact among historians. A postmodern perspective is inclined "to trivialize history by so fragmenting it that it lacks all coherence and focus, all sense of continuity, indeed, all meaning."

[331] As in Derrida, *Of Grammatology*, Baltimore: Johns Hopkins University Press, 1976, 158, who states, "There is nothing outside the text."

[332] Taylor, *Erring*, 179. Lyotard, *The Lyotard Reader*, A. Benjamin, ed., Oxford: Blackwell, 1989, 132.

one of the central literary, philosophical, historical, and theological issues of our contemporary hermeneutical context.

Ricoeur's interests lead him to partake in this discussion, especially with the works of *La métaphore vive*, *Temps et récit*, and his writings on biblical hermeneutics. Already back in 1971, Ricoeur wrote:

> Today I should be less inclined to limit hermeneutics to the discovery of hidden meanings in symbolic language and would prefer to link hermeneutics to the more general problem of written language and texts.[333]

This hermeneutical movement into written language and texts eventually led him into fully developed studies of metaphor and narrative.[334] While metaphor and narrative have traditionally been classified in distinct categories, Ricoeur argues that they should be viewed as related on the level of semantic innovation.[335]

> With metaphor, the innovation lies in the producing of a new semantic pertinence by means of an impertinent attribution: "Nature is a temple where living pillars..." [...]

> With narrative, the semantic innovation lies in the inventing of another work of synthesis – a plot. By means of the plot, goals, causes, and chance are brought together within the temporal unity of a while and complete action.[336]

Ricoeur argues there is a series of links between metaphor and narra-

---

[333] Ricoeur, "From Existentialism to the Philosophy of Language," *Criterion* 10 (1971), 14-18. Reprinted in and quoted from, *The Rule of Metaphor*, 317.

[334] Ricoeur, *La métaphore vive* (*The Rule of Metaphor*) and *Temps et récit, I-III* (*Time and Narrative I-III*).

[335] Ricoeur points out that metaphor has traditionally been considered under a theory of tropes, while narrative has been viewed from the perspective of literary genres. See Ricoeur, *Temps et récit*, I, 11. (*Time and Narrative*, I, ix).

[336] *Time and Narrative*, I, ix (*Temps et récit*, I, 11).

tive, one connection being that both have the capacity to be semantically innovative on the level of discourse: "that is, the level of acts of language equal to or greater than the sentence."[337] Whether in regard to metaphor or narrative, the sentence is the smallest unit out of which discourse arises. This point remains instructive for understanding the direction of Ricoeur's hermeneutical trajectory. Semantics, again for Ricoeur, go beyond semiotics and must be included in an analysis of metaphor and narrative. He is not merely concerned with sign systems, but seeks to discover the intelligible message of the discourse (sentence or beyond) through the world it unfolds.

In other words, a *symbiosis* can be construed in terms of the "meaning effects" of various types of discourse, each understood as language acts and concretized in a text. It is important to underscore that Ricoeur's metaphor - narrative concerns remain hermeneutically oriented. He is committed to the task of hermeneutics, which in his opinion, is necessarily related to the creation, establishing, reception, and reading of the text, and not merely to its semiotic state. Hermeneutics is concerned, not only with configuration, but with prefiguration and refiguration as well. In going beyond a semiotic investigation, restricted to an examination of the internal laws of a literary work, Ricoeur points out:

> It is the task of hermeneutics, in return, to reconstruct the set of operations by which a work lifts itself above the opaque depths of living, acting, and suffering, to be given by an author to readers who receive it and thereby change their acting. For a semiotic theory, the only operative concept is that of the literary text. Hermeneutics, however, is concerned with reconstructing the entire arc of operations by which practical experience provides itself with works, authors, and readers.[338]

---

337 Ibid., ix. (Ibid., 11).

338 Ibid., 86. (*Time and Narrative, I*, 53).

Ricoeur's work on narrativity builds on his explorations into metaphor and thereby offers a hermeneutical perspective of the inventive power of language expressed in texts. A narrative is semantically innovative as it is orchestrated through the vehicle of plot, which brings together a series of events and configures them into a unique and unified whole. In this sense, plots have the capacity to create an order and a time that is not already there. Furthermore, he argues that plots function as a structuring principle, which underlies the resemblances between fictional and historical narratives.[339] Plots and the act of emplotment may explain more about reality, as well as enable a better understanding of it.[340] Along these lines, Ricoeur aims to understand, explain, and newly understand the world, time, human action, texts, self, and God, all through narrative.[341] We suggest that Ricoeur, at least implicitly, has a broader interest in the subject matter of: narrative and world; action and texts; self and God. And all of the previous must be understood as pertinent to his ongoing paradigmatic construction of a general and regional hermeneutics.[342]

In the general hermeneutical sense, narratives have been present and relevant for centuries, forming the bedrock of belief systems, ideologies, utopias, societies, and cultures. These narratives help interpreters to explain and newly understand the world and themselves. At the same time, in the regional hermeneutical sense, historical and fictional narratives are also often textual and must be pondered, understood, explained, and newly understood as texts.[343] Thus, when considering the possibilities of

---

339 Ricoeur, "Narrative and Hermeneutics," in: J. Fisher, ed., *Essays in Aesthetics: Perspectives on the Work of Monroe C. Beardsley*, Philadelphia: Temple University Press, 1983, 149-160. We shall say more about this below.

340 Ricoeur, *Temps et récit, II*, 54. (*Time and Narrative, II*, 32).

341 Ricoeur, *The Philosophy of Paul Ricoeur*, Hahn, ed., 45. The explanation - understanding "debate" remains related to and important for Ricoeur's discussion of narrative. This unfolds in the following manner: "a theory of the text, a theory of human action, and a theory of history. The narrative constituted in this respect a crossroads between the three categories [.....]. It is therefore not surprising that lengthy developments are devoted to the explanation - understanding dialectic."

342 See Introduction.

343 Ricoeur, "Réponse de Paul Ricoeur à ses critiques," in: C. Bouchindhomme et R. Rochlitz, << *Temps et récit* >> *de Paul Ricoeur en débat*, Paris: Cerf, 1990, 202. In a discussion, situating himself with regard to his opponent, who

narrative/world/text relations it is evident that the questions of general and regional hermeneutics continue to pre-occupy Ricoeur.

It is just here, with a general and regional hermeneutic in mind, that Ricoeur proposes a tentative solution to an aporia that was one of his central interests in *Temps et récit*: how a narrative form of discourse deals with the innumerable difficulties pertaining to time. This unfolds in the following manner. A philosophical consideration of time brings forth the problematic of the contrast between phenomenological (subjective perception) time and cosmological (objective measure) time. Both presuppose the other, without however acknowledging their dependence. The latter dimension of time aims to ignore the necessity that time is measured by a subject (someone), while the former lacks the conceptual tools to posit itself as the source of time, without recourse to some objectively preconceived characteristics.[344]

Ricoeur appeals to narrative as a partial, yet incomplete solution to the problematics of the temporal dimension of human existence. Narrative, as both history and fiction under a mimetic act of emplotment, can bring together human expressions of time, which then creates a narrative time that mediates between phenomenological and cosmological time.[345]

Another motivation for Ricoeur's movement into narrative is what we shall refer to as the poetry of the possible.[346] Ricoeur views narratives as *poetic* in the sense that they, like other forms of poetry, are a cre-

---

writes of " 'une herméneutique primaire,' " Ricoeur maintains that truly speaking there is no such thing. Rather, his hermeneutical concerns are focused on the dialectic of "comprendre et expliquer" (understanding and explanation).

344 Ricoeur, *Temps et récit, III*, 19-89. (*Time and Narrative, III*, 12-58).

345 Ricoeur, *The Philosophy of Paul Ricoeur*, Hahn, ed., 42-46. We would add that from a biblical perspective one can also speak more theologically of time as "salvific time." Among many Old and New Testament examples: Genesis 12-22; Exodus 12-15; 1 Corinthians 15: 1-58; Matthew 21:1-46; John 7:1-52. What we have in mind here is the covenant making, Exodus producing, resurrecting, and identity of Jesus make time, in this biblical sense, a time of God's salvation. Narrative time, from our point of view, has a theological component.

346 Vanhoozer, "Philosophical Antecedents to Ricoeur's Time and Narrative," in: D. Wood, ed., *On Paul Ricoeur: Narrative and Interpretation*, London: Routledge, 1991, 34-54, esp. 51. Vanhoozer argues that human possibility is at the center of Ricoeur's narrative theory. "Ricoeur is a philosopher of human possibility, and in this philosophical project literature holds pride of place, for it is by reading stories and histories that we learn what is humanly possible."

ation of the *productive* imagination, which in turn produces a world.³⁴⁷ Poetry has the capacity to open up new ways of seeing the world, new possibilities, and new aspects of reality.³⁴⁸ However, we must point out before moving on that Ricoeur also perceives a distinction needs to be made here. While narratives are indeed poetic, Ricoeur argues not only for reciprocity, but also for contrast between poetry and kerygmatic biblical narratives in particular. The difference between reading a *poetic* text and a *kerygmatic* one is this: poetry leaves its reader in imaginative "play," while the biblical text calls for a commitment—a decision. Ricoeur states:

> So, whereas poetry is play, precisely because I do not have the burden of making a decision – what has been called in traditional Christianity, "conversion." It is not required from poetry, but there is a conversion from one impoverished world of language to an enriched one, but not in the sense of making a decision, taking a stand. So there is an element of promise and commitment in the religious attitude, which is different from the pure play in imagination and through imagination that takes place in poetry. That is why I should preserve a strong kinship and a precise difference between the two.³⁴⁹

Narratives are associated with poetry on the one level, yet kerygmatic biblical narratives are distinguished from being purely poetic on another.³⁵⁰ This relation - distinction dynamic (not ultimately a synthesis) is central to Ricoeur's poetico-narrative thesis of possible worlds being opened up

---

347 Ricoeur, "Poetry and Possibility: An Interview with Paul Ricoeur," in: *The Manhattan Review* 2 (1982), 6-21, reprinted in: Valdés, ed., *A Ricoeur Reader: Reflection and Imagination*, Toronto: University of Toronto Press, 1991, 448-462, esp. 453.

348 Ibid., 455.

349 Ibid., 455.

350 Ibid., 456. It is again evident, that mediation "marks" Ricoeur's work. In our opinion, his whole hermeneutical arc is consciously seeking to mediate between, yet not disintegrate into one, various positions or points of view. In other words, understanding that tensions remain, in spite of mediation, may be highly instructive with regard to Ricoeur's hermeneutical enterprise. See above, Parables, and also the perceptive article by M. Schaldenbrand, "Metaphoric Imagination: Kinship Through Conflict," in: Reagan, ed., *Studies in the Philosophy of Paul Ricoeur*, 1979, 57-81.

for readers to inhabit. Hermeneutically speaking, the poetic world and the kerygmatic, while being related, nevertheless present different worlds of habitation and therefore engender distinct responses from their readers.

A final point that pertains to our investigation of Ricoeur's interest in narrative is connected with his excursions into reading and analyzing the Bible.[351] Ricoeur defines this as a point worth *underscoring* in regard to his long-standing interest in narrative.[352] One of the responses to "why narrative" must then include Ricoeur's specific explorations of the biblical text. There is much to agree with in the conclusion of Don Ihde. Ihde argues that throughout the work of Ricoeur one finds the theme of a *biblically styled* historicity that is sensitive to and draws deeply from Judaic and Christian traditions.[353] Ricoeur's engagement with the biblical text has indeed been a relevant and motivating factor for his work on narrative, a work that in turn, has contributed significantly to biblical hermeneutics.

These reasons for Ricoeur's in-depth study of narrative will be extremely pertinent to an understanding of his particular conception of configuration and refiguration and to his work as a whole. As we have seen, there is a biblical and hermeneutical continuity in Ricoeur's quest, while at the same time there is a new exploration, attempting to creatively expand on and add to the previous orientations and contours of his thought. We shall discuss refiguration in detail below, but before doing so, we now turn to the question of "decoding" narrative.

3.3.2. A "Decoding:" What is Narrative?

Having briefly analyzed a number of explanations pertaining to Ricoeur's movement into narrative, it is important to recognize there

---

351 Ricoeur, "Time and Narrative in the Bible: Toward a Narrative Theology," *Unpublished Sarum Lectures*, Oxford University, 1980, esp. 1-16, views the Bible as a text through which the divine life is disclosed in the dynamic and tensional intersecting of various genres and modes of discourse.

352 Ricoeur, *The Philosophy of Paul Ricoeur*, Hahn, ed., 41.

353 Ihde, "Paul Ricoeur's Place in the Hermeneutic Tradition," in: Hahn, ed., *The Philosophy of Paul Ricoeur*, 59-69, esp. 68-69.

are two pivotal contemporary arguments concerning how narrative is to be described. Our aim is not to enter into a comprehensive historical - chronological analysis of narrative description, but to work with a Ricoeurian conception in dialogue with that of David Carr[354] to show how these two voices speak to a narrative "decoding."[355] This discussion is eminently appropriate in its own right with regard to contemporary narrative altercations, but it also functions as a precursor for our next sections concerning the questions of history and fiction in a narrative context and then the dynamic of refiguration.

We begin with Ricoeur. According to Ricoeur, narratives configure what is pre-figured. In keeping with Heidegger, Ricoeur argues that practical experience, which he calls mimesis I,[356] always precedes emplotment, which he calls mimesis II. A pre-understanding of a world of action exists with the capacity to structurally discern the difference between *action* and mere *physical* movement. Actions relate to motives and goals, which in turn relate to questions such as "who" and "why." Pre-figuration (mimesis I) happens on the level of cultural tradition (symbol recognition and temporal features) and involves actions tethered to this meaning. Any imitation of human action (as in an organized narrative) must first of all have a sense of what is being imitated. Thus, *mimetic* activity is not merely a vacuous exercise, but is rooted in a pre-understanding that has the capacity to conceptually recognize human action, symbols, and temporality.

Following on from this, Ricoeur views narrative as that which reconciles the *heterogeneous* through a specific literary act of emplotted

---

354 Carr, *Time, Narrative, and History*; "Life and the Narrator's Art," in: Silverman and Ihde, eds., *Hermeneutics and Deconstruction*, 108-121; "Narrative As A Form of Life," in: B. P. Dauenhauer, ed., *Textual Fidelity and Textual Disregard*, Bern, New York: Lang, 1990, 3-15; "Ricoeur on Narrative," in: Wood, ed., *On Paul Ricoeur: Narrative and Interpretation*, 160-173; "Narrative and the Real World: An Argument for Continuity," in: B. Fay, P. Pomper, R. T. Vann, eds., *History and Theory: Contemporary Readings*, Oxford: Blackwell, 1998, 137-152.

355 We are aware of the intricacies of the terminological discussion with respect to narrative. What is narrative? Story, plot, history, or discourse, etc.? Modern and post-modern narrative terminology is still finding its way towards a uniform vocabulary. For a fuller discussion of these important details than we shall undertake here see the studies by, G. Genette, *Figures III*, Paris: Seuil, 1972 and S. Chatman, *Story and Discourse*, 1978.

356 For a thorough analysis of mimesis see, E. Auerbach, *Mimesis*, Garden City: Anchor Books, 1957. For the relation between mimesis and hermeneutics see, R. Lundin, C. Walhout and A. C. Thiselton, *The Promise of Hermeneutics*, Carlisle: Paternoster, 1999, esp. "Narrative Hermeneutics," 65-131.

configuration, or mimesis II. Time and narrative are then brought together through this configuring act in the production of narrative discourse. That is, configuration is to be understood as the mediating force between pre-figuration (mimesis I) and refiguration (mimesis III) as it creates the world of the text for its eventual reception by the reader. Ricoeur argues that narrative configuration, through emplotment, orders life by creatively applying a sequential structure to that which was previously unstructured and dis-unified. This sequential emplotment however, is not merely a rote succession of events. Ricoeur states:

> [Plot] is mediation between the individual events or incidents and a story taken as a whole. In this respect, we may say equivalently that it draws a meaningful story from a diversity of events or incidents (Aristotle's *pragmata*) or that it transforms the events or incidents into a story. [... A story] must be more than just an enumeration of events in serial order; it must organize them into an intelligible whole, of a sort such that we can always ask what is the "thought" of this story. In short, emplotment is the operation that draws a configuration out of a simple succession.[357]

Narrative, Ricoeur argues, is capable of creating something new, and thus is a semantic innovation. Configuring the plot of narrative is understood as a synthesis of the heterogeneous in a threefold manner.[358] First, it makes one story out of a multiplicity of incidents. Second, plot organizes unintended circumstances, relationships between actors, planned or unplanned encounters, drawing them together into a single story with a beginning, middle and end. Third, a plot provides a "time" totality in the story, which can be understood as a creative act of a configuration out of succession.

In addition to this tripartite unfolding—his emplotted synthesis of the heterogeneous—Ricoeur offers an "epistemological corollary" to his the-

---

[357] Ricoeur, *Time and Narrative*, I, 65. (*Temps et récit*, I, 102), (*Italics his*).

[358] Ricoeur, "Life in Quest of Narrative," 21-22.

sis.³⁵⁹ He refers to this as the *intelligibility* of the act of configuration. Following Aristotle, Ricoeur argues that a "well told" story is always a useful teaching vehicle offering universal aspects of the human condition.³⁶⁰

Ricoeur offers a further contribution to a contemporary understanding of narrative by drawing out the implications of his epistemological corollary: the intelligibility of the configurative act. In his opinion, there is the possibility of constructing a *science* of narrative, which places narratology on the same level of rational investigation as that of the other sciences of language. Emplotment as the creative center and narratology as the reconstruction of a *rule-governed* understanding of poetry make it possible to "think" narrative.³⁶¹ Thus, narratology, as "second order" discourse, is preceded by a narrative understanding of existence that Ricoeur refers to as "first order," emerging from the *creative* imagination.³⁶²

Apparently, in striving to articulate an epistemological dimension of narrative, Ricoeur does not intend, however, to entirely discount an ontological status. We must recall that Ricoeur's picture of narrative is not merely one of story or literature, of ontological or epistemological bearing. Rather, first and foremost, *hermeneutical* concerns continue to drive his treatment of narrative.

Having briefly summarized Ricoeur's perspective, we shall now turn to concisely explore David Carr's views. The important differences between the two fuel much of the discussion on narrative and life. Carr argues that Ricoeur falsely assumes that human action and narrative discourse reside in two different spheres or realms.³⁶³ Carr asserts:

---

359 Ibid., 22.

360 Ibid., 22. Ricoeur points out that in Aristotle's view this means that poetry is more philosophical than history. Hence, for Aristotle, narrative is closer to practical wisdom than to scientific inquiry.

361 In this instance Ricoeur remains consistent with his orientation concerning the symbol. See Ricoeur, *The Symbolism of Evil*, 347-357, where he argues that the symbol gives rise to thought.

362 Ricoeur, "Life in Quest," 24. Ricoeur is slightly confusing here. Is he discussing texts or oral stories? He uses the terminology of "first order" and "second order" without a great deal of clarification. In addition, the role of the creative imagination is somewhat opaque.

363 Carr, "Narrative As A Form of Life," 3-15, esp. 13.

Configuring time in a narrative way is not something that individuals and communities *do*, it is the way they *are*. It is in this sense, then, that narrative is ontological and not merely epistemological, a form of life and not merely of discourse. Ricoeur, I believe, wants to *reconcile* narrative and time because he begins by accepting the point that they are separate.[364]

Perhaps, Carr has a point? Do human actions in time and narrative have such a disparate character that only an act of narrative configuration can bring them together? Ricoeur's focus on narrative as a written and organizing discourse of the heterogeneous may be too narrow. For Ricoeur, narrative functions as a configuring of human action, whereas for Carr it is simply the way we are. Does then narrative express something that is already there or does it forge something entirely new, in Ricoeur's terms, innovate semantically?

The issue, according to Carr, hinges on whether or not there is a narrative structure and coherence to reality or being that *precedes* the written text, something which Ricoeur and others do not acknowledge.[365] Do life and narrative have an even closer relation that might be understood as the complex narrative structure of human experience and action? In other words, is there such a thing as a *narrative way* of life?[366] Does Carr's critique and proposal offer a valid alternative to the Ricoeurian enterprise?

Following on from these questions, it appears that Carr is correct in his analysis that narrative has become both a "meeting ground" and

---

[364] Ibid., 12. (*Italics his*).

[365] Carr, *Time, Narrative, and History*, 12-13. Carr argues that for these interpreters, "Narrative as a literary artifact produced by historians, reads into the reality of the past a narrative structure that the past does not 'really' have." A clear example of this is found in H. White, *The Content of the Form*, Baltimore: Johns Hopkins University Press, 1987, 24, "What I have sought to suggest is that this value attached to narrativity in the representation of real events arises out of a desire to have real events display the coherence, integrity, fullness, and closure of life that is and can only be imaginary. The notion that sequences of real events possess the formal attributes of the stories we tell about imaginary events could only have its origin in wishes, daydreams, reveries."

[366] Carr, "Narrative," 15. Is it "possible to see narrative as a form of life before it is a form of discourse?"

"battle ground" for the disciplines.[367] He points out that philosophy, history, literature, structuralists, and post-structuralists all have a stake in narrative and approach the subject with differing purposes. Carr concludes that while a diversity of perspectives is not unusual, there still seems to be a *common factor* which binds a number of scholars in these diverse groups together: the relation between *narrative* and the *real world*. He poses the problematic in the following way:

> Simply put, it is the view that real events do not have the character of those we find in stories, and if we treat them as if they did have such a character, we are not being true to them.[368]

Carr substantiates his case through a concise sketch of contemporary narrativists, including such notable figures as F. Kermode, S. Chatman, R. Barthes, L. Mink, H. White and Ricoeur, arguing that in spite of their differences, they are related.[369] What connects this diversity of interpreters? Carr sees the relation in statements such as the following: there are no beginnings, middles and ends; storied events are structured, not actions themselves; stories differ from life, structure orders confusion; stories are not lived, but recounted.[370]

In this scenario, according to Carr, literary form is always understood to be an *imposition* on *unformed* reality. The outcome of this imposing of form results in a distortion of life. In other words, narrativizing brings about a falsification of the events it recounts. Carr states:

> Such form is 'imposed upon' reality, to use the most frequent expression. It distorts life. At best it constitutes an escape, a consolation, at worst an opiate, either as self-delusion, or [...] imposed from without

---

367 Carr, "Ricoeur on Narrative," 160.

368 Ibid., 160.

369 Ibid., 160. See also, Carr, "Life and the Narrator's," 108-121, esp. 109-110.

370 Ibid., 108-113.

by some authoritative narrative voice in the interest of manipulation and power. In either case it is an act of violence, a betrayal, an imposition on reality or life and ourselves.[371]

Carr's critique of this point of view, alongside his admission that "lives are not like the best novels," is his claim that a certain structure of narration exists which emanates from and is dependent on the structure of life. Stories are *lived* before they are *told*. The tremendous amount of work on narrative, in Carr's view, is focused almost entirely on the telling, with little attention being paid to the living. In other words, narrative art is designated to be in a priority position, while life is relegated to an inferior status.

The study of "life," Carr argues, used to be the domain of a valued life philosophy, related to phenomenology and existentialism. In Carr's view, contemporary theories of narrative mentioned above are in danger of leaving behind this valued life philosophy in order to embrace an over-emphasis on literary forms of discourse. Along with a distinction between life and the art of narrative, ought not a viable theory of story telling give equal attention to the one as well as the other? Is it then incorrect to argue that stories are not lived, but told? A better perspective, according to Carr, might be that stories are *told in being lived* and *lived in being told*.[372] He points out:

> I contend that narrative, far from being a distortion of, denial of, or escape from 'reality,' is in fact an extension and confirmation of its primary features.[373]

Carr is proposing, if I understand him correctly, that narrative is an *ontological* state prior to being a *literary* configuration. If narrative is

---

371　Ibid., 110.

372　Carr, *Time, Narrative, and History*, 61.

373　Carr, "Life and the Narrator's," 111.

merely a form of discourse, he argues, it has no choice but to be a distortion of reality. In this case, narrative and reality are argued by some to be entirely distinct. Before saying more about whether narrative is a distortion or not, true to life or not, a literary form or an ontological state, it is important to take another step into the discussion that will hopefully shed more light on these issues.

3.3.2.1. History and Fiction

The problems of "decoding" narrative, as represented by Ricoeur and Carr, left us with unresolved questions.[374] Following on from this lack of resolution and in the interest of clarification, we will now explore how these two proposals are understood to work themselves out in terms of *history* and *fiction*.

In so far as some would suggest that post-modernism has bred a new form of historiography,[375] we should stress that our interest is not primarily in the questions of social memory or identity per se, but rather with questions pertaining to a general theory of historical and fictional narrative.[376]

---

374 The amount of literature on this subject has grown tremendously in recent times. We shall mention only a small selection of contemporary examples on narrative, history, and biblical narratology: G. Gennete, *Figures III, (Poétique)*, Paris: Seuil, 1972 and *Nouveau discours du récit*, Paris: Seuil, 1983. J. M. Adam, La description, Que sais-je 1783, Paris: Presses Univérsitaires de France, 1993 and *Le récit, Que sais-je 2149*, Paris: Presses Univérsitaire, 1984. J. Bres, *La narrativité*, Champs linguistique, Louvain-la-Neuve: Duculot, 1994. U. Eco, *The Limits of Interpretation*, Bloomington: Indiana University Press, 1994 and *Interpretation and overinterpretation*, S. Collini, ed., Cambridge: Cambridge University Press, 1992. H. White, *Metahistory: The Historical Imagination in Nineteenth - Century Europe*, Baltimore: Johns Hopkins University Press, 1973. D. W. Bebbington, *Patterns in History: A Christian View*, Downers Grove, InterVarsity Press, 1979. *History and Theory: Contemporary Readings*, Fay, Pomper, Vann, eds., Oxford: Blackwell, 1998. C. B. McCullagh, *The Truth of History*, London: Routledge, 1998. Jenkins, *On 'What is History?'*, London: Routledge, 1995. B. Southgate, *History: What & Why?, Ancient, Modern and Postmodern Perspectives*, London: Routledge, 1996. *History and the Christian Historian*, R. A. Wells, ed., Cambridge: Eerdmans, 1998. J.-N. Aletti, *L'art de raconter Jésus-Christ: l'écriture narrative de l'évangile de Luc*, Parole de Dieu, Paris: Seuil, 1989 and *Quand Luc raconte, Le récit comme théologie*, Lire la Bible 115, Paris: Cerf, 1998. R. Alter, *The Art of Biblical Narrative*, New York: Basic Books, 1981. P. Bühler and J.-F. Habermacher, *La narration: quand le récit devient communication*, Lieux théologiques 12, Genève: Labor et Fides, 1988. J. Delorme, *Au risque de la parole: lire les évangiles*, Parole de Dieu 31, Paris: Seuil, 1991. M. Sternberg, *The Poetics of Biblical Narrative*, Bloomington: Indiana University Press, 1985. Frei, *The Eclipse of Biblical Narrative*, New Haven: Yale University Press, 1974. V. Philips Long, *The Art of Biblical History*, Grand Rapids: Zondervan, 1994.

375 M. Bentley, *Modern Historiography*, London: Routledge, 1999, 151. B. Southgate, *History: What & Why?* 1-9.

376 C. B. McCullagh, *The Truth of History*, 1, argues that there are two primary questions in today's discussion of history: first, its truth and objectivity and second, its social structures and general processes of social change. Our concern leans in the direction of the former, but is more specifically related to narrative.

What is to be made of the assumption that historical and fictional literature are clearly different? Are works of history "true" in a way that fictional literary works are not? As this field of inquiry is so vast, in an ancient, modern, and post-modern sense, we shall restrict our investigation to a selection of contemporary (mostly, but not entirely Anglo-American) authors who take part in the discussion.[377]

Historian Shirley A. Mullen comments, with regard to what she refers to as a widely shared view in Western "common sense,"

> that history is significantly different from fictional literature and that this difference is linked to its being 'true' in a way that literature is not. It is precisely these convictions - that history is different than literature - and that this difference is linked to history's value and reliability as a discipline, and to its claim to be pursuing truth about the past - that seem to be threatened by much of the discussion today that goes on under the rubric of postmodernism.[378]

In Mullen's view, it is evident that history is different, even considerably different, than literature. While this may be a tenable conclusion, it is not sufficiently clear what Mullen is discussing. What is history?[379] Does history differ from historiography, historical process, or literary framing?[380] What is literature?[381] Is literature (fiction) incapable of expressing and pursuing the truth about the past? In the case of the biblical text, is it to be viewed as "historized fiction" or "fictional-

---

[377] We are certainly not unaware of the parallel discussion in the French speaking world, which in a number of ways is similar to that of the Anglo-American. See Ricoeur, "Philosophies critiques de l'histoire: Recherche, explication, écriture," in: G. Fløistad, ed., *Philosophical Problems Today, I*, Dordrecht: Kluwer Academic, 1994, 139-201, esp. 173-177, who argues that R. Barthes (French), M. Foucault (French), and H. White, (American) have, on one level, similar views of history and fiction.

[378] S. A. Mullen, "Between 'Romance' and 'True History,' " in: R. A. Wells, ed., *History and the Christian Historian*, Grand Rapids: Eerdmans, 1998, 23-40, esp. 24.

[379] See Jenkins, *On What is History? From Carr and Elton to Rorty and White*, London: Routledge, 1995.

[380] Long, *The Art of Biblical History*, 58-87.

[381] D. Barratt, R. Pooley, L. Ryken, eds., *The Discerning Reader: Christian Perspectives on Literature and Theory*, Leicester: InterVarsity Press, 1995.

ized history"?[382] There are claims by some that the Bible is fictional in character,[383] while others portend that biblical history and the genre of fiction are in rigid conflict.[384] What distinction, if any, is to be made between an actual past, a historical report of the past, and literature (narrative fiction)?[385]

There are at least two issues to consider regarding this last question: supportable evidence and the reliability of the historian. First, *evidence*. Normally, historians search for evidence to support and verify their claims about the past. With regard to history and evidence, Ricoeur states his view in the following manner:

> It is in no way my intention to cancel or to obscure the differences between history and the whole set of fictional narratives in terms of their truth-claims. There is a level of analysis and of argumentation for which a conventional concept of truth, defined in terms of empirical verification and falsification, is perfectly valid.
>
> Documents and archives are the 'sources' of evidence for historical inquiry. Fictional narratives, on the other hand, ignore the burden of providing evidences of that kind.[386]

If there is an abundance of evidence for one historical claim, and less evidence for an alternative one, some hold that the first is true.[387] Evidence, however, is also limited by its being situated in time, and the historian is separated from the subject matter of the actual event(s) by

---

[382] Alter, *The Art of Biblical Narrative*, 34, 41 uses these terms without a great deal of clarity or identification as to whether they are the same or different modes of narrating.

[383] B. Halpern, *The First Historians*, San Francisco, Harper & Row, 1988. Alter, *The Art of Biblical Narrative*.

[384] C. J. Hemer, *The Book of Acts in the Setting of Hellenistic History*, Wissenschaftliche Untersuchungen zum Neuen Testament 49, Tübingen: J. C. B. Mohr, 1989, 32 and C. Blomberg, *The Historical Reliability of the Gospels*, Leicester: InterVarsity Press, 1987.

[385] Mullen, "Between," 28, writes, "According to the postmodernist, all narratives - not just the narratives of fiction - are creating worlds and realities and cultures - not reflecting them."

[386] "Ricoeur, "Can Fictional Narratives be True," *Analecta Husserliana* XIV (1983), 3-19, esp. 4-5.

[387] McCullagh, *The Truth of History*, 20-23.

time. Furthermore, no evidence is total and in many contexts, it is often rather sparse or even misleading. Because of this, historians are obliged to work with degrees of probability regarding evidence. Yet, the search for evidence alone may be moving in the wrong direction. Daniel Marguerat, a New Testament scholar, argues that a shift in the notion of historical truth is necessary:

> There is no history apart from the historian's interpretive mediation which supplies the meaning : history is narrative and, as such, constructed from a point of view. Over the multitude of facts at his/her disposal, the historian throws a plot, retaining certain facts that are judged significant, while excluding others, and relating some to others in a relationship of cause and effect.
>
> The truth of history does not depend on the factuality of the event recounted (even though the historian is required to keep to the facts) but, rather, depends on the interpretation the historian gives to a reality that is always in itself open to a plurality of interpretive options.[388]

While this point of view may be defensible, if it is correct, we may need to accept the conclusion that there are simply better and worse interpretations. Would this then result in only being able to speak or write of better or worse histories? If so, on what criteria?[389] Where does the "evidence factor" play a role in this view? How might one discover to *some* verifiable degree, what happened in the past?

The *second* and related problematic is the *historian him/her self*.[390] It is argued that anyone engaged in historical investigation has the task of

---

[388] D. Marguerat, *The First Christian Historian, Writing the Acts of the Apostles*, trans. G. J. Laughery, K. McKinney, R. Bauckham, Cambridge: Cambridge University Press, 2002, 5-6 (ET). *Le première histoire du christianisme. Les Actes des Apôtres*, Paris/Genève: Cerf/Labor et Fides, Lectio Divina 180, 1999, 17-18.

[389] McCullagh, *The Truth of History*, 114, argues that there must be criteria for deciding between interpretations. He suggests that, "interpretations are to be judged for their scope and explanatory power."

[390] Mullen, "Between," 26, points out that postmodernism has "raised crucial questions about the meaningfulness of the historian's self - understanding as someone who seeks to tell 'true' stories about the past."

selecting and ordering the evidence.[391] The historian is affected by the culture, political setting, and personal perspectives, which all relate to one's personality, point of view, and biases.[392] In other words, according to this perspective the historical self of the historian can no longer be conceived of as a neutral observer simply plowing through the facts and recording them with a value free outlook. Hayden White argues that such a position would overlook the historian's aim. White states:

> It is sometimes said that the aim of the historian is to explain the past by "finding," "identifying," or "uncovering," the "stories" that lie buried in chronicles; and that the difference between "history" and "fiction" resides in the fact that the historian "finds" his stories, whereas the fiction writer "invents" his. This conception of the historian's task, however, obscures the extent to which "invention" also plays a part in the historian's operations.[393]

The work of Arnaldo Momigliano offers another, yet related perspective (he argues that a historian is to keep to the facts). The past, in his opinion, is not merely found or uncovered. On the contrary, there is an *active* aim (in ancient times) on the part of the one recording it to constitute something for the readers in the present.[394]

Furthermore, the combined works of Raymond Aron, Paul Veyne and Henri Marrou have contributed to changing the way history and

---

391 Bebbington, *Patterns in History: A Christian View*, 5.

392 J. Scott, "History in Crisis? The Others' Side of the Story," *American Historical Review* (1989), 681, states, "By 'history' I mean not what happened, not what 'truth' is 'out there' to be discovered and transmitted, but what we know about the past, what the rules and conventions are that govern the production and acceptance of the knowledge we designate as history."

393 H. White, Metahistory, 6-7. For White, in a "chronicle" an event is merely "there," whereas in history events are assigned different functions in the story. Also, H. Kellner, *Language and Historical Representation: Getting the Story Crooked*, Madison: University of Wisconsin Press, 1989, 24, writes, "Historians do not 'find' the truths of past events; they create events from a seamless flow, and invent meanings that produce patterns within that flow." Carr, *Time, Narrative, and History*, 49-50, 59-60, esp. 49, would strongly object. Some theorists argue with regard to patterns (structures), "as if they were imposed on meaningless data by the act of narration itself, as if the events of life, experiences and actions, had no structure in themselves and achieved it only at the hand of a literary invention."

394 A. Momigliano, *Essays in Ancient and Modern Historiography*, Oxford: Blackwell, 1977, 365-373.

historiography are understood.[395] These authors have argued that historiography does not uncover mere facts, but is a re-constructive enterprise that deals with interpreted facts. Veyne proposes that historians fix plots and plots select certain facts, while excluding others, and this is history.[396]

In light of the foregoing discussion of the second problematic, it must be acknowledged that the historian is part of a writing of history. The historian has no immediate access to the *actual* past and no historian has the capacity to write a *neutral* narrative.[397] While this may indeed be the case, it is nevertheless debatable what claims or consequences should be drawn from such conclusions.

Historian Keith Jenkins, for example, views history as personal construction and the prospect of truth as a power tool. Jenkins remarks:

> that the historian's viewpoint and predilections still shape the choice of historical materials, and our own personal constructs determine what we make of them. The past we 'know' is always contingent upon our own views, our own 'present' [.....] . Epistemology shows we can never really know the past; that the gap between the past and history (historiography) is an ontological one, that is, is in the very nature of things such that no amount of epistemological effort can bridge it.
>
> We know that such truths are really 'useful fictions' that are in discourse by virtue of power (somebody has to put and keep them there) and power uses the term 'truth' to exercise control.[398]

---

395   R. Aron, *Introduction à la philosophie de l'histoire: essai sur les limites de l'objectivitié historique*, Paris: Gallimard, 1938, (1957). P. Veyne, *Comment on écrit l'histoire*, Paris: Seuil, 1971. H.-I. Marrou, *De la connaissance historique*, Paris: Seuil, 1954. See also Ricoeur, *Temps et récit, I*, 234.

396   Veyne, *Comment on écrit l'histoire*, 70, argues that a historical event is not what happens, but what is able to be narrated. In Ricoeur's perspective, *Temps et récit, I*, 246, (*Time and Narrative, I*, 174). "The force of Paul Veyne's book is to have brought to this critical point the idea that history is only the construction and understanding of plots." Ricoeur, *Temps et récit, I*, 242, (*Time and Narrative, I*, 171), while appreciative of Veyne's work, critiques him for leaving no possibility of distinguishing between narrative, understanding, and explanation.

397   Bebbington, *Patterns*, 16-17. "The historian's outlook, whatever it may be plays a major role in shaping the history [....] ."

398   Jenkins, *Re-Thinking History*, London: Routledge, 1991, 12, 19, 32.

Jenkins makes a strong plea for doing away with *truth* and *objectivity* in history as a result of the historian's inevitable involvement with the subject matter at hand. Historians may indeed consult sources, but in his opinion, history is undeniably and thoroughly a subjective enterprise.

McCullagh, another historian, while viewing historical interpretations as undoubtedly subjective, argues that there can be a case made for them being evenhanded, true, and temperately comprehensive. He states:

> I argue that although historical conclusions are always fallible, when they are well supported by evidence they deserve to be believed very probably true, that is, as telling us something true about the world. Furthermore, it is reasonable to accept as true conclusions inductively inferred from observable evidence, not because one can prove that inductive inferences regularly yield the truth, for one cannot do that without vicious circularity, but because we all conventionally and successfully believe that they do. We should be sceptical of descriptions that are not well supported, but accept as true those which are. Blanket scepticism is disastrous.[399]

What conclusions can be drawn from the involvement of the historian in writing history remains a question open to debate. Are the traditional dualisms of fact/history and fiction/literature to be abandoned or reframed in the light of new perspectives and orientations concerning narrative? How, if at all, is it possible to get closer to the reality of the past? Mullen, for example, is concerned that if the language of the past creates a world rather than reflects it, then language itself, which in some post-modernist views is not "firm" and "univocal," will become elusive and "infinitely malleable." Consider her remarks:

---

399 McCullagh, *The Truth of History*, 5.

If we must assume that all texts are creators of reality rather than reflectors of reality, then there is no way historians can rely on any texts to point beyond themselves to some reality in the past about which they purport to speak.[400]

Mullen writes of the "blurring of the boundaries" between literature (fiction) and history that, in her opinion, has produced various responses.[401] She concludes that the task of the historian is different from that of the writer of fiction.[402]

We now return to the question posed above, prior to examining the two problematics of evidence and the place of the historian. What distinction, if any, is to be made between an actual past, a historical report of the past, and literature (narrative fiction)? In something of a response to these complex questions and before returning more specifically to the problematics of narrative, which have been generally in view throughout this discussion, it is important to give a working definition of history and fiction.[403]

The word history, as we shall use it in agreement with Long and Ricoeur, has the capacity to refer to *actual* past events or to a narrative accounting of these events. Perhaps, the suggestion of Davies is also useful. He reserves the term history for "the events of the past as a continuum" and historiography for "the selective telling of those events."[404]

Fiction, as we have pointed out above, is a term that for some may be thought of as unrelated with and in opposition to history. The word

---

400 Mullen, "Between," 28-29.

401 Ibid., 30-31. See also Ricoeur, "Philosophies critiques," 139-201, esp. 140, for a similar concern. Ricoeur points out that in the contemporary context it is "indéniable" that the literary focus has tended to "déplacé" both research (documentaire) and explanation (epistemology). The valid emphasis on the literary has in turn had a erroneous epistemological effect on the notions of document, archive, and trace. Ricoeur claims that all three (document, explanation, écriture) have a place in a definition of history, and that all three enrich and problematize each other.

402 Ibid., 35. Ricoeur, *Temps et récit*, I, 261. (*Time and Narrative*, I, 186). He concurs, yet presents a more nuanced, and in our opinion, fecund view. Also see below.

403 We are particularly indebted to the work of Ricoeur, "Philosophies critiques," 139-201 and Long, *The Art of Biblical History*, 58-64, for the definitions of history and fiction which are articulated in the following pages.

404 J. Rogerson and P. R. Davies, *The Old Testament World*, Englewood-Cliffs: Prentice Hall, 1989, 218.

fiction, as we shall use it in agreement with Long and Longman, is to be understood in two senses. Fiction is a *genre* and fiction is *artistry, creativity, skill*.[405] If these two senses are kept in mind, then it may be possible to continue to speak of fiction and history as opposites, while at the same time acknowledging that all historiography is fictionalized. Nevertheless, in this scenario, a *tension* between history and fiction does not negate the ability of historiography to recount history.[406] Any textual representation of the past is never the actual past. Thus, it is justifiable to refer to a fictionality of all narratives, while also holding a view that there is a difference between historical narratives (which make a claim to tell what happened) and fictional ones (which are in no way restricted to this, yet may be true to life).[407]

Our position concerning this debate is, for the most part, in agreement with the thought that the task of the historian is different from that of the fiction writer. We, however, would not only want to stress the difference in task, but also confirm the similarity between the two. Ricoeur states it well in his discussion of seeing where the continuity between emplotment and a singular causal imputation resides and where the discontinuity is to be located:

> The continuity resides at the level of the role played by the imagination. [...] The discontinuity has to do with the analysis into factors, the insertion of rules from experience, and, especially, the assignment of degrees of probability that determine adequate causality.

> It is for this reason that historians are not simply narrators: they give reasons why they consider a particular factor *rather than some other* to be the sufficient cause of a given course of events. Poets also create

---

[405] G. J. Wenham, "The Coherence of the Flood Narrative," *Vetus Testamentum* 28 (1978), 336-348, where Wenham convincingly illumines the artistry and talent of the writer of the Flood narrative, while arguing for its unity.

[406] T. Longman, "Storytellers, Poets and the Bible: Can Literary Artifice be True?" in: H. Conn, ed., *Inerrancy and Hermeneutic*, Grand Rapids: Baker, 1988, 137-150.

[407] Long, *The Art of Biblical History*, 62.

plots that are held together by causal skeletons. But these latter are not the subject of a process of argumentation.[408]

There is no doubt a need for *mediation* concerning this relation and distinction, as both pertain to the problematic of history and fiction on the level of imagination and plot. However, as always, mediation is not merely for the sake of mediation, or of arriving at some form of synthesis, that dissolves contrariety. We shall return to this question of a *mediating* function of history and fiction and develop it later.[409]

Ricoeur argues that at the level of sense, there is a common story form that historiography and fictional narrative share. Yet, at the level of what they are referencing, according to certain understandings, they differ. Historical narratives refer to events outside the narrative, though both types of narrative are a reference to human historicity.[410] It could be said that history and fiction are related to each other on the plane of narrative, but they are also distinct from each other on this same plane. Ricoeur states:

> I should want to stress that as 'fictive' as the historical text may be, its claim is to be a representation of reality. And its way of asserting its claim is to support it by the verificationist procedures proper to history as a science. In other words, history is both a literary artifact and a representation of reality. It is a literary artifact to the extent that, like all literary texts, it tends to assume the status of a self-contained system of symbols. It is a representation of reality to the extent that the world it depicts - which is the 'works world' - is assumed to stand for some actual occurrences in the 'real' world.[411]

---

408 Ricoeur, *Temps et récit, I*, 261. (*Italics his.*) (*Time and Narrative, I*, 186).

409 See 4.1.4 An Evaluation for Biblical Hermeneutics, below.

410 Ricoeur, "The Narrative Function," *Semeia* 13 (1978), 177-202, reprinted in: Thompson, ed., *Hermeneutics*, 274-296, esp. 294. "For historicity comes to language only in so far as we tell stories or tell history. *We belong to history before telling stories or writing history.*" (*Italics his.*) ("La fonction narrative," reprinted in: *Etudes théologiques et religieuses* 54 (1979), 209-230, esp. 228,).

411 Ibid., 291. Also "Ricoeur, "Can Fictional Narratives be True," 3-19, esp. 7.

Ricoeur's point is that while history is story, as fiction, it too is related to and through the imagination, yet history is not solely fiction in that its field of operation is indebted to include other considerations than merely the imagination.[412]

3.3.2.2. A "Re-Decoding" of Narrative

Now that we have addressed the question of history and fiction, as well as the key issues of evidence and the historian's involvement with telling a story, we return more specifically to narrative—a "re-decoding" of narrative; notably the crucial debate between Carr and Ricoeur.

Carr's position is that narrative is a form of life. In this scenario, narrative is fiction or history, but it is understood as primarily an *ontological* state of structured existence prior to becoming a literary expression. He critiques Ricoeur for missing the relevance of narrative configuration in *life* itself and thus relegating it to a retrospective *literary act* discharged by historians and novelists. In Carr's view, Ricoeur focuses narrative too one sidedly on great literature, ignoring the narrative structure of lived human time, whether or not it ever finds its way into a text. Ricoeur's over-emphasis on the text, in Carr's perspective, leaves him in a position that is closer to the structuralists and the discontinuity theorists of narrative, than it may seem.[413]

However, Carr also points out that Ricoeur does not go quite as far as to say that the real world is one of a mere sequence of *physical movement*, as he does speak of a pre-narrative structure that can then

---

412 Ricoeur, "The Creativity of Language," in: Kearney, ed., *Dialogues with Contemporary Continental Thinkers*, Manchester: Manchester University Press, 1984, 17-36. Reprinted in and cited from: Valdés, ed., *A Ricoeur Reader: Reflection and Imagination*, 463-481, esp. 464. Ricoeur points out, "For history is not only the story (histoire) of triumphant kings and heroes, of the powerful; it is also the story of the powerless and dispossessed. The history of the vanquished dead crying out for justice demands to be told."

413 Carr, "Narrative and the Real World: An Argument for Continuity," 137-152, esp. 139, mentions L. Mink and H. White as two examples of such theorists. See Mink, for example, in his "History and Fiction as Modes of Comprehension," *New Literary History*, 1 (1970), 541-558, for a representation of this theory. He states: "to say that narratives qualities are transferred to art from life seems a *hysteron proteron*. Stories are not lived but told. Life has no beginnings, middles or ends [.......]. So it seems truer to say that narrative qualities are transferred from art to life." (*Italics his*).

be configured.[414] Yet, Carr is not convinced. In his opinion, this is still not a narrative structure and it does not allow Ricoeur to escape the discontinuity position, which Carr characterizes in the following way:

> Things simply happen, one after the other, randomly or according to their own laws. Any significance, meaning or value ascribed to events is projected onto them by *our* concerns, prejudices and interests and in no way attaches to the events themselves.[415]

A real world experience of time for Ricoeur, Carr argues, is in a state of confusion and chaos. In short, following Augustine, a state of discord. Structurally distinct from the "real world," literary narrative through emplotment is what brings concord to human experience. In contrast to this, Carr's position stresses that life has a *narrative quality and structure* all its own. It is not *dependent* on literature. Therefore, narrative is first and foremost a *life*, before it becomes *art*. Carr states:

> The art of narrative is not the mirror of life but its confirmation and in some cases its completion and perfection. In fiction it can make things come out right, it can produce a wholeness and closure that life, it is true, never achieves. In history and other truth-telling genres it has the advantage of hindsight, it tells stories that are finished and can see in them and relate contours and significance unavailable to those who participated in them. The products of the narrator's art neither simply imitate nor distort life but confirm it and enrich it. But they do so by borrowing the structure, indeed the narrative structure, from their source.[416]

---

414 Ibid., 137. Also, Ricoeur, *Temps et récit, I*, 113. (*Time and Narrative, I*, 74).

415 Carr, "Life and the Narrator's," 111. (*Italics his*).

416 Ibid., 121.

Having clarified Carr's position, we can now move on to look more carefully at Ricoeur's narrative point of view. Does Ricoeur invite the label of a discontinuity theorist? He states:

> […] it is because the ideas of beginning, middle, and end are not taken from experience. They are not features of some real action but the effects of the ordering of the poem.[417]

In his work on the problematic of the relation between narrative and life, Ricoeur speaks of the maxim of Socrates; a life unexamined is not worth living.[418] What Ricoeur seems to be arguing for, against Carr, is that in order to be able to speak of the continuity or lack thereof between life and narrative, an interpreter must acknowledge that access to either one does not happen via a *direct* encounter, but through *mediation*. Thus, one must first take a *detour* through the text or the other (Lévinas) in order to be able to narrate one's own story.

Yet, perhaps Carr is correct to view Ricoeur as a discontinuity theorist. What is the relation between life and narrative and narrative and life from Ricoeur's standpoint? Does Carr's outline, in the description of a *direct* ontological connection between life and narrative, become the only way of framing such a connection? After a brief, but necessary detour into plot, we shall define Ricoeur's narrative - life - narrative orientations and assess them in light of Carr's proposal.

Ricoeur, following Aristotle's *Poetics*, views the act of plotting as essential to the nature of narrative. Plots, generally speaking, synthesize heterogeneous experience. A plot makes a single story out of numerous events or scenarios, not merely in terms of a succession, but in the sense that it forms them into an intelligible whole. Plot also organizes a diversity of characters and actors, actions and those acted upon, circumstances of intended and unintended results, into a unity. Ricoeur

---

417 Ricoeur, *Temps et récit, I*, 67. (*Time and Narrative, I*, 39).

418 Ricoeur, "Life in Quest of Narrative," in: Wood, ed., *On Paul Ricoeur*, 20-33, esp. 20.

refers to this as "discordant concord" or "concordant discord."[419] Furthermore, Ricoeur argues that plot brings together two types of time: disappearing time and enduring time. Thus, narrative is a *mediation* between these two types of time.

Two further clarifications on Ricoeur's notion of narrative must be mentioned before going on more directly to the problematic of narrative - life - narrative. First, the activity of creating a plot is not to be thought of as static, but rather as an *intelligible* dynamic. Ricoeur refers to this, in the epistemological sense, as a "narrative intelligence."[420] Such a narrative intelligence, which emanates from the *creative imagination* "always precedes" narratology (a study of narrative). Narratives have the capacity to teach and to communicate, which gives them a level of *rationality* that is comparable to the credible scientific investigations in the fields of the human sciences.

Second, there is the phenomenon of tradition recognized as, in Ricoeur's terms, a "living transmission" of both *innovation* and *sedimentation*. Thus, a tradition is that which comprises certain models or methods of interpretation and ways of identifying literary genres. However, since innovation already exists in the production of such models, the rules governing the models are necessarily open to modification and change.

Following the detour into plot and the two clarifications on narrative intelligibility, related to epistemology and tradition stated, we shall now further unpack Ricoeur's position. In his work on narrative, Ricoeur is concerned with the question of the relation of narrative and life, but he seeks to respond to the problematic in a different way than Carr.

Ricoeur appeals to *mimesis* in order to argue that he is not unaware of the ontological dimension of narrative. His aim, however, as we

---

[419] Ricoeur, "Life: A Story in Search of a Narrator," in: M. C. Doeser and J. N. Kraaj, eds., *Facts and Values: Philosophical Reflections from Western and Non-Western Perspectives*, Dordrecht: Nijhoff, 1985, 121-132, reprinted in: Valdés, ed., *A Ricoeur Reader: Reflection and Imagination*, 423-437, esp. 424.

[420] Ibid., 428-429.

would view it, is to present a "life" as not merely ontological, but also as one that is epistemological and hermeneutical—one which is *mediated* by this necessity for interpretation. He states:

> I think that my suggestion of a triple mimesis constitutes an attempt to address this difficulty. If, according to Mimesis I, every narrative configuration has a kind of retroactive reference, it is because life itself is an inchoate narrative; this is what I call the pre-narrative character of life. I wonder, consequently, if the circularity between prefiguration, configuration and refiguration may facilitate my escape from the dilemma which will surround me, and the terms amongst which I am constrained to choose: history is either a distortion of life, or it represents it.[421]

It is in this manner that Ricoeur seeks to develop a project that is not constrained to the above either/or, between life as chaos or life as immediately accessible narrative, which he detects in Carr's framework. For Ricoeur, these problematics are always more *arduous* than either - or solutions can provide. Perhaps, it is too facile a conclusion to argue that narrative is either a *distortion* of life or a *representation* of it. This framework assumes a direct ontology and a clear view of life with the ability to readily perceive the two options of either distortion or representation. More likely, so it seems, is that there are necessary mediations on both sides of this equation.

Ricoeur sees mimesis as a *creative imitation* of human action. In so doing, he has sought to evade the predicament of narrative being either a falsification or a reflection of life. His position is that such alternatives, through the potent scope and orbit of mimesis can be accepted, and in doing so produce something like: "a life in search of its own history."[422] If I understand Ricoeur correctly, he is again underscor-

---

[421] Ricoeur, "Discussion: Ricoeur on Narrative," in: Wood, ed., *On Paul Ricoeur*, 160-187, esp. 180.

[422] Ibid., 181.

ing the implausibility that a life, in order to understand itself, can be merely in dialogue with itself. This, if this is the case, the question of falsifying or reflecting must be reframed.

In terms of this debate, what Ricoeur attempts to delineate is a "theory of action" and a "theory of history," arguing that while they are related, they are not the same thing. Let us take history as an example. A history is concerned not with just actions, but also effects, both of which may take on the characteristics of *positive* and *negative*. A theory of action focuses on thoughts, perspectives, intentions, but life has broader horizons. Ricoeur states:

> Thus today, when we attempt to understand Lenin, we cannot base this understanding solely on what he thought before the Bolshevik Revolution, but must also take into account that it was this Revolution that produced Stalin. The historian's problem is then to ascertain to what extent Lenin's thought and actions contain the necessary, but of course not the sufficient, conditions for Stalin's emergence. But this is no longer a question of a theory of actions alone; it also has to do with a theory of history. History tears itself away from life; it is constituted through the activity of comprehension that is also the activity of configuration.[423]

Ricoeur argues strongly for the case that life and narrative are not the same thing. Does life need literature to understand itself? For Ricoeur, the literature of *history* and *fiction* are both expressions and references to human existence in time. It is true that these two types of texts have different aims. And yet, they have the same goal: expressing and referring to human existence. Life cannot be understood without both of them. In this sense, the world we enter is a world that precedes us, rife with the narratives of our predecessors. We might say we are already, to some degree at least, "configured" by the refigurations that have taken

---

423 Ibid., 181.

place in the lives of others. In addition to this, Ricoeur has articulated his conviction that it is the "Parole de Dieu" that has preceded the "parole de l'homme." [424]

In this sense, Ricoeur writes of a narrative identity. We learn through the narratives that precede us to become "narrators of our own stories without completely becoming the author of our life."[425] Thus, as *storied subjects,* we are never given at the beginning, and if we were, we would be in peril of becoming self-contained, self-centered selves - "and it is just this from which literature can liberate us."[426]

We conclude with the following observations. It is clear from our investigation of narrative and history and fiction that neither Ricoeur, nor Carr for that matter, have modernist or post-modernist perspectives. Either interpreter may offer a way forward between "sharp boundaries" and "radical indeterminacy" as we have defined them in this study. Granted, history is always interpreted by the historian, but this does not necessitate an extreme *suspicion* toward the idea that the events recounted *actually took place* in some sense and affected the world in specific ways. Thus, Ricoeur and Carr avoid the extremes of both archetypes, arguing that history and fiction are related, yet distinct ways of expressing and recounting life. Each in their own way seeks to formulate narrative without collapsing the distinction between fiction and history. At the same time, there is a recognition of a degree of symmetry that exists between the two.

The real difference here between Ricoeur and Carr is an important one: the nature of life and the nature of narrative. We affirm the validity of Carr's point that life is structured and time ordered, at least to some degree, prior to being configured in a literarily narrated fashion. However, Ricoeur's point that narrative is a semantic innovation is also valid. If it is apparent that we inherit the narratives of our predecessors,

---

[424] Ricoeur, *Réflexion faite,* 14. "Word of God." "word of man."

[425] Ricoeur, "Life: A Story in Search of a Narrator," 437.

[426] Ibid., 437.

does this necessarily exclude the possibility that a narrative structure exists in life prior to taking on a literary form? In our opinion, both these positions are relevant in their own ways and there is no reason why they cannot contribute to each other in order to give a limitedly appropriate description for the nature of narrative. We shall explain this in the following manner.

We return now to our image of a *prism*.[427] As we have already mentioned with regard to our examination of the views of Ricoeur and Harnisch on biblical parables, this metaphor is able to comprise both something that previously existed (raw narrative structure) and something new (a structured narration in literature), without canceling out either and allowing both to remain relevant. Thus, the metaphor of a prism allows for both *reflection* and *creation*, without taking sides as to an either - or constraint. In this sense, life may have a narrative structure of beginning, middle and end; yet narrative literature retains its capacity to bring something new to life that was not already there. Narrative is both a *mirroring* and a *novelty*. It is *related* to life, but *distinct* from it. On the one hand, the roles of redescription and transformation need not imply that the old description and formation have not existed with striking effects. On the other hand, these predecessors are not all that are necessary for an understanding of human existence in time. Furthermore, if this is the case, narrative retains both its *ontological* and *epistemological* fecundity, remaining valid for and capable of expressing an understanding, explanation, and new understanding for *living* hermeneutics.

3.3.3. An Evaluation for Biblical Hermeneutics

After analyzing the narrative positions of both Ricoeur and Carr, and investigating the problem of history and fiction, we turn to evaluate the relevance of this debate for biblical hermeneutics. The force of Ricoeur's position on historical and fictional narrative and its potential

---

427 See above, footnote 320. We shall again refer to the imagery of light. A prism, in the sense we are using it, is both a reflector and a creator of light. As existing light strikes the prism from the outside, it creates a new light from the inside.

contribution to biblical hermeneutics is striking.

While interests in the *aesthetic* narrative dimensions of the text have become more prominent in the contemporary hermeneutical context, Ricoeur has maintained an emphasis on the *historical* dimension. In so doing, he forges a way through the perplexing hermeneutical poles of the Bible belonging solely to either the historian or the artist (the theological is not our concern at the present).[428] Ricoeur has no dispute with the artistry of biblical narrative and affirms its literary and fictional character. At the same time, however, he is not willing to reduce the Bible to the status non - historical.[429]

A non-referential literary focus on biblical narrative is challenged by Ricoeur, who shows that the historian's interest relates to what happened, and not only with a good story.[430] Rather than only a new construction, there is also a reconstruction of the past. Ricoeur states this in the following manner:

> A robust conviction animates historians. Whatever may be said about the selective aspect of the gathering, conserving, and consulting of documents, or about their relationship to the questions historians put to them, or even about the ideological implications of all these maneuvers, the recourse to documents does indicate a dividing line between history and fiction. Unlike novels, historians' constructions do aim at being *re*constructions of the past. Through documents and their critical examination of documents, historians are subject to what once was.[431]

---

[428] Ricoeur, "Le récit interprétative. Exégèse et théologie dans les récits de la Passion," *RSR* 73 (1985), 17-38, esp. 20-21, makes, from our hermeneutical point of view, an intriguing parallel here between, "Jésus de l'histoire et le Christ de la foi." (Jesus of history and Christ of faith). He points out that the "kérygme christologique" is something "qui demande récit." (that demands story). There is not something preceding that which is narrativised. Ricoeur appeals to 1 Corinthians 15:3-8, "that Christ died for our sins according to the Scriptures, that he was buried, that he was raised on the third day according to the Scriptures, and that he appeared to Peter and then to the Twelve."

[429] Ricoeur, "Toward a Narrative Theology: Its Necessities, Its Resources, Its Difficulties," in: Wallace, ed., *Figuring the Sacred*, 236-248.

[430] See also E. V. McKnight, "Presuppositions in New Testament Study," in: J. Green, ed., *Hearing the New Testament*, Carlisle: Paternoster, 1995, 278-300, esp., 290-291, who argues that reference remains essential to Ricoeur's hermeneutical program.

[431] Ricoeur, *Temps et récit, III*, 203-204, (*Italics his*). (*Time and Narrative, III*, 142-143).

In Ricoeur's efforts to reveal the interlacing (entrecroisement) of fiction and history within the text, he does not reduce narrative to either one. He argues that these two *great* modes of narrative can never be entirely synthesized.[432] In this scenario, both concordance and discordance between history and fiction are found in the interlacing of each mode with the other. Yet this exploration is precisely what allows their contrariety to appear.

Ricoeur also argues for the reality of the epistemological component of narrative. With an over literary-izing of the biblical narrative, there may be a loss of the necessary division between a speculative philosophy of history and a history of historians.[433] What Ricoeur wants to alert interpreters to is the contemporary misconception of a declassification of history. He remarks:

> [....] c'est la parenté entre les paradigmes organisateurs du champ historique et ceux qui président à la composition des fictions littéraires qui a provoqué le déclassement de l'histoire comme connaissance à prétention scientifique et son reclassement comme artifice littéraire et, à titre de corollaire, suscité l'affaiblissement des critères épistémologiques de différenciation entre histoire proprement dite et philosophie de l'histoire.

> [...] it is the relationship between the organizing paradigms of the field of history and those that govern the composition of literary fiction which has provoked a declassification of history as knowledge with scientific pretentions and its reclassification as literary artifice and, as a corollary, caused the weakening of epistemological criteria that differentiates history proper and the philosophy of history.[434]

---

432 Ricoeur, *Temps et récit*, I, 315. (*Time and Narrative*, I, 226, note 1, 267).

433 Ricoeur, "Philosophies critiques," 139-201, esp. 171.

434 Ibid., esp. 172. (My translation).

Under this declassification, history no longer has any real connection with the events recounted. In Ricoeur's opinion, this point of view has *unjustly collapsed* history into fiction. Thus, a history that has lost its epistemological status can no longer be spoken of as history.[435] When the writing of history is considered constitutive of historical knowledge itself, history and fiction have synchronized rendering the two undecipherable.[436] History construed solely as literature is in jeopardy of losing its *scientific* status.

Furthermore, the aim of historians is not only related to the real. Rather, this real, according to Ricoeur, is connected with the "debt" that those in the present have to those of another time (autrefois): the dead. Debt, in this context, refers to a passive reception, an inheritance from those who have preceded the present generation.[437] Biblical narratives are often about people like us, in Ricoeur's terms, those who act, interpret, and suffer as we do. While there remains a differentiation, it is not so great that we in the present cannot understand the intentionality of historical discourse manifested in the documentations, the explanations, and the writings of history. Historians receive a past before they create a story. Biblical narrative, from this Ricoeurian perspective, can be said to be both a "mark" and a "sign of passing." In other words, we are speaking of the "trace" of the past in the text, which places the present reader in its debt.

---

435 While it is true that there is a problem with a positivist barrier between historical and fictional narrative (Ricoeur does critique such a positivism), the dismantling of this barrier nevertheless does not result in a complete blurring of the two narrative modes (which Ricoeur also critiques). See Ricoeur, *Temps et récit, I,* 123, 315, (*Time and Narrative, I,* 82, 226 and 267). The realistic novel and "l'effet du réel" according to Ricoeur, "ne prend pas en compte le fait que la réalité prétendûment représentée porte sur le caractère proprement temporel du passé." ("Philosophies critiques," 185). (does not take into account the fact that the supposedly represented reality concerns the truly temporal character of the past). (My translation).

436 Ricoeur, "Philosophies critiques," 139-201, esp. 176-177, is unyielding in his refusal to abandon an opposition between fiction and non-fiction in spite of there not being a "certain" criterion for the truth of a representation of the past. Also 143, "Autant il faudra résister, [........], à la tentation de dissoudre le fait historique dans la narration et celle-ci dans une composition littéraire indiscernable de la fiction, autant il faut refuser d'entrée de jeu la confusion entre fait historique et événement réel." (As much as one must resist, [....], the temptation to dissolve the historical fact into the narration and the latter into a literary composition indistinguishable from fiction, one must also immediately refuse a confusion between historical fact and real event). (My translation).

437 Ricoeur, "Philosophies critiques," 139-201, esp. 186-194. Also, *Temps et récit, III,* 227-228, 279. (*Time and Narrative, III,* 156-157, 192) and "Herméneutique. Les finalités de l'exégèse biblique," in: *La Bible en philosophie. Approaches contemporaines*, Paris: Cerf, 1993, 27-51, esp. 32.

In conclusion, we would argue that Ricoeur's work on narrative contributes to biblical hermeneutics by embodying a fine balance between the récit of fiction and the récit of history. In our opinion, this balance has the potential to avoid both the "radical indeterminacy" of post-modernism with its tendency to dissolve history into fiction, and the "sharp boundaries" of modernism with its tendency to naively suppose that historical fact equals access to the event itself. Ricoeur's point of view offers an *alternative* to the biblical text being viewed as merely a historical, or in contradistinction, a literary text.

Biblical hermeneutics then, in our opinion, can profit from Ricoeur's nuanced treatment of historical and fictional narrative, since it begins to move away from a tendency to reduce the Bible to one or the other, without at the same time seeing their relationship. As we have pointed out, this relationship does not necessarily *dissolve* history into fiction, nor does it give *direct* access to the events themselves. If this is the case, then it is possible to refer to the Bible as being historical, and not merely literature. In so doing, it can therefore be argued that the text does not lose its epistemological status as a vehicle of explanation of traces of the past.

In addition, Ricoeur's narrative enterprise, especially his conception of mimesis I-III, opens up the possibility of affirming the value of a biblical hermeneutics understood as a *living hermeneutics* in motion. This motion proposes the wager of the productive versus destructive, positive versus negative, and pro-meaning versus anti-meaning. Perhaps, a concept/image of motion need not imply meaninglessness, ceaseless flux, or the radical indeterminacy of biblical texts, but is instead capable of offering a critique of the *illusion* of either absolute meaning or total non–meaning.[438] If so, this opens a passage through which biblical hermeneutics might now be challenged to move forward.

---

438 W. V. Harris, *Interpretive Acts: In Search of Meaning*, Oxford: Oxford University Press, 1988, ix. "There is a great difference between saying that constructions of meaning can never be more than probable and saying that meaning is necessarily indeterminable."

REFIGURATION

4. Trajectories toward Closure

4.1. Authors, Readers, and Texts

With the configuring investigation of the narrative section now behind us, we enter into the final stages of our research: the exploration of authors, readers, and texts.

Why authors, readers, and texts? While an investigation into this triad may seem to veer away from the motion between configuration and *refiguration*, we would argue that this is not the case. The analysis of authors, readers, and texts is in fact a necessary *bridge* from configuration to refiguration in this hermeneutical venture. In other words, an examination of authors, readers, and texts is paramount to understanding Ricoeur's view of refiguration, although we are not quite there yet. Thus, this section moves gradually out of a configuration of Ricoeur's work and progressively into an exploration of his notion of refiguration.[1]

The notion of refiguration (mimesis III) will be articulated through the debate[2] over authorial intention and reader response.[3] Indeed, Seán

---

1   Ricoeur, *Temps et récit, III*, 9-14. (*Time and Narrative, III*, 3-6).

2   This subject has received a tremendous amount of discussion in our contemporary context. We mention only a few examples: E. D. Hirsch, Jr., *Validity in Interpretation*, New Haven: Yale University Press, 1967. W. Iser, *The Act of Reading: A Theory of Aesthetic Response*, Baltimore: Johns Hopkins University Press, 1978. U. Eco, *The Role of the Reader: Explorations in the Semiotics of Texts*, Bloomington: Indiana University Press, 1979. J. P. Tompkins, ed., *Reader-Response Criticism: From Formalism to Post-Structuralism*, Baltimore: Johns Hopkins University Press, 1980. F. Lentricchia, *After the New Criticism*, London: Metheun, 1983. W. V. Harris, *Literary Meaning: Reclaiming the Study of Literature*, London: Macmillan, 1996. For an excellent bibliography on recent work in the field of reader-response criticism see Tompkins, *Reader-Response Criticism*, 233-272.

3   See E. Freund, *The Return of the Reader: Reader-Response Criticism*, London: Metheun, 1987, 7, who points out that reader-response theory or criticism, is a term with manifold representations: the implied reader (Iser), the model reader (Eco), the ideal reader (Culler), the actual reader (Jauss), the informed reader (Fish). Our concern is...

Burke suggests that the crisis of post-modernism is a crisis of authorship.[4] Where is the author in the contemporary hermeneutical enterprise? According to Roland Barthes:

> the modern scriptor ... is not the subject with the book as predicate; there is no other time as that of the enunciation and every text is eternally written *here and now* ... For him, on the contrary, the hand cut off from any voice, borne by a pure gesture of inscription (and not of expression) traces a field without origin - or which, at least, has no other origin than language itself, language which ceaselessly calls into question all origins.
>
> Succeeding the Author, the scriptor no longer bears within him passions, humours, feelings, impressions, but rather the immense dictionary from which he draws a writing that can know no halt: life never does more than imitate the book, and the book itself is only a tissue of signs, an imitation that is lost, infinitely deferred. Once the Author is removed, the claim to decipher a text becomes quite futile.[5]

Do authors, in our contemporary hermeneutical context, have rights, aims, and purposes, or are they merely ideological fabrications?[6] In

---

limited to the general theoretical component which considers the flesh and blood reader. We shall not focus, for example, on the dimension of readers in the text per se. Within our limited field of inquiry however, the role of the text, from what might be referred to on a sliding scale as more or less of a concern for the text, remains an interest. In other words, the text can play a greater or lesser role in the readerly interpretive effort depending on where it is situated on the scale. Two examples of this would be: Fish, *Doing What Comes Naturally*, (less textual), and Iser, *The Act of Reading: A Theory of Aesthetic Response*, (more textual).

4   S. Burke, "Introduction: Reconstructing the Author," in: S. Burke, ed., *Authorship: From Plato to the Postmodern*, Edinburgh: Edinburgh University Press, 1995, xv-xxx, esp. xxix. "When we consider that the war on totalities must be a war waged on the transcendental / impersonal subject through whose putative construction totalities emerge, it becomes clear that the great crises of postmodernism are crises of authorship even if they still disdain to announce themselves as such."

5   Barthes, "The Death," in: *Image-Music-Text*, Paris, reprinted in: Burke, *Authorship*, 125-130, esp. 127-128, (parenthesis and *Italics* his). Harris, *Literary Meaning*, 30-35, argues that Barthes is strong on rhetoric, yet weak on explanation. Harris claims that Barthes assumes and does not argue or demonstrate, the death of the author.

6   Moore, *Literary Criticism and the Gospels: The Theoretical Challenge*, New Haven: Yale University Press, 1989, 38. Moore clearly sides with the latter. "If he is not simply to be regarded as a historical figure inefficiently managing our scholarly discourse in absentia, from some remote point antecedent and external to it, who or what is he in addition?"

many cases today, authors seem to be ejected from texts as quickly as survivors might attempt to parachute from burning airplanes. But, if authors are mortally wounded can vital meaning survive? J. S. Croatto, for example, argues that authors die with the inscribing of their message. In this sacrificial "act" one lays down one's life.[7] We might also reflect back to the work of Stanley Fish and his famous statement with regard to the interpretation of a text: "the reader's response is not to the meaning, it is the meaning."[8] Others argue, however, that up until recently, authors and their intentions were considered just as important for hermeneutics as the text itself. Kevin Vanhoozer states:

> [...] premodernity and modernity alike shared a similar aim in interpretation: to recover the meaning of the text, understood in terms of the intention of the author [...] up until fairly recently there was a near consensus on the importance of the author's intention.[9]

Perhaps, on taking Croatto's understanding of an "act" further, we might query whether there is yet a place for the *resurrection* of the author and his/her intention with regard to textual interpretation? If the total focus of meaning is located in the reader reading the text, what is the role of author and text in the hermeneutical trajectory?

Attempting to work with this question is monumental, since within both literary theory and biblical interpretation[10] there is the contemporary notion that readers, by decree, requisition the primary place and become the ultimate consideration with regard to textual - biblical - meaning and interpretation.[11] It is argued that this has led to the reader

---

7 J. S. Croatto, *Biblical Hermeneutics: Toward a Theory of Reading as the Production of Meaning*, New York: Orbis, 1987, 16-17.

8 Fish, *Is There a Text?* 3.

9 Vanhoozer, *Is There A Meaning in This Text?* 74.

10 Moore, *Literary Criticism*, 107. Moore argues "reader theory in literary studies is a Pandora's box into which we, infant literary critics of the Bible, have barely begun to peer."

11 For some of the implications with regard to biblical texts see, N. Petersen, "The Reader in the Gospel," *Neotestamentica* 18, (1984), 38-51. E. V. McKnight, *The Bible and the Reader: An Introduction to Literary Criticism,...*

achieving something of a celebrity ranking within hermeneutics. Susan Suleiman states:

> The words *reader* and *audience*, once relegated to the status of the unproblematic and obvious, have acceded to a starring role.
>
> Today, one rarely picks up a literary journal on either side of the Atlantic without finding articles (and often a whole special issue) devoted to the performance of reading, the role of feeling, the variability of individual response, the confrontation, transaction or interrogation between texts and readers, the nature and limits of interpretation - questions whose very formulation depends on a new awareness of the audience as an entity indissociable from the notion of artistic texts.[12]

What are we to make of the role of authors and the relatively recent emphasis on readers in response to the text?[13] How is it possible for texts, the biblical text - narratives, to refigure readers' lives? Do authors count? Have God and Author been sacrificed on the altar of the reader?

Our primary interest here, having sketched something of the wider context of the discussion, is with how Ricoeur views authors and readers in relation to refiguration (mimesis III). However, we must point out that our analysis is not so much focused on the *textual* landscape of sense and reference (although this remains a consideration), as it is on the general question of how Ricoeur envisions the *authors* and *readers* of narrative texts.[14]

Philadelphia: Fortress, 1985. R. Detweiler, ed., *Reader Response Approaches to Biblical and Secular Texts*, Semeia 31, Decatur: Scholars Press, 1985. R. M. Fowler, *Let the Reader Understand. Reader Response Criticism and the Gospel of Mark*, Minneapolis: Fortress, 1991. Vanhoozer, *Is There A Meaning in This Text?* 1998.

12   S. R. Suleiman, "Introduction: Varieties of Audience-Orientated Criticism," in: S. R. Suleiman and I. Crosman, eds., *The Reader in the Text: Essays on Audience and Interpretation*, Princeton: Princeton University Press, 1980, 3-45, esp. 3-4. (*Italics* hers).

13   R. A. Reese, *Writing Jude: The Reader, the Text, and the Author*, Sheffield: Unpublished PhD Thesis, 1995, 3. She states, "I am not interested in discovering *the* meaning of the text. Instead, I want to see the text expand its meaning potential as it interacts (through me) with other texts in the textual sea."

14   We have already dealt with the problematic of the sense and reference of a text in 3.1 above.

First, let us examine the act of reading and the role of readers. According to Ricoeur, hermeneutics is focused on the text, but also concerned with more than just the text. Within the task of hermeneutics, as opposed to that of semiotics, both author and reader have a legitimate place and must be included in the operational trajectory of text interpretation.[15] In other words, mimesis II cannot be disconnected from the two sides of mimesis I (l'amont) and mimesis III (l'aval). Ricoeur states the following with regard to hermeneutics:

> It does not confine itself to setting mimesis II between mimesis I and mimesis III. It wants to characterize mimesis II by its mediating function. [...] the reader is that operator par excellence who takes up through doing something – the act of reading – the unity of the traversal from mimesis I to mimesis III by way of mimesis II.[16]

In this hermeneutical scenario, the passage from mimesis II to mimesis III takes place through the *act* of reading.[17] Ricoeur appeals to Roman Ingarden, Wolfgang Iser, and Hans Robert Jauss for a reception theory of reading a text.[18] Such a theory, according to Ricoeur, must still be preoccupied with the problematic of the reference of the text, yet the reader now has to be taken into consideration.[19] However, at this juncture, we need to take a relevant detour into a Ricoeurian shift. It is important to point out that Ricoeur, while continuing to use the term "reference" in *Temps et récit*, also modifies it with the term "refiguration." This is the case for at least the following reasons.

---

15 We shall see more clearly what role Ricoeur attributes to "author" and "reader" below.

16 Ricoeur, *Temps et récit, I*, 86. (*Time and Narrative, I*, 53).

17 Ricoeur, *Temps et récit, III*, 246-247. (*Time and Narrative, III*, 168-169), argues with respect to the act of reading, that there is a triple dialectic in a phenomenology of reading: discordant concordance, lack of determinacy and excess of meaning, familiar and unfamiliar.

18 R. Ingarden, *Das literarische Kunstwerk*, Second Edition, Tubingen: M. Niemeyer, 1961, (*The Literary Work of Art*, Evanston: Northwestern University Press, 1974, ET). W. Iser, *The Act of Reading: A Theory of Aesthetic Response*. H. R. Jauss, *Towards an Aesthetic of Reception*, Minneapolis: University of Minnesota Press, 1982, and *Aesthetic Experience and Literary Hermeneutics*, Minneapolis: University of Minnesota Press, 1982.

19 Ricoeur, *Temps et récit, I*, 117-124. (*Time and Narrative, I*, 77-82, ET).

In *La métaphore vive*, Ricoeur wrote of metaphorical reference as extralinguistic.[20] In his opinion, such statements have a capacity to refer outside the closed boundaries of language itself. This perspective also holds true for narrative, yet with regard to *Temps et récit*, Ricoeur, states:

> I would say today that a connecting link was missing between reference, considered the intention belonging to the metaphorical statement, and hence still to language, and the being-as detected by the latter. This intermediary link is the act of reading [.....] . Now the act of the poet is abolished in the poem uttered. What alone is relevant is the act of the reader who in a certain way makes the metaphor, by grasping the new semantic relevance along with its impertinence in the literal sense.[21]

For Ricoeur, metaphor is not limited to the innovation of meaning, but it extends to the power of the redescription of the real, more generally speaking, to our being-in-the-world on the level of both language and ontology. In re-working the conception of metaphorical reference, Ricoeur now extends it to narrative, but because of the complications of reference (which is described below as to tied to existential logic or analytic philosophy for example),[22] he underscores:

> I came to say that metaphorical and narrative statements, taken in hand by reading, aim at refiguring reality, in the twofold sense of *uncovering* the concealed dimensions of human experience and of *transforming* our vision of the world. [...] refiguring seemed to me [....] to constitute an active reorganization of our being-in-the-world, performed by the reader following the invitation of the text.[23]

---

20 Ricoeur, *La métaphore vive*, 273-324. (*The Rule of Metaphor*, 216-256).

21 Ricoeur, *The Philosophy of Paul Ricoeur*, Hahn, ed., 29.

22 Ibid., Hahn, ed., 47. Also, *Time and Narrative III*, 6, "The hermeneutic of the 'real' and the 'unreal' goes beyond the framework assigned by analytic philosophy to the question of reference." (*Temps et récit, III*, 13).

23 Ricoeur, *The Philosophy of Paul Ricoeur*, Hahn, ed., 47. (*Italics* his.)

From this point of view, a reader is not just dealing with text meaning (sense), but also the text reference transmitted through its meaning (sense). However, what Ricoeur now considers essential to the hermeneutical equation is the *reader*, who becomes one of the key reasons for the move from *reference* to *refiguration*.

It is only because text and reader each have a world that there can potentially be a confrontation and intersection between the two, which then has the possibility of leading to a refiguration of the reader's life and the world of action.[24] In other words, the configured text/narrative has a world and the reader has a world. Refiguration takes place through the effect the plot (configuration) generates on the reader reading (mediation) and acting on this plot in time.[25]

We now end the detour, but keeping this shift in mind is important. A valid reading theory, according to Ricoeur, now transfigures the question of reference into one of refiguration. Refiguration incorporates both the reader and the phenomenon of reading, neither of which were taken into sufficient consideration in *La métaphore vive*.[26]

A Ricoeurian hermeneutics, as noted previously, pays very close attention to how the world of the text unfolds in *front* of itself, and is less concerned with restoring the author's intentions, which lie behind the text.[27] The vis-à-vis of the text is not its author, but its sense and reference; its configured world. Thus, a readerly appropriation of a text is to understand oneself in front of the world the text projects.[28] Without this *mediation* by the reader, according to Ricoeur, the text cannot *refigure*

---

24   See also Petersen, "The Reader in the Gospel," 38-51, esp. 42-43 for another perspective on text, world, and reader.

25   Ricoeur, *Temps et récit, I*, 116-117. (*Time and Narrative, I*, 77).

26   Ricoeur, *Temps et récit, III*, 229-231. (*Time and Narrative, III*, 158-160).

27   Ricoeur, *Temps et récit, I*, 122. (*Time and Narrative, I*, 81). Also, A. Thomasset, *Paul Ricoeur: Une poétique de la morale*, Bibliotheca Ephemeridum Theologicarum Lovaniensium CXXIV, Leuven: Leuven University Press, 1996, 271-272, who also alludes to this motion in Ricoeur's hermeneutics.

28   Ricoeur, "The Hermeneutical Function," *From Text to Action*, 75-88, esp. 87-88. (*Italics* his). "Ultimately, what I appropriate is a proposed world. The latter is not *behind* the text, as a hidden intention would be, but *in front of* it, as that which the work unfolds, discovers, reveals." ("La fonction herméneutique de la distanciation," *Du texte à l'action*, 101-117, esp. 116-117). Also, *Interpretation Theory: Discourse and the Surplus of Meaning*, 92-94.

human action in time. Furthermore, with regard to both historical and fictional narrative, the former through reference by traces and the latter through metaphorical reference, there is an interface with human action in time. The result of this interface is that read narratives have the capacity to refigure the temporality of readerly human action.[29]

As has been shown, in *Time and Narrative* (*Temps et récit*), Ricoeur accentuates the role of the reader in the hermeneutical trajectory. His awakening to the necessary mediation of the reader can be understood from the perspective that Ricoeur has now given recognition, not only to the epistemological criteria of the text/narrative, but also to its ontological dimension.[30] This new apperception came about because the *world* of the text had previously remained, in his opinion, a *world* exceeding the text's structure, yet with the result that there was no way of linking it up with the *world* of the reader. Ricoeur states:

> To be sure, in adopting in this way, as I also did in *The Rule of Metaphor*, the thesis that the literary text transcends itself in the direction of a world, I removed the literary text from the closure imposed upon it – legitimately, moreover – by the analysis of its immanent structures. At that time I said that the world of the text marked the opening of the text to its "outside," to its "other," in that the world of the text constitutes an absolutely original intentional object in relation to its "internal' structure. It must be admitted, however, that considered apart from reading, the world of the text remains a transcendence in immanence. Its ontological status remains in suspension – an excess in relation to structure, an anticipation in relation to reading.[31]

In our opinion, it appears that Ricoeur joins the contemporary hermeneutical movement with its emphasis on the reader. While Ricoeur

---

29 Ricoeur, *Time and Narrative*, III, 158-179 and 259-261. (*Temps et récit*, III, 229-263 and 371-374).

30 Ibid., 100-101. "It is by way of reading that literature returns to life, that is, to the practical and affective field of existence." Ricoeur points out that both history and fiction affect their readers and both relate to the "reel." Ontological criteria return at this stage of *Temps et récit*, showing that both history and fiction pose a "représentance" ("standing-for"), which has possible positive affects on readers. (*Temps et récit III*, 148-150, esp. 149).

31 Ibid., 158-159. (*Italics* his). (*Temps et récit III*, 230).

practices a form of *reader-response* theory, his following of Iser and Jauss shows that his is of a milder form than that of Fish or Barthes. However, Ricoeur leaves us with several questions here. What prohibitions prevent readers from simply devising or creating their own meaning(s) of the text - narrative? Do readers determine, constitute, or discover textual meaning? Is it possible for a reader to misinterpret a text?

Ricoeur has written above that, the world of the text remains *latent* when not read. If this is the case, using his terminology, is it more appropriate to speak of the world of the text becoming a world "for me" when I read it? Perhaps, it is possible to distinguish between a text's "world – meaning," and its "meaning - world" for me. Does the latency of the world of the text affect its truly being a world? If a narrative is configured at the level of mimesis II, would it still remain a world in itself whether or not it is read?[32] Is it not possible for a text to be complete without being dependent on its reader to complete it?[33] For example, is a piece of music a piece of music, if it is never played?[34] Ricoeur's readerly point of view, at this stage, is more *aesthetic* than *rhetorical*, and as such, it favors a reader's *response* to the text over a reader's *responsibility* to the intent of its author.[35]

The questions in the previous paragraph merit further investigation. Whether a more recent phenomenon, or originating in a previous era, an "anti-authorial" project has recently constituted itself as a prominent component within the interpretive landscape.[36] It has already been demonstrated in our research that Ricoeur affirms that texts always have authors. However, at the same time, he argues that texts must be understood as having autonomy at the level of the original author's intention.[37] Ricoeur points out:

---

32 Ibid., 164. Ricoeur states, "Without the reader who accompanies it, there is no configuring act at work in the text; and without a reader to appropriate it, there is no world unfolded before the text." *(Temps et récit III*, 239).

33 Ricoeur, *From Text to Action*, "What is a Text?" 105-124, esp. 124, "[...] reading is the concrete act in which the destiny of the text is fulfilled." (*Du texte à l'action*, "Qu'est-ce qu'un texte?" 137-159, esp. 159).

34 Ibid., 119. "Reading is like the execution of a musical score; it marks the realization, the enactment, of the semantic possibilities of the text." (Ibid., 153).

35 Ricoeur, *Temps et récit, III*, 243-245. (*Time and Narrative, III*, 166-167). See M. Warner, "The Fourth Gospel's Art of Rational Persuasion," in: M. Warner, ed., *The Bible as Rhetoric: Studies in Biblical Persuasion and Credibility*, Warwick Studies in Philosophy and Literature, London: Routledge, 1990, 153-177, for a useful discussion of rhetoric.

36 For a fuller discussion see, Burke, "Introduction: Reconstructing the Author", in: *Authorship*, xv- xxx.

37 See above, From Speaking to Writing and The Text.

[....] writing renders the text autonomous with respect to the intention of the author. What the text signifies no longer coincides with what the author meant; henceforth, textual meaning and psychological meaning have different destinies.[38]

The text's career escapes the finite horizon lived by its author. What the text means now matters more that what the author meant when he wrote it.[39]

For Ricoeur, a text or narrative has an author, but this author's intent is neither retrievable, nor is it significant for the reader. According to Ricoeur's understanding of text as a discourse fixed by writing and the event of a speech act with preservable meaning, it is the *event* that disappears along with the *author's intent*, while the meaning remains fixed by the text.[40] In other words, the saying vanishes (event), while the said endures (meaning). Ricoeur attempts to preserve the "said," while eschewing what he presumes is a psychological moment related to the intent of an author.

In the 1998 collaborative volume with A. LaCocque *Penser la Bible* (*Thinking Biblically*),[41] one of Ricoeur's more recent efforts, this becomes even clearer. He continues to devalue authorial intention as a valid part of the hermeneutical endeavor. With regard to the biblical text, it is argued, that there is a "dynamisme textuel" at every level of biblical literature, however, this dynamism has no recourse to an author's intent, but rather is related to the original authors being aware of an incompleteness of their work, which seeks to be "remembered" and which, "asks to be, re-modeled, re-actualized by the community that is

---

38 Ricoeur, "The Hermeneutical Function," cited from, *Hermeneutics and the Human Sciences*, 131-144, esp. 139. While this may or may not be the case, Ricoeur shows his assumption that an author's intention is psychological. Might it not be otherwise? See the discussion below on author's intent.

39 Ricoeur, *Interpretation Theory*, 30.

40 See above Explanation and Understanding and Discourse and the Dialectic.

41 Ricoeur and LaCocque, *Penser la Bible*, (*Thinking Biblically: Exegetical and Hermeneutical Studies*).

the only agent of these texts."⁴² The authors state:

> [...] the first effect of reading is to confer an autonomy, an independent existence on a text, which thereby opens it to subsequent developments and subsequent enrichments, all of which affect its very meaning.
>
> Le premier effet de l'écriture (la lecture?) est de conférer au texte une autonomie, une existence indépendante, qui l'ouvre ainsi à des développements, à des enrichissements ultérieurs, lesquels affectent sa signification même.⁴³

Ricoeur and LaCocque portray the autonomy of the biblical text.⁴⁴ But this autonomy of the text comes into tension with its reliance on a reading community for its completion, or for its actual transfer of meaning. From this point of view, it is argued that the autonomy of the text is connected to its *author*, while the audience challenges its total independence. In this sense, the authors contend:

> The text exists, in the final analysis, thanks to the community, for the use of the community, with a view to giving shape to the community.⁴⁵

However, if the text itself is plurivocal, then it must be read at several levels. As interest in the biblical text varies between readers and reading communities, receptions of its meaning will certainly, also differ. The many voices contained in the text, as well as the many kinds of recep-

---

42   Ibid., xiii. (*Penser la Bible*, 11-12).

43   Ibid., xi. (*Penser la Bible*, 9). Parenthesis mine. The reason for this parenthesis is that the English reads, "The first effect of 'reading' [...]"

44   See Ricoeur, "Herméneutique et critique des idéologies," *Démythisation et Idéologie*, 25-64, reprinted in: *Du texte à l'action*, 333-377, esp. 366. ("Hermeneutics and the Critique of Ideology," in: *From Text to Action*, 270-307, and in: Thompson, ed., *Hermeneutics*, 63-100, esp. 91, ET), for a fuller statement on the autonomy of the text.

45   Ricoeur and LaCocque, *Thinking Biblically*, xiii. (*Penser la Bible*, 12). Does the biblical text exist solely because of its community of readers? See D. Stewart, "Ricoeur on Religious Language," Hahn, ed., *The Philosophy of Paul Ricoeur*, 423-442, esp., 438, for another point of view. Stewart sets forth the perspective that Ricoeur would affirm that without a historical event there is no "text" to confront a community of readers.

tions enacted by readers, both underscore the need to read this complex textual situation at more than one level.

In reference to the biblical text and what is identified by these authors as, "the communities of reading and interpretation," they see the hermeneutical circle functioning in an insular manner. What happens in the interpretation of "Les Écritures" is that the community interprets *itself*.[46] What is of import to us here is again the affirmation and emphasis on the text and the place it is given within this discussion of thinking biblically.

> If this [hermeneutical] circle is not vicious to the eyes of the faithful belonging to such communities, it is because the founding role attached to the sacred texts and the founded condition of the historical community do not designate interchangeable places. The founding text *teaches* – this is what the word *torah* means. And the community receives instruction.[47]

While the text and the community of readers remain central and authorial intention is underplayed, Ricoeur and LaCocque argue that the function of the text and the function of the community are not the same.[48] The First Testament, for example, took a priority position in the founded community of readers. Thus, on the reader's part, there was a necessary recognition of an asymmetry between authoritative text and the community reading it. Within this hermeneutical proposition, *biblical content* obliges the reader to enter the circle of its thought. According to LaCocque and Ricoeur,

---

46 See L. Fisher, "Mediation, Muthos, and the Hermeneutical Circle in Ricoeur's Narrative Theory," in: M. Joy, ed., *Paul Ricoeur and Narrative: Context and Contestation*, Calgary: University of Calgary Press, 1997, 207-219, for a useful discussion of what, in her opinion, is the crucial importance of the hermeneutical circle in Ricoeur's thought.

47 Ricoeur and LaCocque, *Thinking Biblically*, xvi-xvii. (*Penser la Bible*, 15).

48 Ibid., xi. In relation to the text's autonomy there is the added inference of a renunciation of what these authors refer to as "characteristic of Romanticist hermeneutics," which seeks to discover the intention of the author. While Ricoeur and LaCocque do not entirely deny the appropriateness of biblical research having a legitimate concern for an author, date, and placing of a biblical text, they do argue: "we do hold that the meaning of a text is in each instance an event that is born at the intersection between, on the one hand, those constraints that the text bears within itself and that have to do in large part with its *Sitz im Leben* and, on the other hand, the different expectations of a series of communities of reading and interpretation that the presumed authors of the text under consideration could not have anticipated." (*Italics theirs*). (Ibid. 9).

this entry requires reading the text *imaginatively* and *sympathetically*, as an act of adhesion through which a dynamic community of readers is then founded. It is suggested that it is only within this *sharing* that there is a possibility of accessing the meaning of these texts.

In summary, Ricoeur's work continues to hinge on its prioritization of the text, and especially since *La métaphore vive*, on the reader. Furthermore, he is determined to refute the psychological excesses of the authorial intent approach, which reduces hermeneutics to the search for connection with another mind; and yet Ricoeur also opposes the thought that the text is a *closed system* of signs.

While Ricoeur's position may offer a *valid* critique of some modernist interpretation theories mentioned above, it has several *weaknesses*. When Ricoeur argues that a discourse (text) is "somebody saying something to someone"[49] his tendency is to downplay the knowability of the intent of the "somebody" when it comes to the written text. However, is it not possible to critique a rationalist, structuralist, or Romanticist hermeneutics, without resorting to the exclusion of authorial intent? In addition, how does Ricoeur's view square with his own position and intent? How shall we read, for example, Ricoeur's written discourse defending an integral independence between philosophy and theology? He writes:

> I hope that my readers will agree that I have gone to such lengths not to mix these genres that I might well be accused of personal inconsistency. All things considered, I am more willing to be the target of this suspicion than of that of confusionism, mixing crypto-theology on the philosophical plane and crypto-philosophy on the plane of exegesis and theology![50]

---

49 Ricoeur, *Interpretation Theory*, 30. With respect to the view of Ricoeur and LaCocque mentioned above, we propose the following question: Why would imagination and sympathy not also be necessary readerly components when it comes to someone's acts of reading somebody's intended text?

50 Ricoeur, *The Philosophy of Paul Ricoeur*, Hahn, ed., 449.

One of the major weaknesses of Ricoeur's views of authorial intention is that he tends to undermine his own *intentionality* as an author. It is certainly true that the intentionality of an author may not always be transparent; nevertheless, an active concern for the Other demands an interpreter's attention to the one speaking and writing. In our opinion, there is evidence of the practical necessity of including the author's intentions in a viable hermeneutics—surely, more so than Ricoeur seems to allow for. We shall argue that this is the case with respect to Ricoeur's own work, as well as to his perspective of the texts of others.

Ricoeur, in our point of view, is not entirely consistent. There are a number of occurrences in his own work, at least on the implicit level (if not the explicit), of a different perspective. *Penser la Bible* (*Thinking Biblically*),[51] for example, shows an effort on the part of each author included to write in light of an awareness of the other's work:

> The exegete first wrote out his contribution, then the philosopher responded to it. Next, they both revised their respective contributions in such a way that the final redaction would yield a book in which each author's work took account of that of the other.[52]

In order for such a venture to meet its goal, it would seem that the *intentions* of the other author could not be entirely ignored in the process of working together to produce a single volume.[53] These authors also write of their shared *conviction* with regard to certain points of view that they have written about in this particular book.[54] However, in taking their contention about the autonomy of the text seriously, one must ask if it is rather the text that has conviction, and not per se the authors?

---

51 Ricoeur and LaCocque, *Thinking Biblically*. (*Penser la Bible*).

52 Ibid., ix. (*Penser la Bible*, 7).

53 We acknowledge that the scenario is different with a living author. However, why should it be presupposed that a once living author's literary act is to be minimized when it comes to reading his/her text?

54 Ricoeur and LaCocque, *Thinking Biblically*, xvii-xviii. (*Penser la Bible*, 16-17).

Ricoeur writes, in another context, of the practical articulations related to narrative and how Heidegger's existential analysis in *Being and Time* can play a central role, although this must be framed in certain way. Ricoeur seems to presuppose first, a correct understanding of Heidegger's *intended* existential analysis and then second, his own capacity to be able to frame this, "under certain conditions that must be clearly laid out."[55] Ricoeur, at least, implicitly accepts both Heidegger's and his own intentions as authors, and we would surmise their relevance for interpreting *Being and Time* and *Time and Narrative*. One further example of Ricoeur's, at least implicit concession to authorial intention, is found in the context of his discussion of the work of Genette on narrative in *Temps et récit II*. Ricoeur writes of the "intention" of Genette, rather than merely what the text says.[56]

We contend for the possibility that the author's intentions more specifically, as well as texts and readers, must be taken into consideration in the hermeneutical enterprise. Generally speaking, it is ironic, how authors often demand the right to defend what they have written in a text, in spite of maintaining that the author's intentions are unrecoverable or even unnecessary.[57] This is also most noticeable, either when authors are asked what they meant by a reader who is trying to understand their work, or when they are accused, for example by a critic, of meaning something they never intended. The response is frequently, "I meant to say [...] in regard to that argument or that person's position, or I did not mean that and have been misunderstood; what I really meant was [...]"[58]

---

55   Ricoeur, *Time and Narrative*, I, 60. (*Temps et récit*, I, 96).

56   Ricoeur, *Time and Narrative*, II, 180. "In fact Genette had himself referred to Plato's famous text [...]. His intention, then, however was polemical." (*Temps et récit*, II, 121).

57   A most simple example of this is in copyright laws which recognize the "rights" of authors.

58   See Ricoeur, "Poetry and Possibility: An Interview with Paul Ricoeur," in: *The Manhattan Review*, 6-21, reprinted in: Valdés, ed., *A Ricoeur Reader: Reflection and Imagination*, 448-462, esp. 459-460. We have already mentioned several instances of this ambiguity in Ricoeur's work. Two further examples: First, in a response to the question of the subject and society, Ricoeur argues for a subject who is responsible for his/her words. If this is not the case, we are no longer in a position to speak of freedom and the "rights of man." If this is the case, might it not be appropriate to speak of the "rights" of authorship also? Ricoeur calls for an *"ethic of the word"* and the basic moral duty "that people be responsible for what they say." (*Italics his*). "The Creativity of Language," in: Kearney, ed., *Dialogues with Contemporary Continental Thi*nkers, 17-36, reprinted in and cited from: *A Ricoeur Reader*, 463-481, esp. 477. In an age with such a profound and certainly correct emphasis on human rights, should not the rights of an author also be taken into consideration in the interpretation of the text? Second, Ricoeur comments that, "Thompson is right" concerning the emphasis of the "operative concept of the text" in four of Ricoeur's essays.

The previous argument is clearly based on the possibility of questioning "living authors," but would this not also equally apply to deceased authors whose voice continues to live on through their texts? No one denies, for example, that the biblical writers have passed from the scene. However, we would argue that what remains is the author's literary action (not so much now being there, but having been there). In Ricoeur's terminology, perhaps the question could be addressed to him in this manner: is the text not the "trace" or "testimony" of an author intending something to someone? Does not Ricoeur admit as much in the following statement?

> The witness is witness to things that have happened. We can think of the case of recording Christian preaching in the categories of story, as narration about things said and done by Jesus of Nazereth, as proceding from this intention of binding confession-testimony to narration-testimony. This conjunction is preformed in different ways by the four Evangelists and we could form a typology on this basis. At one extreme of the range we would have Luke; on the other John.[59]

Do authors and testimony have a link that readers have a responsibility to pay attention to? Kevin Vanhoozer makes a helpful observation with regard to testimony in arguing that:

> [...] testimony, of all literary forms, is least welcoming to deconstruction and radical reader-response criticism. For the reader to impose his own meaning or to affirm indeterminate multiple meanings is to deny the very nature of testimony; it is to subject testimony to inter-

---

He goes on to write that "[....] this concept had been introduced with the express intention [....] ." "A Response by Paul Ricoeur," in: Thompson, ed., *Hermeneutics*, 32-40, esp. 37. This seems to imply that there could be a getting it "wrong" and an authorial intent.

59   Ricoeur, "The Hermeneutics of Testimony," in: *Essays on Biblical Interpretation*, 119-154, esp. 134-137. ("L'herméneutique du témoignage," *Archivio di Filosofia* 42, (1972), 35-61, reprinted in *Lectures III*, 107-139, esp. 121-123). One wonders if the author continues to have a voice in testimony.

pretative violence. Rightly to receive testimony, I shall argue, means to attend to and respect the voice of the author.[60]

In addition to Vanhoozer, several other recent works take the intentional *act* of the author seriously.[61] Ricoeur himself has explored and given careful attention to *intended human action*, yet not drawn out the significance of this when it comes to the written. Rather than equating authorial intention with a purely psychological phenomenon, as he often seems to do, authorial intention should be focused on *intention as act*.[62] Thus, a text can and should be considered an author's literary act and as such be shown the due attention and care of the interpreter's act. Just as it would be inappropriate, or perhaps even disastrous to ignore a speaker's intention, so also to some degree at least, it would be problematic to disregard the intentional act of an author.

It is true that textual interpretation is always mediate and indirect—a task of seeking sense as opposed to one that is immediate and direct, with a readily seen complete sense. However, a text is never entirely semantically autonomous.[63] Texts are author intended entities, not necessarily enclosed within the psychological constraints of their author; rather they are opened up to interpretation as literary acts, the unfolding of a world out into the world and it is this phenomenon that invites a reader's engagement.

---

60 See Vanhoozer, "The Hermeneutics of I-Witness Testimony: John 21.20-24 and the Death of the 'Author'," in: A. Graeme Auld, ed., *Understanding Poets and Prophets: Essays in Honour of George Wishart Anderson*, Sheffield: Journal of Old Testament Studies Press, 1993, 366-387, esp. 367-368, for a fuller critique of modern and postmodern perspectives on the author.

61 See for example, M. Sternberg, *The Poetics of Biblical Narrative*. N. Wolterstorff, *Divine Discourse: Philosophical Reflections on the Claim that God Speaks*, Cambridge: Cambridge University Press, 1995. W. V. Harris, *Interpretive Acts*.

62 Vanhoozer, *Is There A Meaning in This Text?* 225.

63 Sternberg, *The Poetics of Biblical Narrative*, 9-11, argues, "As interpreters of the Bible, our only concern is with 'embodied' or 'objectified' intention   [......] . In my own view, such intention fulfils a crucial role, for communication presupposes a speaker who resorts to certain linguistic and structural tools in order to produce certain effects on the addressee; the discourse accordingly supplies a network of clues to the speaker's intention. The text's autonomy is a long-exploded myth: the text has no meaning, or every kind of meaning, outside the coordinates of discourse that we usually bundle into the term 'context' ."

We have argued that there is an ambiguity with regard to Ricoeur's position on the author's intention. Is it warranted, or even appropriate to continue to refer to "the author," while at the same time arguing that "the author's intent" can be excluded when interpreting a text? Perhaps, in the light of this ambiguity, Ricoeur might have considered a modification of his point of view that an author's intentions are by and large irrelevant to the interpretation of texts. Authors' intentions must be considered pertinent to textual interpretation, as it is their communicative actions that set the literary genre and content of the text.[64] The search for the meaning of biblical texts must be concerned with what authors have accomplished as an *act* of communication. This perspective, therefore, is not a return to a psychological intentionality, which Ricoeur rightly critiques, but a turn to the author's literary act.[65]

4.2. Refiguration and Beyond

Having opened up the exploration of authors, readers, and texts, and offered another perspective to that of Ricoeur, we are now ready to continue our hermeneutical trajectory through to his notion of *refiguration* (mimesis III). Thus, at this final stage of our investigation we are moving towards the completion of the hermeneutical enterprise, at least as far as this is possible in this authored text. A refiguring of Ricoeur's work brings closure to our prefiguration - configuration modes of description, analysis, and evaluation. How does refiguration fit into Ricoeur's hermeneutical project, and how can we evaluate this dimension in light of Ricoeur's concept of appropriation?[66]

---

64 D. Dutton, "Why Intentionalism Won't Go Away," in: A. J. Cascardi, ed., *Literature and the Question of Philosophy*, London: Johns Hopkins University Press, 1987, 192-209.

65 In personal discussion and correspondence, the present author posed the following question to Ricoeur: "how is it possible, in your hermeneutics, to speak of a necessary love for the Other/other, yet ignore the intention of the author of a text?" Ricoeur agreed that it is important to be sympathetic to authorial intention (here the concern was the Bible) and responded in the following way: "The question is not to deprive the authors from their commitment, but to wonder to what extent the authority of the author on his/her text is part of the meaning." Personal correspondence with Ricoeur, 28 May, 1999.

66 See Ricoeur, "Appropriation," in: Thompson, ed., *Hermeneutics*, 182-193.

It must first of all be pointed out that, for Ricoeur, refiguration is connected to the problematic of time and narrative,[67] but includes broader implications as well.[68] Our reflection, at this juncture, is more specifically focused on time and narrative, which concerns the relevance of *refiguration* and *beyond*, in the wider and more general context of Ricoeur's hermeneutics.

In an expansion of Aristotle, Ricoeur writes that mimesis III (refiguration) is what connects the world of the text and the world of the reader.[69] It is important to recall again, as it is central to Ricoeur's notion of refiguration, that refiguration and configuration are linked through the *act of reading*. Ricoeur states:

> The act of reading is thus the operator that joins mimesis III to mimesis II. It is the final indicator of the refiguring of the world of action under the sign of the plot.[70]

As the reader reads the text, this in turn brings an end to the act of configuration, whereby the mode of refiguration then takes place.[71] When refiguration happens or is achieved, the reader has reached the end of the hermeneutical trajectory.[72] It is, according to Ricoeur, in the reader that *mimesis* reaches its accomplishment. We have already pointed out that Ricoeur moves away from the terminology of "reference" in *Temps et récit*.[73] Keep in mind he modifies reference with refiguration, but also chooses to employ Gadamer's vocabulary of "application," which he states he has written of elsewhere as

---

67   Ricoeur, *The Philosophy of Paul Ricoeur*, Hahn, ed., 47, points out "[....] it was the temporal dimension of action that was subject to refiguration [...] refiguration contained a different sense, even an opposite one, in the case of historical and that of fictional narrative."

68   Ibid., 47.

69   Ricoeur, *Temps et récit*, *I*, 109. (*Time and Narrative, I,* 71).

70   Ibid., 117. (*Time and Narrative, I,* 77).

71   Ibid., 110. (*Time and Narrative I,* 71).

72   Ricoeur, *Temps et récit, III,* 255. (*Time and Narrative, III,* 274).

73   Section 4.2 above is explicitly relevant for an understanding of refiguration in the present context of our discussion. It also offers a fuller explanation of Ricoeur's shift from the terminology of "reference" to "refiguration" in *Temps et récit*.

"appropriation."[74] This latter conception merits further consideration, which we undertake below.

Before exploring appropriation, it is important to note that a Ricoeurian modification of reference and his motion towards refiguration in *Temps et récit* also takes place in response to what Ricoeur refers to as the influence of a post-Heideggerian theory of truth. According to Ricoeur, this theory rejects *correspondence*, while appealing to truth as *manifestation*.[75] It is in this latter sense, Ricoeur argues, that metaphor and narrative, through the mediation of the reader, aim at a refiguration of reality.

This brings us to a key question. What does Ricoeur mean by *refiguring* reality, and does it have any connection with his concept of *appropriation*? We would wager it does and the response to this is twofold. A refiguration of reality affirms at least: *uncovering* the hidden in human experience and a *transformation* of one's vision of the world.[76] Ricoeur states that this refiguring of reality pertains to:

> an active reorganization of our being-in-the-world, performed by the reader following the invitation of the text, [...] to become the reader of oneself.[77]

He describes appropriation as:

> Far from saying that a subject, who already masters his own being-in-the-world, projects the *a priori* of his own understanding and interpolates this *a priori* in the text, I shall say that appropriation is the process by which the revelation of new modes of being - or, if you prefer Wittgenstein to Heidegger, new 'forms of life' - *gives* the subject new capacities for knowing himself. If the reference of a text is the projec-

---

74 Ricoeur, *Temps et récit*, III, 229. (*Time and Narrative*, III, 158). See also Ricoeur, "Appropriation," 182-193. "Qu'est-ce qu'un texte?" in: *Du texte à l'action*, 151-159. ("What is A Text?" in: *From Text to Action*, 118-124). "La fonction herméneutique," in: *Du texte à l'action*, 115-117. ("The Hermeneutical Function," in: *From Text to Action*, 87-88).

75 Ricoeur, *The Philosophy of Paul Ricoeur*, Hahn, ed., 47. "Appropriation," 182-193, esp. 193.

76 Ricoeur, *The Philosophy of Paul Ricoeur*, Hahn, ed., 47. See also, *Temps et récit*, III, 229. (*Time and Narrative*, III, 158).

77 Ricoeur, *The Philosophy of Paul Ricoeur*, Hahn, ed., 47. Also see 4.2 above.

tion of a world, then it is not in the first instance the reader who projects himself. The reader is rather broadened in his capacity to project himself by receiving a new mode of being from the text itself.[78]

Thus, Ricoeur's perspective of "refiguration," in our opinion, resembles his notion of "appropriation" on the level of a text - narrative - world being given to a reader and leading to new self-understanding (refiguring reality). We, therefore, envision these two terms in a similar manner, while nevertheless recognizing that a major difference in the context of refiguration and appropriation also needs to be articulated. That is, the *act* of reading has become primary for the former, while *interpretation*[79] is referred to as the device for the latter.[80]

We now turn briefly, yet more specifically, to investigate Ricoeur's notion of appropriation. Ricoeur's description follows his translation of the German expression *Aneignung*. Aneignen, he argues, means to make one's own what was initially foreign.[81] According to this understanding of appropriation, the aim of hermeneutics is to battle against *estrangement* as evidenced in "historical alienation" and "cultural distance," with interpretation playing a definitive role in giving the world of the text to the present world of the reader. In order for this to be realized there must be a "reading," a "giving up" of the self, as well as a "reception" of the world of text. This unfolds in the following manner. Ricoeur states:

---

78   Ricoeur, "Appropriation," 192. (*Italics his*). While it is true that Ricoeur's primary combat in this article is with the problematics of historicism (he now writes of the objectification of meaning as a necessary mediation between writer and reader which requires the existential component of the appropriation of meaning, 185) and the illusions of the subject (appropriation of the meaning of the text implies a dispossession of the narcissistic *ego* and the possibility of new *self*-understanding, 191-192, (*Italics his*) we can nevertheless recognize the connection with refiguration.

79   Ricoeur, "What is A Text?" in: *From Text to Action*, 105-124, esp. 118. ("Qu'est-ce qu'un texte?" in: *Du texte à l'action*, 137-159, esp. 152). It is important to clarify here. Interpretation and appropriation have a complex intersignification in Ricoeur's work. On the one hand, interpretation and appropriation are related to understanding and therefore more subjective. "By 'appropriation,' I understand this: that the interpretation of a text culminates in the self-interpretation of a subject who thenceforth understands himself better, understands himself differently, or simply begins to understand himself." On the other hand, interpretation and appropriation are related to explanation (bringing out the structure of the text) and therefore more objective. esp. 122, (156, FT). "The text seeks to place us in its meaning. [...] to interpret is to follow the path of thought opened up by the text, to place oneself en route toward the *orient* of the text." (*Italics his*). Several pages later in the same essay, 124, (159, FT), Ricoeur concludes, "Appropriation loses its arbitrariness insofar as it is the recovery of that which is at work, [...], within the text. What the interpreter says is a resaying that reactivates what is said by the text."

80   Ricoeur, *Time and Narrative, III*, 158, suggests, "[...] it is only through the mediation of reading that the literary work attains complete significance [...]." (*Temps et récit, III*, 230). See also, "Appropriation," 185, "Interpretation brings together, equalises, renders contemporary and similar. This goal is attained only insofar as interpretation actualises the meaning of the text for the present reader. Appropriation is the concept which is suitable for the actualisation of meaning as addressed to someone."

81   Ibid., 185.

> Relinquishment is a fundamental moment of appropriation and distinguishes it from any form of 'taking possession.' Appropriation is also and primarily a 'letting-go.' Reading is an appropriation-divestiture. How can this letting-go, this relinquishment, be incorporated into appropriation? Essentially by linking appropriation to the revelatory power of the text which we have described as its referential dimension. It is in allowing itself to be carried off towards the reference of the text that the *ego* divests itself of itself [. . .] [82]

Ricoeur's idea of appropriation is fixed on a *reception* and *acceptance* of the world of the text, which in turn functions as a critique of the illusion of the subject (reader) being in any sense the refigurer or possessor of itself. It is the *act* of reading that both appropriates and divests the environment of a meeting between two worlds. It is not the reader who projects him/herself onto the text. On the contrary, the reader is given a *new self* in being challenged by the *otherness* of the text, whose meaning is then appropriated.[83] The reader *surrenders* to the power of the text and through its reception is able to read him/herself.

Having now elucidated something of Ricoeur's perspective on refiguration and appropriation, we are left with a number of queries. How does refiguration make any difference in the world? Does reading and the act of connecting the world of the text with the world of the reader, in turn, make the world? What world? Whose world? Is Ricoeur's description of appropriation a satisfactory account of what appropriation actually means and how it functions in the hermeneutical adventure? How does Ricoeur's view, if at all, lead us beyond an interpretative acquiescence?

In beginning to respond to these questions, we turn now to assess

---

82 Ibid., 191. (*Italics his*). Also see, Wallace, "Can God be Named Without Being Known? The Problem of Revelation in Thiemann, Ogden, and Ricoeur," *JAAR* 59/2 (1991), 281-308, for an exposition of Ricoeur's view of the revelatory power of the biblical text. Also, S. M. Schneiders, *The Revelatory Text*, San Francisco: Harper, 1991.

83 Ricoeur, "Appropriation," 192, points out, "I should like to contrast the *self* which emerges from the understanding of the text to the *ego* which claims to precede this understanding. It is the text, with its universal power of unveiling, which gives a *self* to the *ego*." (*Italics his*).

Ricoeur's concept of appropriation, which has come under useful analysis and questioning by Stephen Prickett.[84] Prickett shows how Ricoeur has avoided and apparently dissociated *appropriation* from any *negative* representations, many of which, Prickett argues, possessed pejorative connotations and realities.[85]

In a Prickettian perspective, for example, appropriation - "to make one's own" has also been used to refer to the looting of monasteries and to the usurping of another's property.[86] Historically speaking, appropriation has often had a negative dimension. The problem, for Prickett, is not so much with the thought that hermeneutics is a battle against "historical alienation" and "cultural distance," but rather with *how* such a combat is conducted. In practicing a hermeneutics of *suspicion* with regard to Ricoeur's description of appropriation, Prickett maintains that Ricoeur is at pains to entirely eliminate the forensic horizon of appropriation as violence, i.e. one of "taking possession."[87]

According to Prickett, Ricoeur's process of appropriation is identified as a "cease and surrender" to the text, and never as a "capture and control" of what the text has to say. Ricoeur's gesture of *abdication* to this other of the text rests on the creative possibility of *revelation*, a revelation not merely of something, but also of self-critique and new understanding. Ricoeur affirms this in the following:

> The link between appropriation and revelation is, in my view, the cornerstone of a hermeneutics that seeks to overcome the failures of historicism and to remain faithful to the original intention of Schleiermacher's hermeneutics. To understand an author better than he understood himself is to unfold the revelatory power implicit in his discourse, beyond the limited horizon of his own existential situation.

---

84   S. Prickett, *The Origins of Narrative*, Cambridge: Cambridge University Press, 1996, 26-33, for a critique of Ricoeur's views.

85   Ibid., 26-28.

86   Ibid., 26-28.

87   Ibid., 30.

Only the interpretation that satisfies the injunction of the text, follows the 'arrow' of meaning, and endeavors to 'think in accordance with' it engenders a new *self*-understanding.[88]

However, Prickett argues that there are *dangers* in seeing self-discovery as a result of the process of appropriation. Hermeneutics on its own, in Prickett's view, does not necessarily guarantee self-understanding. Some level of *suspicion* should be retained when reading texts simply because the endeavor of hermeneutics has limits. Moreover, Prickett asserts that Ricoeur's attempt to remain faithful to the original intention of Schleiermacher's hermeneutics incurs difficulties.[89]

According to Prickett, Ricoeur's reframing of appropriation is questionable, in so much as it dehistorizes the concept and is too subjective.[90] Thus, there is in Ricoeur's type of appropriation, a reductionistic *positivity* with regard to the exchange between reader and text. However, his notion of refiguration in *Temps et récit* may provide something of a corrective to the previous by emphasizing the stakes involved in the act of reading. Yet, the reader's relation to the text is still primarily one of *surrender* and *letting-go*, which naively risks being exposed to the possibility of deception that may function on the level of the text. Perhaps, the possibility of textual deception thus puts refiguration or appropriation under a hermeneutics of trust and suspicion. If so, another way of putting this would be that Ricoeur's perspective is, ironically, too trusting, but also too passive. Once suspicion has a role, it may turn out that the text should be actively embraced and made one's own. Do texts *mean*? How inherently significant is reading? Does "what" is read make any difference to self-understanding? From our point of view, "what" is read,

---

88   Ricoeur, "Appropriation," 191, 192-193. (emphasis and *italics his*).

89   Prickett, *The Origins of Narrative*, 31-32, esp. 32, argues that the original intention of Schleiermacher's hermeneutics is a much debated question. In his opinion, Ricoeur's attempting to move past historicism may be commended, but "for many of his critics there is a dangerous hubris implicit in the idea that the interpreter can remain faithful to the original intention of Schleiermacher's hermeneutics."

90   Ibid., 32.

and not just the act of reading itself, is an important factor in refiguration, appropriation, and the entire hermeneutical trajectory. Concerning Ricoeur's outlook on texts and appropriation, Gerald Bruns remarks:

> What Ricoeur proposes is something like a magical-looking-glass theory of textual meaning. Texts mean, not by corresponding to states of affairs, not by satisfying truth conditions, but by manifesting or opening up a region of existence whose reality is not simply matter for analysis but is, on the contrary, matter for appropriation, that is, for intervention and action. The looking-glass theory of meaning presupposes an ontological turn away from epistemology toward a hermeneutics of praxis and action.[91]

At this stage, Ricoeur's more ontological notions of refiguration and appropriation seem more concerned with a reading of oneself (which takes place through an interaction between the world of the narrative - text and the world of the reader) than with "what" is read. The figure of self-understanding is vital for Ricoeur, as is the act - event of reading the text, which contributes to it. Yet, in keeping with Ricoeur's own hermeneutical trajectory, refiguration or appropriation cannot become the sole consideration of hermeneutics. Truer self-understanding is not a projection of self onto the text, but through the engagement with a trustworthy "what" of the text, receiving and embracing a new capacity of self-knowledge from it.[92]

Understandably, we have learned much from Ricoeur, but we would now like to turn to the "beyond," and to unpack what we have referred to in this study as a *living hermeneutics* in motion. Our aim in concluding this section is to explain a *living hermeneutics* in motion, specifically in relation to biblical hermeneutics. It seems to us that reading is

---

[91] G. Bruns, "Against Poetry: Heidegger, Ricoeur, and the Originary Scene of Hermeneutics," in: D. E. Klemm and W. Schweiker, eds., *Meanings in Texts and Actions: Questioning Paul Ricoeur*, Charlottesville: The University of Virginia Press, 1993, 26-46, esp. 36.

[92] Ricoeur, *Temps et récit*, III, 247. (*Time and Narrative*, III, 169).

a *passive* act, rather than an *active* act. By this, we mean that reading is more imaginative[93] and less an action-taking place in the animate world (not that the latter kind of action excludes the imagination). A living hermeneutics in motion only comes to its realized, yet provisionally mediated closure, when the configured text is acted or performed out into the world. Following such an engagement with the world, there is then a movement back to the three modes of prefiguration, configuration, and refiguration, all of which create anew this deepening of the previous dialogue. It is only in this sense that a refiguring of reality (not just the reader's internal reality), can be brought to finite closure.

In other words, the motion from the *world of the text* to the *world of the reader* must be carried out a step further by being lived out into the animate world. Hermeneutics does not culminate with the linking of author and reader,[94] or with the connecting of the world of text and world of reader,[95] but rather with the hermeneutical "what" that is read and then acted upon in the world. Such action demonstrates the power of a living hermeneutics to *refigure reality* as it continues its motion through the text to the reader and through the reader out into the animate world. It is only when this motion reaches the world, not just the world of the reader, that a living hermeneutical motion is reanimated, spiraling forward through the process of prefiguration, configuration, and refiguration in the broadest sense. The animate world, in its relation and distinction to both text and reader, is a hermeneutical factor that demands consideration. That is, the world of the text and the world of the reader must finally be in dialogue with the world. This

---

93   Ricoeur, "The Bible and the Imagination," in: Wallace, ed., *Figuring the Sacred*, 144-166, esp. 145, points out, "By placing myself at the very heart of the act of reading, I am hoping to place myself at the starting point of the trajectory that unfolds into the individual and social forms of the imagination."

94   Against Walhout, "Narrative Hermeneutics," in: R. Lundin, C. Walhout, and A. C. Thiselton, *The Promise of Hermeneutics*, 107.

95   Ricoeur, "Qu'est-ce qu'un texte?" in: *Du texte à l'action*, 137-159, esp. 153-156. ("What is A Text?" in: *From Text to Action*, 105-124, esp. 118-122). Ricoeur, "Life: A Story in Search of a Narrator," 423-437, esp. 430-431, argues, "My thesis here is that the process of composition, of configuration, does not realize itself in the text but in the reader, and under this condition configuration makes possible reconfiguration of a life by way of the narrative. More precisely: the meaning or the significance of a story wells up from *the intersection of the world of the text and the world of the reader*. The act of reading becomes the crucial moment in the entire analysis." (*Italics his*).

hermeneutics in motion, however, is envisaged as stratified, neither static, nor iniquitous.[96] In this context, hermeneutics must be understood as indeed living, and having the capacity to affect the world.

While it is true that the goal of understanding and explanation is what has been done in the text, which then for a reader has the possibility of becoming new understanding (Ricoeur's passionate claim), this new understanding also calls for an engagement with the world in order to evaluate and cultivate its authenticity and trustworthiness. If this is the case, the hermeneutical venture is not entirely a private matter between text and reader; hermeneutics constitutes an interaction with the world, which is distinct from, yet related to both.

We shall now briefly, yet hopefully in a fecund manner, make a transition into the question of biblical hermeneutics. How is a living hermeneutics necessarily a biblical hermeneutics? If the primary aim of biblical interpretation is concerned only with the text or its effect on the reader, what happens to the world? The question here is not with the irrelevance of "effect," but with the possibility of an additional necessary detour through the world in order for responsible reading to take place.

No doubt the dynamics of the interpretation of the biblical text are not facile. Stefan Collini remarks:

> Interpretation is not, of course, an activity invented by twentieth century literary theorists. Indeed, puzzles about how to characterize that ability have a long history in Western thought, provoked above all by the enormously complicated task of establishing the meaning of the Word of God.[97]

Meanings have been and continue to be produced through the arduous marvel of the interpretation of "the Word of God." In this case, as

---

96 Ricoeur, "Phénoménologie de la Religion," *Revue de l'Institut Catholique de Paris* 45 (1993), 59-75, esp. 65, contends that the hermeneutical circle is not vicious, but can be "portant et vivifiant."

97 S. Collini, "Introduction," in: S. Collini, ed., U. Eco, *Interpretation and overinterpretation*, Cambridge: Cambridge University Press, 1992, 3.

meaning is mined from the biblical text, our understanding, explanation, and new understanding should not stop with the transformation of the reader, although this is crucial, but with the transformation of the world. If the world is God's world outside of text and reader, then this world has a hermeneutical exigency.

Perhaps, another way of asserting this would be to refer to the action of re-narrating[98] or performing the text of the Bible[99] out into the world, which then contributes to a refiguration of reality. In this sense, the biblical text, through its readers, must be acted out into an animate world that speaks back, if anything other than self-transformation is to be hoped for that world. Ricoeur's use of the biblical realities of new Covenant, the Kingdom of God, and new creation are not merely poetic possibilities, nor are they solely concerned with self-understanding (they do pertain to and are for both) in the biblical text.[100] Such biblical realities, however, also aim at refiguring the totality of reality, not just the internal reality of the reader.

Afer exploring authors, readers, and texts, and evaluating refiguration and appropriation and its relation to biblical hermeneutics in Ricoeur's hermeneutical trajectory, we have discovered some helpful insights. The stress that Ricoeur puts on readers and texts is instructive, but his notion of authorial intent could have been re-formulated in better ways. In doing so, he would have been more consistent with the whole hermeneutical enterprise.

---

98   J. Milbank, *The Word Made Strange*, Oxford: Blackwell, 1997, 31-32.

99   S. C. Barton, "New Testament Interpretation as Performance," *Scottish Journal of Theology*, 52/2 (1999), 179-208, following N. Lash, appeals to a performance model of hermeneutics where Scripture is related to a musical score being performed with creative fidelity allowing it to come alive again in the contemporary context.

100   Ricoeur, "Toward a Hermeneutic of the Idea of Revelation," *Harvard Theological Review* 70 (1977), 1-37, reprinted in and cited from: *Essays on Biblical Interpretation*, 74-118, esp., 103. "The proposed world that in biblical language is called new creation, a new Covenant, the Kingdom of God, is the 'issue' of the biblical text unfolded in front of this text." (emphasis his).

5. Conclusion

We conclude with a recap of the major points of our exploration of Ricoeur's contribution to biblical hermeneutics. Our aim was to discover if Ricoeur's work could offer biblical hermeneutics an alternative; a way forward between the hermeneutical polarization's of "sharp boundaries" and "radical indeterminacy." This inquiry lead us into diverse, yet interlacing examinations of modernism and post-modernism, regional and general hermeneutics, a theory of the text, the methodological archetypes of historical criticism, structuralism, and into parables, and narrative. Here is where we have come.

First, in the contemporary hermeneutical maze, it is important to accentuate that Ricoeur's hermeneutics centers on the text. In his concentration on the text, its configured sense, and extra-linguistic referent, Ricoeur argues that not all interpretations are equal, either on the level of uniformity or plurality. This means that neither the modernist utopia of uniformity (sharp boundaries) or the post-modernist paradise of plurality (radical indeterminacy), concerning the interpretation of texts is hermeneutically feasible.

Thus, one of Ricoeur's major contributions, in moving us beyond the modernist - post-modernist controversy of "sharp boundaries" and "radical indeterminacy," is to be found in his insistence on the inclusion of the text, and a theory of the text, (as a meaningful and referring, yet not totalizing text), in the hermeneutical enterprise. In elucidating and highlighting the import of Ricoeur's contribution to general and regional hermeneutics and a theory of the text, we in turn have seen how his work combats the excesses of immoderate extremes.

Second, in the current discussion, regarding the divergence of philosophical - general and biblical - regional hermeneutics, we have seen how Ricoeur effectively re-positions and re-habilitates the text in a general hermeneutics and how related to this, he establishes an effective theory of the text, and how in turn both of these articulations engineer and fortify a critique of "sharp boundaries" and "radical indeterminacy." However, Ricoeur's contribution to biblical hermeneutics goes further. He argues that a specific text, the biblical text, is the *organon* for philosophical - general hermeneutics. Thus, his position stands against, in particular, the so-called "Yale school," which argues that for Ricoeur, the opposite is the case. According to Ricoeur, however, it is the biblical text that informs, evaluates, and governs a philosophical hermeneutics, and not the other way around.

Third, with the text in place in general hermeneutics, and more specifically, at this juncture, the biblical text as the organon of general hermeneutics, and with both in their *related*, yet *distinct* ways taking us beyond intemperate extremes, we opened up a dialogue with methodology. We devoted a good deal of space to the question of methodology and its pertinence to biblical hermeneutics. Ricoeur's contribution here, as we shall articulate it, is to offer a *pertinent* methodological analysis, which interconnects, albeit in a modified fashion, three methods related to interpreting the biblical text. In Ricoeur's biblical hermeneutics, there is a place for the historical-critical, structural, and hermeneutic methods. The uniqueness of the hermeneutic method, as Ricoeur defines it, is its capability of comprising the former two, which are often perceived to be in exclusive opposition to each other, while at the same time it is also capable of including the reader as a valid hermeneutical concern.

There may be objections here to Ricoeur's synthesizing efforts, in that he is not regarded as highly *systematic*, however, a significant contribution of our research has elucidated and demonstrated that Ricoeur prefers to act, if we may say so, as an *architect of mediation*; as one who mediates various positions in order to create new ones, to open new possibilities for viewing biblical hermeneutics in new ways and from new perspectives. This is not to affirm that Ricoeur should not be more systematic, but only to argue that in the material we have worked with, it is not his goal and neither has it been ours. Ricoeur's interests, as we have read him, are frequently sophisticated orientations, contours, framings, and options, not systems.

Fourth, we moved into an application of our previous sections with an analysis of Ricoeur's work on biblical parables. Initially, as evidenced in our comparing Ricoeur with the post-modernist orientation of the work of Crossan's, we concluded that there is a radical difference between the two, which culminates in parabolic *meaning-fullness* versus *meaning-lessness*. Ricoeur's work on Jesus' parables resists Crossan's pessimism, affirming through a parabolic sense and reference, their capacity to *re-orient*, not merely *dis-orient* their readers.

Another pertinent discussion on narrative parables was the *tension theory of metaphor*. Parables and metaphors have the capacity to refer to and refigure reality, while not necessarily being identified as the same thing. A parable, strictly speaking, is not a metaphor, but engenders a semantic impertinence that creates, in Ricoeur's vocabulary, a metaphoric process. We brought into this context the work of Harnisch, an exegete who investigates the problematic of metaphor and parable, bringing to Ricoeur's work a complement and a critique. Ricoeur and Harnisch agree that metaphor is not grounded in a theory of substitution, but a theory of tension. It is, however, more specifically when the parable itself enters the discussion that Harnisch rightly calls for an emendation of a Ricoeurian perspective in drawing attention to the tensional significance *inside* the parable itself and thus not just between the reader who is *outside* and the story. In seeking to make a valid contribution to biblical hermeneutics in regard to the parables of Jesus, our own proposal highlights the image of a "prism," which attempts to integrate the Ricoeurian and Harnischian parabolic perspectives, yet also go beyond them both.

Fifth, we next turned to an investigation of narrative. We addressed the debate about narrative and its relation to life. We explored the positions of Ricoeur and Carr and sought a way through their opposing points of view. Our conclusion was to appeal to a mediating position again employing the image of a "prism." Narratives *both* reflect life *and* create something new at the same time.

We also undertook an analysis of the problematic of *historical* and *fictional* narrative, learning that Ricoeur, in contrast to some postmodern understandings, does not abandon history on the narrative register. In demonstrating that there is an interweaving (entrecroisement) of fiction and history and history and fiction at some levels in the text, Ricoeur is opposed to collapsing the two forms of narrative into one, without distinction.

The results of our investigation and analysis of this were then applied to an evaluation for biblical hermeneutics. We showed the significance of a Ricoeurian contribution in a balanced narrative approach, which has the potential of avoiding the "radical indeterminacy" of post-modernism and its tendency to dissolve history into fiction, and the "sharp boundaries" of modernism with its tendency to naively suppose that historical fact equals access to the event itself. There is an *alternative* to the biblical text being viewed as merely history, or in contradistinction, solely literature. Such an alternative presents a path through unproductive extremes, which tend to *polarize* biblical hermeneutics in a reductionistic fashion.

Following on from these conclusions on narrative and an evaluation for biblical hermeneutics, our portrayal of authors, readers, and texts proposed a reflection on Ricoeur's views of this triad, especially focusing on authors and readers and the question of authorial intention and reader's response. Ricoeur, notably in *Temps et récit* and *Penser la Bible*, has underscored the *act of reading* in interpreting a text in general, and the biblical text in particular. He has adopted, in contrast to his work in *La métaphore vive*, a form of reader response that, in keeping with much contemporary literary theory, highlights the reader in the interpretation of narrative - text. He tends to privilege a reader's response over that of the reader's accountability to an author's intention. Working from his own writings we aimed to show his avoidance of authorial intention was untenable and inconsistent. We endorsed, following recent developments on authorial intention, that it be viewed as a literary act: intended human action, not merely a psychological phenomenon.

Our last exploration, in order to bring our study to closure, concerned *appropriation*, and *beyond*. In the attempt to delineate Ricoeur's description of the end of the hermeneutical venture in the wider context of his hermeneutics, we directed our attention to refiguration as the act of reading, which appropriates the world of the text enabling the reader to read her/himself. Refiguration and appropriation have to do with the text giving modes of being to our being-in-the-world. We then turned to a more specific investigation of Ricoeur's concept of appropriation, arguing from the work of Prickett that it dismisses any pejorative dimension. Appropriation, for Ricoeur, is a passive "letting-go," when it should also be concerned with an active embrace of the trustworthy Other. In this case, the text can provide new self-understanding and new self-knowledge.

We then aimed for the "beyond" in more precisely describing living hermeneutics in motion, as that which moves through the text and the reader out into the world. Our appeal was to biblical orientations that are concerned with the refiguration of the totality of reality, not merely that of the reader.

On the whole, our trajectory was to prefigure, configure, and refigure something of Ricoeur's creative action, detours and all. The world of *his* text and the world of *this* reader have met, while the *beyond* has been and is being worked out into the *world* through text and reader.

SELECT BIBLIOGRAPHY

As Ricoeur's comprehensive bibliography numbers into the hundreds we have decided to establish a select bibliography of his books and articles. For a more complete bibliography see Frans D. Vansina, *Paul Ricoeur: Bibliographie systématique de ses écrits et des publications consacrées à sa pensée* (1935-1984), Leuven - Louvain-la-Neuve: Peeters - Editions de l'Institut Supérieur de Philosophie, 1985 and Bibliography of Paul Ricoeur: A Primary and Secondary Systematic Bibliography compiled by Frans D. Vansina and Paul Ricoeur, in: *The Philosophy of Paul Ricoeur*, L. E. Hahn, ed., Chicago: Open Court, 1995. In addition, we have included a select bibliography of secondary sources on Ricoeur's work and a list of other books and articles relevant to our research.

1) Selected list of Writings by Paul Ricoeur

Books

Ricoeur, P. et Dufrenne, M., *Karl Jaspers et la philosophie de l'existence*, Paris: Seuil, 1947.

Ricoeur, P. *Gabriel Marcel et Karl Jaspers, Philosophie du mystère et philosophie du paradoxe*, Paris: Temps Présent, 1948.

———. *Philosophie de la volonté, I: Le volontaire et l'involontaire*, Paris: Aubier, 1950, (*Freedom and Nature*, Evanston: Northwestern University Press, 1966, English Translation, trans. E. V. Kohak).

———. *Histoire et vérité*, Paris: Seuil, 1955 (*History and Truth*, Evanston: Northwestern University Press, 1965, ET, trans. C. A. Kelbley).

———. *Philosophie de la volonté. Finitude et culpabilité I, L'homme* faillible, Paris: Aubier, 1960 (*Fallible Man*, Chicago: Henry Regnery, 1965, ET, trans. C. A. Kelbley).

———. *Philosophie de la volonté. Finitude et culpabilité II, La symbolique du mal*, Paris: Aubier, 1960 (*The Symbolism of Evil*, New York: Harper & Row, 1967, ET, trans. E. Buchanan).

———. *De l'interprétation: Essai sur Freud*, Paris: Seuil, 1965, (*Freud and Philosophy: An Essay on Interpretation*, New Haven: Yale University Press, 1970, ET, trans. D. Savage).

———. *Husserl: An Analysis of his Phenomenology*, Evanston: Northwestern University Press, 1967.

———. *Le conflit des interprétations: Essais d'herméneutique*, Paris: Seuil, 1969, (*The Conflict of Interpretations: Essays in Hermeneutics*, D. Ihde, ed., Evanston: Northwestern University Press, 1974, ET, trans. K. McLaughlin, D. Savage, and others).

———. *La métaphore vive*, Paris: Seuil, 1975, (*The Rule of Metaphor*, Toronto: University of Toronto Press, 1977, ET, trans. R. Czerny, with K. McLaughlin, J. Costello, SJ).

———. *Interpretation Theory: Discourse and the Surplus of Meaning*, Fort Worth: Texas Christian University Press, 1976.

———. *The Philosophy of Paul Ricoeur*, C. E. Reagan and D. Stewart, eds., Boston: Beacon, 1978.

———. *Essays on Biblical Interpretation*, L. S. Mudge, ed., Philadelphia: Fortress, 1980.

———. *Hermeneutics and the Human Sciences*, J. B. Thompson, ed. and trans., Cambridge: Cambridge University Press, 1981.

———. *Temps et récit*, 3 tomes., Paris: Seuil, 1983-1985, (*Time and Narrative*, 3 Vols., Chicago: University of Chicago Press, 1984-1987, ET, trans., K. McLaughlin and D. Pellauer; Vol. 3, K. Blamey and D. Pellauer).

———. *A l'école de la phénoménologie*, Paris: Vrin, 1986.

———. *Du texte à l'action. Essais d'herméneutique II*, Paris: Seuil, 1986, (*From Text to Action, Essays in Hermeneutics II*, Evanston: Northwestern University Press, 1991, ET, trans., K. Blamey and J. B. Thompson).

———. *Amour et justice*, Tübingen: Mohr, 1990.

———. *Soi-même comme un autre*, Paris: Seuil, 1990, (*Oneself as Another*, Chicago: University of Chicago Press, 1992, ET, trans., K. Blamey).

———. *A Ricoeur Reader: Reflection and Imagination*, M. J. Valdés, ed., Toronto: University of Toronto Press, 1991.

———. *Lectures I-III*, Paris: Seuil, 1991-1994.

———. *Le Juste*, Paris: Seuil, 1995.

———. *Réflexion faite: Autobiographie intellectuelle*, Paris: Seuil, 1995.

———. *Figuring the Sacred: Religion, Narrative, and Imagination*, M. I. Wallace, ed., Minneapolis: Fortress, 1995.

———. *The Philosophy of Paul Ricoeur*, L. E. Hahn, ed., Chicago: Open Court, 1995.

———.
Penser la Bible, en collaboration avec A. LaCocque, Paris: Seuil, 1998, (*Thinking Biblically: Exegetical and Hermeneutical Studies*, Chicago: University of Chicago Press, 1998, ET, trans., D. Pellauer).

Articles

———.
"Le christianisme et le sens de l'histoire. Progrès, ambiguité espérance," *Christianisme social* 59 (1951), 261-274, reprinted in: *Histoire et vérité*, 81-98, ("Christianity and the Meaning of History: Progress, Ambiguity, Hope," reprinted in: *Journal of Religion* 21 (1952), 242-253, reprinted in: *History and Truth*, 81-97, ET).

———.
"Herméneutique des symboles et réflexion philosophique I," *Archivio di Filosofia* 31 (1961), 51-73, reprinted in: *Le conflit des interprétations: Essais d'herméneutique*, Paris: Seuil, 1969, 283-310, ("The Hermeneutics of Symbols and Philosophical Reflection I," reprinted in: D. Ihde, ed., *The Conflict of Interpretations*, Evanston: Northwestern University Press, 1974, 287-314, ET).

———.
"Structure et herméneutique," *Esprit*, novembre 1963, 596-627, reprinted in: *Le conflit*, 31-63, ("Structure and Hermeneutics," reprinted in: *The Conflict*, 27-61).

———.
"Le langage de la foi," *Bulletin du Centre Protestant d'Etudes* 16 (1964), 17-31, ("The Language of Faith," reprinted in: *Union Seminary Quarterly Review* 28 (1973), 203-212, reprinted in: C. E. Reagan and D. Stewart, eds., *The Philosophy of Paul Ricoeur: An Anthology of his Work*, Boston: Beacon, 1978, 223-238, ET).

———.
"Existence et herméneutique," in: H. Kuhn, H. Kahlefeld, K. Forster, eds., *Interpretation der Welt, Festschrift für R. Guardini zum achtzigsten Geburtstag*, Würzburg: Echter-Verlag, 1965, 32-51, reprinted in: *Le conflit*, 7-28, ("Existence and Hermeneutics," reprinted in: *The Conflict*, 3-26).

———.
"La structure, le mot, l'événement," ("Structuralisme. Idéologie et méthode"), *Esprit*, mai 1967, 801-821, reprinted in: *Le conflit*, 80-97, ("Structure, Word, Event," reprinted

in: *Philosophy Today* 12 (1968), Summer, 114-129, reprinted in: *The Conflict*, 79-96).

———.
"Préface à Rudolf Bultmann," in: *Jésus. Mythologie et démythologisation*, Paris: Seuil, 1968, 9-28, reprinted in: *Le conflit*, 373-392 ("Preface to Bultmann," reprinted in: *The Conflict*, 381-400, reprinted in: L. Mudge, ed., *Essays on Biblical Interpretation*, Philadelphia: Fortress, 1980, 49-72, ET).

———.
"Qu'est-ce qu'un texte? Expliquer et comprendre," in: R. Bubner, ed., *Hermeneutik und Dialektik*, Tübingen: Mohr, 1970, 181-200, reprinted in: *Du texte à l'action*, Paris: Seuil, 1986, 137-159. ("What is a Text?" Explanation and Understanding," reprinted in: *From Text to Action*, Evanston: Northwestern University Press, 1991, 105-125, ET).

———.
"Événement et sens," in: E. Castelli, éd., *Révélation et histoire. La théologie de l'histoire*, Paris: Aubier, 1971.

———.
"Du conflit à la convergence des méthodes en exégèse biblique," in: X. Léon-Dufour, éd., *Exégèse et herméneutique*, Paris: Seuil, 1971, 35-53.

———.
"Sur l'exégèse, de Genèse 1,1 - 2,4a," in: *Exégèse et herméneutique*, 67-84.

———.
"Esquisse de conclusion," in: *Exégèse et herméneutique*, 285-295.

———.
"Contribution d'une réflexion sur le langage à une théologie de la parole," in: *Exégèse et herméneutique*, 301-319.

———.
"Preface," in: D. Ihde, *Hermeneutic Phenomenology: The Philosophy of Paul Ricoeur*, Evanston: Northwestern University Press, 1971, xiii-xvii.

———.
"The Model of the Text: Meaningful Action Considered as a Text," *Social Research* 38/3 (1971), 529-562, reprinted in: *From Text to Action*, 144-167, ("Le modèle du texte: l'action sensée considérée comme un texte," reprinted in: *Du texte à l'action*, 183-211, French Translation).

———.
"From Existentialism to the Philosophy of Language," *Criterion* 10 (1971), 14-18,

reprinted in: *The Rule of Metaphor*, 315-322.

———. "La métaphore et le problème central de l'herméneutique," *Revue philosophique de Louvain* 70 (1972), 93-112.

———. "L'herméneutique de témoignage," *Archivio di Filosofia* 42, (1972) 35-61, reprinted in *Lectures III*, 107-139. ("The Hermeneutics of Testimony," reprinted in: *Anglican Theological Review* 61 (1979), 435-461, and *Essays on Biblical Interpretation*, 119-154).

———. "Herméneutique et critique des idéologies," in: *Démythisation et Idéologie*, éd., E. Castelli, Paris: Aubier, 1973, 25-61. ("Hermeneutics and the Critique of Ideology") reprinted in: J. B. Thompson, ed., *Hermeneutics and the Human Sciences*, Cambridge: Cambridge University Press, 1981, 63-100, ET).

———. "The Task of Hermeneutics," *Philosophy Today* 17 (1973), Summer, 112-128, reprinted in: *From Text to Action*, 53-74, ("La tâche de l'herméneutique," reprinted in: F. Bovon et G. Rouiller, éds., *Exegesis. Problèmes de méthode et exercices de lecture*, Neuchâtel: Delachaux, 1975, 179-200, reprinted in: *Du texte à l'action*, 75-100, FT).

———. "The Hermeneutical Function of Distanciation," *Philosophy Today* 17 (1973), Summer, 129-141, reprinted in: *From Text to Action*, 75-88, ("La fonction herméneutique de la distanciation," reprinted in: F. Bovon et G. Rouiller, éds., *Exegesis. Problèmes de méthode et exercices de lecture*, 201-215, reprinted in: *Du texte à l'action*, 101-115, FT).

———. "Philosophy and Religious Language," *Journal of Religion* 54 (1974), 71-85, ("La philosophie et la spécificité du langage religieux," reprinted in: *Revue d'histoire et de philosophie religieuses* 55 (1975), 13-26, FT).

———. "Biblical Hermeneutics," *Semeia* 4 (1975), 29-148.

———. "Herméneutique philosophique et herméneutique biblique," in: *Exegesis. Problèmes de méthode*, 216-228, reprinted in: *Du texte à l'action*, 119-133, ("Philosophical Hermeneutics and Biblical Hermeneutics," reprinted in: *Exegesis. Problems of Method*, Pittsburgh: Pickwick Press, 1978, 321-339, reprinted in: *From Text to Action*, 89-101, ET).

———. "Objectivation et aliénation dans l'expérience historique," *Archivio di Filosofia*, 45 (1975), 27-38, reprinted in: E. Castelli, éd., *Temporalité et aliénation*, Paris: Aubier, 1975, 27-38.

———. "Préface," in: A. LaCocque, *Le livre de Daniel, Commentaire de l'Ancien Testament*, Xb, Neuchâtel: Delachaux, 1976, 5-11.

———. "Le 'Royaume' dans les paraboles de Jésus," *Etudes théologiques et religieuses* 51 (1976), 15-20.

———. "Expliquer et comprendre," *Revue philosophique de Louvain*, 75 (1977), 126-147, reprinted in: *Du texte à l'action*, 161-182, ("Explanation and Understanding," reprinted in: *From Text to Action*, 125-143).

———. "Nommer Dieu," *Etudes théologiques et religieuses* 52 (1977), 489-508, reprinted in: *Lectures III*, Paris: Seuil, 1994, 281-305 ("Naming God," reprinted in: *Union Seminary Quarterly* 34 (1979), 215-227, reprinted in: M. I. Wallace, ed., *Figuring the Sacred: Religion, Narrative, and Imagination*, Minneapolis: Fortress, 1995, 217-235, ET).

———. "Herméneutique de l'idée de révélation," in: *La révélation*, Bruxelles, Facultés universitaires Saint-Louis, 1977, 15-54, ("Towards a Hermeneutic of the Idea of Revelation," reprinted in: *Harvard Theological Review* 70 (1977), 1-38, reprinted in: *Essays in Biblical Interpretation*, 73-118).

———. "Philosophie et langage," *Revue philosophique de la France et de l'Etranger* 103 (1978), 449-463.

———. "Listening to the Parables," *Criterion* 13 (1974), 18-22, reprinted in: C. E. Reagan and D. Stewart, eds., *The Philosophy of Paul Ricoeur: An Anthology of His Work*, 1978, 239-245.

———. "The Narrative Function," *Semeia* 13 (1978), 177-202, reprinted in: *Hermeneutics and the Human Sciences*, 274-296, ("La fonction narrative," reprinted in: *Etudes théologiques et religieuses* 54 (1979), 209-230, FT).

———. "Time and Narrative in the Bible:

Toward a Narrative Theology," Unpublished manuscript, Sarum Lectures, Oxford University, 1980.

———.
"La logique de Jésus," *Études théologiques et religieuses* 55 (1980), 420-425.

———.
"A Response by Paul Ricoeur," in: *Hermeneutics and the Human Sciences*, 1981, 32-40.

———.
"The Conflict of Interpretations: Debate with H. G. Gadamer," in: *Phenomenology: Dialogues and Bridges*, R. Bruzina and B. Wilshire, eds., Albany: State University of New York Press, 1982, 299-320, reprinted in: M. J. Valdés, ed., *A Ricoeur Reader, Reflection and Imagination*, 216-241.

———.
"The Bible and the Imagination," in: H. D. Betz, ed., *The Bible as a Document of the University*, Chico: Scholars, 1981, 49-75, reprinted in: *Figuring the Sacred*, 144-166 ("La Bible et l'imagination," reprinted in: *Revue d'histoire et de philosophie religieuses* 62 (1982), 339-360, FT).

———.
"Poetry and Possibility: An Interview with Paul Ricoeur," in: *The Manhattan Review*, 2 (1982), 6-21, reprinted in: A Ricoeur Reader, 448-462.

———.
"On Interpretation," in: Alan Montefiore, ed., *Philosophy in France Today*, Cambridge: Cambridge University Press, 1983, 175-197, reprinted in: *From Text to Action*, 1-20 ("De l'interprétation," reprinted in: *Du texte à l'action*, 11-35, FT).

———.
"Can Fictional Narratives be True?" *Analecta Husserliana* 14 (1983), 3-19.

———.
"Narrative and Hermeneutics," in: J. Fisher, ed., *Essays in Aesthetics: Perspectives on the Work of Monroe C. Beardsley*, Philadelphia: Temple University Press, 1983, 149-160.

———.
"From Proclamation to Narrative," *Journal of Religion* 64 (1984), 501-512.

———.
"The Creativity of Language," in: R. Kearney, ed., *Dialogues with Contemporary Continental Thinkers*, Manchester: Manchester University Press, 1984, 17-36, reprinted in: *A Ricoeur Reader*, 463-481.

———.
"Temps biblique," *Archivio di filosofia* 53 (1985), 23-35, reprinted in: M. I. Wallace, ed., *Figuring the Sacred*, 167-180.

———.
"Le récit interprétatif: Exégèse et Théologie dans les récits de la Passion," *Recherches de science religieuse* 73 (1985), 17-38.

———.
"Life: A Story in Search of a Narrator," in: M. C. Doeser and J. N. Kraaj, eds., *Facts and Values: Philosophical Reflections from Western and Non-Western Perspectives*, Dordrecht: Nijhoff, 1985, 121-132, reprinted in: *A Ricoeur Reader*, 423-437.

———.
"Eloge de la lecture et de l'écriture," *Etudes théologiques et religieuses* 64 (1989), 395-405.

———.
"Life in Quest of Narrative," in: D. Wood, ed., *On Paul Ricoeur: Narrative and Interpretation*, London: Routledge, 1991, 20-33.

———.
"D'un Testament à l'autre: essai d'herméneutique biblique," in: D. Marguerat et J. Zumstein, éds., *La mémoire et le temps, Mélanges offerts à Pierre Bonnard*, Genève: Labor et Fides, 1991, 299-309; also, *Collana Dialogo di Filosofia* 9, Rome: Herder, 1991, reprinted in: *Lectures III*, 355-366.

———.
"L'enchevêtrement de la voix et de l'écrit dans le discours biblique," in: *Religion, Parole, Ecriture*, Milan: Biblioteca dell'Archivio di Filosofia, 1992, 233-247, reprinted in: *Lectures III*, 307-326.

———.
"Talking Liberties," London: *Channel 4 Television*, 1992, 36-40.

———.
"Herméneutique. Les finalités de l'exégèse biblique," in: *La Bible en philosophie. Approaches contemporaines*, Paris: Cerf, 1993, 27-51.

———.
"Phénoménologie de la Religion," *Revue l'Institut Catholique de Paris* 45 (1993), 59-75.

———.
"Philosophie critiques de l'histoire: Recherche, explication, écriture," in: G. Fløistad, ed., *Philosophical Problems Today*, 1, Dordrecht: Kluwer Academic Publishers, 1994, 139-201.

2) Selected list of Secondary Works on Paul Ricoeur's Thought

Abel, O. *La promesse et la règle*, Paris: Michalon, 1996. Alexandre, J. "Notes sur l'esprit des paraboles. Une réponse à Paul Ricoeur," *Etudes théologiques et religieuses* 51 (1976), 367-372.
Azouvi, F. et de Launay, M. *Entretien avec Paul Ricoeur, La critique et la conviction*, Paris: Calmann-Lévy, 1995. Blocher, H. "Paul Ricoeur dans le conflits des interprétations," *Ichthus* 10 (1971), 24-27.

____.
"L'herméneutique selon Paul Ricoeur," *Hokma* 3 (1976), 11-57. Bouchard, G. "Sémiologie, sémantique, et herméneutique selon Paul Ricoeur," *Laval théologique et philosophique* 36 (1980), 255-288.
Bouchindhomme, C. et Rochlitz, R. << *Temps et récit* >> *de Paul Ricoeur en débat*, Paris: Cerf, 1990.
Bourg, D. "Pour une grammaire chrétienne," *Esprit* 140-141 (1988), 238-246.
Bourgeois, P. L. *Extension of Ricoeur's Hermeneutic*, The Hague: Nijhoff, 1973.

____.
"From Hermeneutics of Symbols to the Interpretation of Texts," in: C. E. Reagan, ed., *Studies in the Philosophy of Paul Ricoeur*, Athens (Ohio): Ohio University Press, 1979, 84-95.

____.
"Semiotics and the Deconstruction of Presence: A Ricoeurian Alternative," *The American Catholic Philosophical Quarterly* 66 (1992), 361-406.
Bourgeois, P. L. and Schalow, F. *Traces of Understanding: A Profile of Heidegger's and Ricoeur's Hermeneutics*, Amsterdam: Rodopi, 1990.
Bovon, F. et Rouiller, G. éds., *Exegesis. Problèmes de méthode et exercices de lecture*, Neuchâtel: Delachaux, 1975.
Brès, Y. "Le règne des herméneutique ou 'Un long détour' ," *Revue philosophique de la France et de l'Etranger* 94 (1969), 425-429.
Bruns, G. "Against Poetry: Heidegger, Ricoeur, and the Originary Scene of Hermeneutics," in: *Meanings in Texts and Actions: Questioning Paul Ricoeur*, D. E. Klemm

and W. Schweiker, eds., Charlottesville: University of Virginia Press, 1993, 26-46.
Carr, D. "Ricoeur on Narrative," in: D. Wood, ed., *On Paul Ricoeur: Narrative and Interpretation*, London: Routledge, 1991, 160-173.
Ciamarelli, F. "Herméneutique et créativité. A propos de Paul Ricoeur," *Revue philosophique de Louvain* 83 (1985), 410-412.
Clark, S. H. *Paul Ricoeur*, London: Routledge, 1990.
Comstock, G. "Truth or Meaning: Ricoeur versus Frei on Biblical Narrative," *Journal of Religion* 66 (1986), 117-140.

____.
"Two Types of Narrative Theology," *Journal of the American Academy of Religion* 55/4 (1986), 687-717.
Czarneck, J. "L'Histoire et la vérité selon Paul Ricoeur," *Foi et vie* liii (1955), 548-555.
DiCenso, J. *Hermeneutics and the Disclosure of Truth: A Study of the Work of Heidegger, Gadamer, and Ricoeur*, Charlottesville: University Press of Virginia, 1990.
Dornisch, L. A. *Theological Interpretation of the Meaning of Symbol in the Theory of Paul Ricoeur*, Milwaukee: Microfilms, 1973.

____.
"Symbolic Systems and the Interpretation of Scripture: An Introduction to the Work of Paul Ricoeur," *Semeia* 4 (1975), 1-21.

____.
"The Book of Job and Ricoeur's Hermeneutics," *Semeia* 19 (1981), 3-21.
Dumouchel, P. "Paul Ricoeur. tension de la vérité," *Esprit* 51 (1983), 46-55.
Fialkowski, A. "Paul Ricoeur et l'herméneutique des mythes," *Esprit* 35 (1967), 73-89.
Fisher, L. "Mediation, Muthos, and the Hermeneutical Circle in Ricoeur's Narrative Theory," in: M. Joy, ed., *Paul Ricoeur and Narrative: Context and Contestation*, Calgary: University of Calgary Press, 1997, 207-219.
Fodor, J. *Christian Hermeneutics: Paul Ricoeur and the Refiguring of Theology*, Oxford: Clarendon Press, 1995.

____.
"The Tragic Face of Narrative Judgement: Christian Reflections on Paul Ricoeur's Theory of Narrative," in: *Paul Ricoeur and Narrative: Context and Contestation*, Calgary: University of Calgary Press, 1997, 153-173.

Gisel, P. "Le conflit des interprétations (étude de l'herméneutique dans la pensée de P. Ricoeur)," *Esprit* 38 (1970), 776-784.

____. "Paul Ricoeur," *Etudes théologiques et religieuses* 49 (1974), 31-50.

Gerhart, M. "Paul Ricoeur's Notion of 'Diagnostics': Its Function in Literary Interpretation," *Journal of Religion* 56 (1976), 137-156.

____. *The Question of Belief in Literary Criticism: An Introduction to the Hermeneutical Theory of Paul Ricoeur*, Stuttgart: Verlag, 1979.

____. "Paul Ricoeur," in: M. Marty and D. Peerman, eds., *A Handbook of Christian Theologians*, Cambridge: Lutterworth, 1984, 608-624.

Greisch, J. "Bulletin de philosophie: La tradition herméneutique aujourd'hui (H.-G. Gadamer, P. Ricoeur, G. Steiner)," *Revue des sciences philosophiques et théologiques* 61 (1977), 289-300.

____. "Bulletin de philospfhie herméneutique: Les limites de l'interprétation," *Revue des sciences philosophiques et théologiques* 77 (1993), 255-288.

Greisch, J. and Kearney, R. *Paul Ricoeur, Les métamorphoses de la raison herméneutique*, Paris: Cerf, 1991.

Ihde, D. *Hermeneutic Phenomenology: The Philosophy of Paul Ricoeur*, Evanston: Northwestern University Press, 1971.

Javet, P. "Imagination et réalité dans la philosophie de Paul Ricoeur," *Revue de théologie et de philosophie* 16 (1967), 145-165.

Jervolino, D. *The Cogito and Hermeneutics*, Dordrecht: Kluwer, 1990.

Joy, M. ed., *Paul Ricoeur and Narrative: Context and Contestation*, Calgary: University of Calgary Press, 1997.

Kearney, R. ed., *Paul Ricoeur: The Hermeneutics of Action*, London: Sage Publications, 1996.

Kemp, T. P. and Rasmussen, D. M. eds., "The Narrative Path: The Later Works of Paul Ricoeur," *Philosophy and Social Criticism* 14 (1988), 1-120, reprinted in: *The Narrative Path: The Later Works of Paul Ricoeur*, Cambridge, Mass. MIT Press, 1989.

Klemm, D. E. *The Hermeneutical Theory of Paul Ricoeur. A Constructive Analysis*, Toronto: Associated University Presses, 1983.

Klemm, D. E. and Schweiker, W. eds., *Meanings in Texts and Action: Questioning Paul Ricoeur*, Charlottesville: University of Virginia Press, 1993.

Laughery, G. J. *Living Hermeneutics in Motion: An Analysis and Evaluation of Paul Ricoeur's Contribution to Biblical Hermeneutics*, New York/Lanham: University Press of America, 2002.

____. "Language at the Frontiers of Language," in: *After Pentecost: Language and Biblical Interpretation*: Scripture and Hermeneutics Series, C. Bartholomew, ed., Grand Rapids/Carlisle: Zondervan/Paternoster, 2001, 171-194.

____. "Ricoeur on History, Fiction, and Biblical Hermeneutics," in: *'Behind' the Text: History and Biblical Interpretation*, Scripture and Hermeneutics Series, C. Bartholomew, ed., Grand Rapids/Carlisle: Zondervan/Paternoster, 2003, 339-362.

____. "Evangelicalism and Philosophy," in: *The Futures of Evangelicalism*, C. Bartholomew, ed., Leicester: IVP, 2003; Grand Rapids: Kregel, 2005, 246-270.

____. "Scripture, Science, and Hermeneutics," *European Journal of Theology*, M. Elliott, ed., 15.1 (2006), 35-49, co-writer G. Diepstra.

____. "Interpreting Science and Scripture: Genesis 1-3," *European Journal of Theology*, J. Grant, ed., 18.1 (2009), 5-16, co-writer G. Diepstra.

____. *Living Reflections: Theology, Philosophy, and Hermeneutics*, Huémoz, Destinée, 2010.

____. "Sculpting in Time: The Drama of A Narrative-based Hermeneutical Approach to the Early Chapters of Genesis," *The Evangelical Quarterly: An International Journal of Theology*, I. H. Marshall, ed., October (2011), 291-307 co-writer, G. Diepstra.

____. "Postmodernism, History, and Biblical Hermeneutics: Interacting with the Thought of Paul Ricoeur," *Theofilos*, S. Lindholm, ed., December (2012), 2-25.

____. "Exploring the Possible World of Genesis 2-3 with Paul Ricoeur," *The Evangelical Quarterly: An International Journal of*

Theology, J. Wilks, ed., October (2013), 309-327, co-writer G. Diepstra.
Lawlor, L. *Imagination and Chance: The Difference between the Thought of Ricoeur and Derrida*, Albany: State University of New York Press, 1992.
Lowe, W. J. "The Coherence of Paul Ricoeur," *Journal of Religion* 61 (1981), 384-402.

———. *Introduction to Fallible Man*, New York: Fordham University Press, 1986, rev. edition.
Madison, G. B. *Sens et Existence. En hommage à Paul Ricoeur*, Paris: Seuil, 1975.

———. "Ricoeur's Philosophy of Metaphor," and " Ricoeur and the Hermeneutics of the Subject," in: *The Hermeneutics of Postmodernity*, Bloomington: Indiana University Press, 1988.
Michaël, P. "Entretien avec Paul Ricoeur," *Bulletin du Centre Protestant d'Etudes* 43, 1991.
Moore, H., "Paul Ricoeur: Action, Meaning and Text," in: C. Tilley, ed., *Reading Modern Culture*, Oxford: Blackwell, 1990, 85-120.
Mongin, O. *Paul Ricoeur*, Paris: Seuil, 1994.
Okonda, O. "L'herméneutique chez Paul Ricoeur. Instances et méthode sur les trois moments de l'herméneutique ricoeurienne," *Cahiers philosophiques africains*, (1974), 33-61.
Pellauer, D. "The Significance of the Text in Paul Ricoeur's Hermeneutical Theory," in: C. E. Reagan, ed., *Studies in the Philosophy of Paul Ricoeur*, Athens (Ohio): Ohio University Press, 1979, 97-114.

———. "Paul Ricoeur on the Specificity of Religious Language," *Journal of Religion* 61 (1981), 264-284.
Petit, J. L. "Herméneutique et sémantique chez Paul Ricoeur," *Archives de philosophie* 48 (1985), 575-589.
Philibert, M. *Paul Ricoeur ou la liberté selon l'espérance*, Paris: Seghers, 1971.
Placher, W. C. "Paul Ricoeur and Postliberal Theology: A Conflict of Interpretations?" *Modern Theology* 4 (1983), 35-52.
Reagan, C. E. and Stewart, D. eds., *The Philosophy of Paul Ricoeur: An Anthology of his Work*, Boston: Beacon, 1978.
Reagan, C. E. ed., *Studies in the Philosophy of Paul Ricoeur*, Athens: Ohio University Press, 1979.
Riggio, P. "Paul Ricoeur et l'herméneutique des mythes," *Dialogue* 35 (1967), 73-89.
Robert, J. D. "La coupure épistémologique entre sciences de la nature et sciences de l'homme d'après Paul Ricoeur," *Revue des questions scientifiques* 152 (1981), 111-113.
Sales, M. "Recension de la Préface de P. Ricoeur au 'Jésus' de Bultmann," *Archives de philosophie* 32 (1969), 156-160.
Schaldenbrand, M. "Metaphoric Imagination: Kinship Through Conflict," in: C. E. Reagan, ed., *Studies in the Philosophy of Paul Ricoeur*, Athens (Ohio): Ohio University Press, 1979, 57-81.
Schillebeeckx, E. "Le philosophe Paul Ricoeur, docteur en théologie," *Christianisme social* 75 (1968), 639-645.
Secretan, P. "Paradoxe et conciliation dans la philosophie de Paul Ricoeur," *Studia Philosophica* 21 (1961), 187-198.

———. "L'interprétation selon Paul Ricoeur," *Studia Philosophica* 25 (1965), 182-198.

———. "Herméneutique et verité. Hommage à Paul Ricoeur à l'occasion de son 60ᵉ anniversaire," in: F. Bovon et G. Rouiller, éds., *Exegesis. Problèmes de méthode et exercices de lecture*, Neuchâtel: Delachaux, 1975.
Spiegleberg, H. *The Phenomenological Movement*, The Hague: Nijhoff, 1982.
Stevens, B. "Herméneutique philosophique et herméneutique biblique dans l'oeuvre de Paul Ricoeur," *Revue théologique de Louvain* 20 (1989), 178-193.

———. *L'apprentissage des signes: Lecture de Paul Ricoeur*, Dordrecht: Kluwer, 1991.
Stewart, D. "Ricoeur on Religious Language," in: L. E. Hahn, ed., *The Philosophy of Paul Ricoeur*, 423-442, 1995.
Thomasset, A. *Paul Ricoeur: Une poétique de la morale*, Bibliotheca Ephemeridum Theologicarum Lovaniensium CXXIV, Leuven: Leuven University Press, 1996.
Thompson, J. B. *Critical Hermeneutics: A Study in the Thought of Paul Ricoeur and Jürgen Habermas*, Cambridge: Cambridge University Press, 1981.
Van Den Hengel, J. *The Home of Meaning: The Hermeneutics of the Subject of Paul Ricoeur*, Washington, D. C.: University Press of America, 1982.
Vanhoozer, K. J. *Biblical Narrative in the Philosophy of Paul Ricoeur*, Cambridge: Cambridge University Press, 1990.

———. "Philosophical Antecedents to Ricoeur's Time and Narrative," in: D. Wood, ed., *On Paul Ricoeur: Narrative and Interpretation*, London: Routledge, 1991, 34-54.
Van Leeuwen, T. M. *The Surplus of Meaning, Ontology and Eschatology in the Philosopy of Paul Ricoeur*, Amsterdam: Rodopi, 1981.
Vansina, F. D. *Paul Ricoeur: Bibliographie systématique de ses écrits et des publications consacrées à sa pensée (1935-1984)*, Leuven - Louvain-la-Neuve: Peeters - Editions de l'Institut Supérieur de Philosophie, 1985.

———.
Bibliography of Paul Ricoeur: A Primary and Secondary Systematic Bibliography compiled by Frans D. Vansina and Paul Ricoeur, in: L. E. Hahn, ed., *The Philosophy of Paul Ricoeur*, Chicago: Open Court, 1995.
Van Riet, G. "Paul Ricoeur." *Philosophie et religion*, Louvain-Paris: Publications universitaire de Louvain, 1970, 57-61.
Wallace, M. I. *The Second Naiveté: Barth, Ricoeur, and the New Yale Theology*, Macon: Mercer University Press, 1990.

———.
"Can God Be Named Without Being Known? The Problem of Revelation in Thiemann, Ogden and Ricoeur," *Journal of the American Academy of Religion* 59/2 (1991), 281-308.
Wood, D. ed., *On Paul Ricoeur: Narrative and Interpretation*, London: Routledge, 1991.

3) Other Works

Adam, J. M. *La description, Que sais-je* 1783, Paris: Presses Univérsitaires de France, 1993 and *Le récit, Que sais-je* 2149, Paris: Presses Univérsitaire, 1984.
Aletti, J.-N. *L'Art de raconter Jésus Christ: l'écriture narrative de l'évangile de Luc, Parole de Dieu*, Paris: Seuil, 1989.
Quand Luc raconte. Le récit comme théologie, Lire la Bible 115, Paris: Cerf, 1998.
Alter, R. *The Art of Biblical Narrative*, New York: Basic Books, 1981.

———.
The Art of Biblical Poetry, New York: Basic Books, 1985.
Altizer, T. ed., *Deconstruction and Theology*, New York: Crossroad, 1982.
Amerding, C. "Structural Analysis," *Themelios* 4 (1979), 96-104.

Aron, R. *Introduction à la philosophie de l'histoire: essai sur les limites de l'objectivitié historique*, Paris: Gallimard, 1938, (1957).
Austin, J. L. eds., J. O. Urmson and M. Sbisa, *How to do Things with Words*, Oxford: Clarendon Press, 1962.
Bailey, K. E., Grand Rapids: *Poet and Peasant and Through Peasant's Eyes: A Literary Cultural Approach to the Parables in Luke*, Eerdmans, 1983.
Barr, J. *The Semantics of Biblical Language*, London: SCM, 1961.

———.
Holy Scripture, Philadelphia: Westminster, 1983.
Barratt, D. Pooley, R. Ryken, L. eds., *The Discerning Reader: Christian Perspectives on Literature and Theory*, Leicester: InterVarsity Press, 1995.
Barthes, R. "Introduction à l'analyse structurale des récits," *Communications* 8 (1966), 1-27.

———.
"L'Effet de Réel," *Communications* 11 (1968), 84-89.

———.
"The Death of the Author," in: *Image-Music-Text*, London: Fontana, 1984.
Barton, S. C. "New Testament Interpretation as Performance," *Scottish Journal of Theology* 52/ 2 (1999), 179-208.
Barton, J. and Morgan, R. *Biblical Interpretation*, Oxford: Oxford University Press, 1988.
Beardslee, W. A. *Literary Criticism of the New Testament*, Philadelphia: Fortress, 1970.
Benjamin, A. ed., *The Lyotard Reader*, Oxford: Blackwell, 1989.
Bentley, M. *Modern Historiography*, London: Routledge, 1999.
Black, M. and Geach, P. eds., *Translations from the Philosophical Writings of Gottlob Frege*, Oxford: Blackwell, 1970.
Blocher, H. "Biblical Narrative and Historical Reference," *Scottish Bulletin of Evangelical Theology* 3 (1989), 102-122.
Blomberg, C. L. *The Historical Reliability of the Gospels*, Leicester: InterVarsity Press, 1987.

———.
Interpreting the Parables, Leicester, InterVarsity Press, 1990.
Booth, W. C. *The Rhetoric of Fiction*, Chicago: University of Chicago Press, 1961.
The Company We Keep: An Ethics of Fiction, Berkeley: University of California Press, 1988.

Bourgeois, P. L. and Rosenthal, S. B. *Thematic Studies in Phenomenology and Pragmatism*, Amsterdam: Grüner, 1983.
Bozeman, T. D. *Protestants in an Age of Science*, Chapel Hill: University of North Carolina Press, 1977.
Breech, J. *Jesus and Postmodernism*, Minneapolis: Fortress, 1989.
Bres, J. *La narrativité, Champs linguistique*, Louvain-la-Neuve: Duculot, 1994.
Brossier, E. Dire *la Bible. Récit bibliques et communication de la foi*, Paris: Centurion, 1986.
Brown, F. B. and Malbon, E. S. "Parabling as Via Negativa: A Critical Review of the Work of John Dominic Crossan," *Journal of Religion* 64 (1984), 530-538.
Bühler, P. and Habermacher, J.- F. éds., *La narration. Quand le récit devient communication*, Lieux théologiques 12, Genève: Labor et Fides, 1988.
Bultmann, R. *Kerygma and Myth*, H. W. Bartsch, ed., New York: Harper, 1961.
Burke, S. ed., *Authorship: From Plato to the Postmodern*, Edinburgh: Edinburgh University Press, 1995.
Burnett, F. W. "Postmodern Biblical Exegesis: The Eve of Historical Criticism," *Semeia* 51 (1990), 40-64.
Carr, D. "Life and the Narrator's Art," in: H. J. Silverman and D. Ihde, eds., *Hermeneutics and Deconstruction*, New York: State University Press of New York, 1985, 108-121.

———. *Time, Narrative, and History*, Bloomington: Indiana University Press, 1986.

———. "Narrative as a Form of Life," in: B. Dauenhauer, ed., *Textual Fidelity and Textual Disregard*, New York: Peter Lang, 1990, 3-15.

———. "Narrative and the Real World: An Argument for Continuity," in: B. Fay, P. Pomper, R. T. Vann, eds., *History and Theory: Contemporary Readings*, Oxford: Blackwell, 1998, 137-152.

Carson, D. A. and Woodbridge, J. D. eds., *Scripture and Truth*, Leicester: InterVarsity Press, 1983.
Carson, D. A. *The Gagging of God*, Leicester: InterVarsity Press, 1996.
Carson, D. A. ed., *Biblical Interpretation and the Church: The Problem of Contextualization*, Nashville: Nelson, 1984.

Cascardi, A. J. ed., *Literature and the Question of Philosophy*, London: Johns Hopkins University Press, 1987.
Castelli, E. *Débat sur le Langage théologique*, Paris: Aubier, 1969.
Chatman, S. *Story and Discourse: Narrative Structure in Fiction and Film*, Ithaca: Cornell University Press, 1978.
Clines, D. J. A. Fowl, S. E. and Porter, S. E. eds., *The Bible in Three Dimensions*, Sheffield: Sheffield Academic Press, 1990.
Cooper, J. W. "Reformed Apologetics and the Challenge of Post-Modern Relativism," *Calvin Theological Journal* 28 (1993), 108-120.
Crossan, J. D. "The Good Samaritan: Towards a Generic Definition of Parables," *Semeia* 2 (1974), 82-107.

———. *The Dark Interval. Towards a Theology of Story*, Niles: Argus, 1975.

———. *Raid on the Articulate*, New York: Harper & Row, 1976.

———. "A Metamodel for Polyvalent Narration," *Semeia* 9 (1977), 105-147.

———. *Finding the First Act: Trouve Folktales and Jesus' Treasure Parables*, Philadelphia: Fortress, 1979.

———. *Cliffs of Fall: Paradox and Polyvalence in the Parables*, New York: Seabury, 1980.

———. "Stages in Imagination," in: *The Archaeology of the Imagination*, ed., C. E. Winquist, JAAR Thematic Studies 48/2, Chico: AAR, 1981, 56.
Dauenhauer, B. ed., *Textual Fidelity and Textual Disregard*, New York: Peter Lang, 1990.
Delorme, J. *Au risque de la parole: lire les évangiles*, Parole de Dieu 31, Paris: Seuil, 1991.
Derrida, J. *La voix et le phénomène*, Paris: Presses Universitaires de France, 1967.

———. *L'écriture et la différence*, Paris: Seuil, 1967.

———. *De la grammatologie*, Paris: Editions de Minuit, 1967.

Detweiler, R. ed., *Reader Response Approaches to Biblical and Secular Texts*, Semeia 31, Decatur: Scholars Press, 1985.
Docherty, T. ed., *Postmodernism: A Reader*,

New York: Columbia University Press, 1993.
Dodd, C. H. *The Parables of the Kingdom*, London: Nisbet, 1935.
Donahue, J. R. The Gospel in Parable, Philadelphia: Fortress, 1988.
Dutton, D. "Why Intentionalism Won't Go Away," in: A. J. Cascardi, ed., *Literature and the Question of Philosophy*, London: Johns Hopkins University Press, 1987, 192-209.
Eagleton, T. "Capitalism, Modernism, and Postmodernism," *New Left Review* 152 (1985), 70-71.
Echeverria, E. J. *Criticism and Commitment*, Amsterdam: Rodopi, 1981.
Eco, U. *The Role of the Reader*, Bloomington: Indiana University Press, 1979.

____. *The Limits of Interpretation*, Bloomington: Indiana University Press, 1994.

Ellingsen, M. *The Integrity of Biblical Narrative: Story in Theology and Proclamation*, Minneapolis: Fortress, 1990.
Evans, Stephen, C. "Critical Historical Judgement and Biblical Faith," in: R. A. Wells, ed., *History and the Christian Historian*, Cambridge: Eerdmans, 1998.
Fay, B. Pomper, P. Vann, R. T. eds., *History and Theory: Contemporary Readings*, Oxford: Blackwell, 1998.
Fish, S. *Is There a Text in This Class? The Authority of Interpretative Communities*, Cambridge, Mass. Harvard University Press, 1980.

____. *Doing What Comes Naturally: Change, Rhetoric, and the Practice of Theory in Literary and Legal Studies*, Oxford: Clarendon Press, 1987.

____. "Why No One's Afraid of Wolfgang Iser?" in: *Doing What Comes Naturally*, 68-86.

Fowl, S. E. "The Ethics of Interpretation or What's Left Over After the Elimination of Meaning," 379-398, in: D. J. A. Clines, S. E. Fowl, and S. E. Porter, eds., *The Bible in Three Dimensions*, Sheffield: Sheffield Academic Press, 1990.
Fowler, R.M. *Let the Reader Understand. Reader Response Criticism and the Gospel of Mark*, Minneapolis: Fortress, 1991.
France, R. T. "The Church and the Kingdom of God: Some Hermeneutical Issues," in: D. A. Carson, ed., *Biblical Interpretation and the Church*, Nashville: Nelson, 1985, 30-44.

Frege, G. "On Sense and Reference," in: M. Black and P. Geach, eds., *Translations from the Philosophical Writings of Gottlob Frege*, Oxford: Blackwell, 1970.
Frei, H. *The Eclipse of Biblical Narrative*, New Haven: Yale University Press, 1974.

____. "The Literal Reading of Biblical Narrative in the Christian Tradition: Does It Stretch or Will It Break?" in: F. McConnell, ed., *The Bible and the Narrative Tradition*, Oxford: Oxford University Press, 1986, 36-77.

Freund, E. *The Return of the Reader: Reader-Response Criticism*, London: Metheun, 1987.
Friedrich, C. J. ed., *The Philosophy of Kant*, New York: Modern Library, 1949.
Furnish, V. P. "Historical Criticism and the New Testament: A Survey of Origins," *BJRL* 56 (1974), 368.
Gadamer, H. G. *Wahreit und Methode*, Tübingen: Mohr, 1960. (*Truth and Method*, London: Sheed and Ward, 1975, reprinted *Truth and Method*, 2nd ed., New York: Continuum, 1989, ET, trans., J. Weinsheimer and D. Marshall).
Gellner, E. *Legitimation of Belief*, Cambridge: Cambridge University Press, 1974.
Genette, G. *Figures III (Poétique)*, Paris: Seuil 1972 (partial English trans.: *Narrative Discourse*, Ithaca: Cornell University Press, 1980.
Gisel, P. and Evrard, P. éds., *La théologie en postmodernité*, Genève: Labor et Fides, 1996.
Green, J. ed., *Hearing the New Testament*, Carlisle: Paternoster, 1995.
Greenwood, D. C. *Structuralism and The Biblical Text*, Berlin: Mouton, 1985.
Grenz, S. J. *A Primer on Postmodernism*, Cambridge: Eerdmans, 1996.
Gruenler, R. G. *New Approaches to Jesus and the Gospels: A Phenomenological Study of Synoptic Christology*, Grand Rapids: Baker, 1982.
Gunton, C. *Enlightment and Alienation*, Basingstoke: Marshalls, 1985.
Halpern, B. *The First Historians*, San Francisco, Harper & Row, 1988.
Harris, W. V. *Interpretive Acts: In Search of Meaning*, Oxford: Clarendon Press, 1988.

____. *Literary Meaning: Reclaiming the Study of Literature*, London: Macmillan, 1996.

Heidegger, M. *Being and Time*, New York: Harper & Row, 1962.
Hemer, C. J. *The Book of Acts in the Setting*

*of Hellenistic His*tory, Wissenschaftliche Untersuchungen zum Neuen Testament 49, Tübingen: J. C. B. Mohr, 1989.

Himmelfarb, G. "Revolution in the Library," *The Key Reporter*, Spring (1997), 1-5.

———. "Telling it as you like it: postmodernist history and the flight from fact," in: K. Jenkins, ed., *The Postmodern History Reader*, London: Routledge, 1997, 158-174.

Hirsch, E. D. *Validity in Interpretation*, New Haven: Yale University Press, 1967.

Hodge, C. *Systematic Theology*, I, New York: Scribners, 1921.

Husserl, E. *Cartesian Meditations: An Introduction to Phenomenology*, The Hague: Nijhoff, 1960.

Huyssen, A. *After the Great Divide: Modernism, Mass Culture, Postmodernism*, Bloomington: Indiana University Press, 1986.

Ingarden, R. *Das literarische Kunstwerk*, Second Edition, Tubingen: M. Niemeyer, 1961, (*The Literary Work of Art*, Evanston: Northwestern University Press, 1974, ET).

Ingraffia, B. D. *Postmodern Theory and Biblical Theology*, Cambridge: Cambridge University Press, 1995.

Iser, W. The *Implied Reader: Patterns of Communication in Prose Fiction from Bunyan to Beckett*, Baltimore: Johns Hopkins University Press, 1974.

———. *The Act of Reading, A Theory of Aesthetic Respons*e, London: John Hopkins University Press, 1978.

Jabès, E. *The Book of Yukel, Return to the Book*, Middletown: Wesleyan University Press, 1977.

Jasper, D. ed., *Postmodernism, Literature and the Future of Theo*logy, Basingstoke/New York: Macmillan/St. Martin's Press, 1993.

Jauss, H. R. *Towards an Aesthetic of Reception*, Minneapolis: University of Minnesota Press, 1982.

———. *Aesthetic Experience and Literary Hermeneutics*, Minneapolis: University of Minnesota Press, 1982.

Jenkins, K. ed., *The Postmodern History Reader*, London: Routledge, 1997.

———. *On "What is History": From Carr and Elton to Rorty and White*, London: Routledge, 1995.

Jenkins, K. *Re-Thinking History*, London: Routledge, 1991

Jeremias, J. The Parables of Jesus, Revised Edition, London: SCM, 1963.

Jülicher, A. *Die Gleichnisreden Jesu*, 2 Vols., Tübingen: Mohr, 1910.

Kant, I. *Religion within the Limits of Reason Alone*, Greene and Hudson, New York: Harper, 1794/1960, ET.

———. "What is Enlightenment?" in: C. J. Friedrich, ed., *The Philosophy of Kant*, New York: Modern Library, 1949.

———. *What is Enlightenment?* New York: Liberal Arts Press, 1959.

Kearney, R. Dialogues with Contemporary Continental Thinkers, Manchester: Manchester University Press, 1984.

———. *The Wake of the Imagination*, London: Hutchinson, 1988.

Kellner, H. *Language and Historical Representation: Getting the Story Crooked*, Madison: University of Wisconsin Press, 1989.

Kerby, A. P. *Narrative and the Self*, Bloomington: Indiana University Press, 1991.

Kermode, F. *A Sense of Ending: Studies in the Theory of Fiction*: London: Oxford University Press, 1966.

Klemm, D. E. ed., *Hermeneutical Inquiry*, 2 Vols., Atlanta: Scholars, 1986.

LaCocque, A. *Le livre de Daniel*, Commentaire de l'Ancien Testament, XVb, Neuchâtel: Delachaux, 1976.

Ladd, G. E. *The Presence of the Future*, Grand Rapids: Eerdmans, 1974.

Lakeland, P. *Postmodernity*, Minneapolis: Fortress, 1997.

Lanser, S. S. *The Narractive Act: Point of View in Prose Fiction*, Princeton: Princeton University Press, 1981.

Lentricchia, F. After the New Criticism, London: Methuen, 1983.

Lindbeck, G. *The Nature of Doctrine*, Philadelphia: Westminster, 1984.

Locke, J. *An Essay Concerning Human Understanding*, New York: Dover, 1690/1959, Book IV, xix, 14.

Long, Phillips V. *The Art of Biblical History*, Grand Rapids: Zondervan, 1994.

Longman, T. "Storytellers, Poets and the Bible: Can Literary Artifice be True?" in: H. Conn, ed., *Inerrancy and Hermeneutic*, Grand Rapids: Baker, 1988, 137-150.

Louw. J. P. and Nida, E. A. *Greek - English Lexicon of the New Testament: Based on Semantic Domains*, New York: United Bible Societies, 1988.

Lundin, R. *The Responsibility of Hermeneutics*, Grand Rapids: Eerdmans, 1985, with C. Walhout and A. C. Thiselton.

———. *The Promise of Hermeneutics*, Carlilse: Paternoster, 1999, with C. Walhout and A. C. Thiselton.

Lyotard, J-F. *The Postmodern Condition: A Report on Knowledge*, Manchester: Manchester University Press, 1984.

———. "A Conversation," in: *Flash Art*, 921, 1985, 32-35.

———. *The Lyotard Reader*, ed. A. Benjamin, Oxford: Blackwell, 1989.

Madison, G. B. *The Hermeneutics of Postmodernity*, Bloomington: Indiana University Press, 1988.

Marguerat, D. *Le première histoire du christianisme. Les Actes des Apôtres*, Paris/Genève: Cerf/Labor et Fides, Lectio Divina 180, 1999. (*The First Christian Historian, Writing the Acts of the Apostles*, trans. G. J. Laughery, K. McKinney, R. Bauckhaum, Cambridge: Cambridge University Press, 2002, ET).

Marin, L. "Essai d'analyse structurale d'un récit-parabole: Matthieu 13/1-23," *Etudes théologiques et religieuses* 46 (1971), 35-74.

———. "Les femmes au tombeau: Essai d'analyse structurale d'un texte évangélique," in: C. Chabrol, and L. Marin, éds., *Sémiotique narrative: récits bibliques*, Paris: Didier/Larousse, 1971, 39-50, ("The Women at the Tomb: A Structural Analysis of a Gospel Text," reprinted in: D. Patte, ed., *The New Testament and Structuralism*, Pittsburgh: Pickwick, 1976, 73-96, ET).

Marrou, H.-I. *De la connaissance historique*, Paris: Seuil, 1954.

McConnell, F. ed., *The Bible and the Narrative Tradition*, Oxford: Oxford University Press, 1986.

McKnight, E. V. *The Bible and the Reader: An Introduction to Literary Criticism*, Philadelphia: Fortress, 1985.

———. "Presuppositions in New Testament Study," in: J. Green, ed., *Hearing the New Testament*, Carlisle: Paternoster, 1995, 278-300.

Mercer, N. "Postmodernity and Rationality: the Final Credits or just a Commercial Break?" in: A. Billington, T. Lane, and M. Turner, eds., *Mission and Meaning*, Carlilse: Paternoster, 1995, 319-338.

Milbank, J. *The Word Made Strange*, Oxford: Blackwell, 1997.

Momigliano, A. *Essays in Ancient and Modern Historiography*, Oxford: Blackwell, 1947, reprinted 1977.

Moore, S. D. "The 'Post-' Age Stamp: Does It Stick? Biblical Studies and the Postmodern Debate," *JAAR* 57 (1989), 543-559.

———. *Poststructuralism and the New Testament*, Minneapolis: Fortress, 1994.

Mullen, S. A. "Between 'Romance' and 'True History'," in: R. A. Wells, ed., *History and the Christian Historian*, Grand Rapids: Eerdmans, 1998, 23-40.

Nietzsche, F. *The Will to Power*, ed., W. Kaufmann, New York: Vintage Books, 1968.

Norris, C. *What's Wrong with Postmodernism: Critical Theory and the Ends of Philosophy*, Baltimore: Johns Hopkins University Press, 1990.

Patte, D. *Semiology and Parables*, ed., Pittsburgh: Pickwick, 1976.

———. *The New Testament and Structuralism*, Pittsburgh: Pickwick, 1976.

Perrin, N. "The Parables of Jesus as Parables, as Metaphors, and as Aesthetic Objects," *Journal of Religion* 47 (1967), 340-347.

———. *Rediscovering the Teaching of Jesus*, New York: Harper, 1967.

———. *Jesus and the Language of the Kingdom*, Philadelphia: Fortress, 1976.

Poland, L. *Literary Criticism and Biblical Hermeneutics: A Critique of Formalist Approaches*, Chico: Scholars, AAR Academy Series 111, 1985.

Poythress, V. S. *Science and Hermeneutics*, Grand Rapids: Zondervan, 1988.

Prickett, S. *The Origins of Narrative: The Romantic Appropriation of the Bible*, Cambridge: Cambridge University Press, 1996.

Ramsey, I. T. *Religious Language*, New York: Macmillian, 1957.

Reese, R. A. *Writing Jude: The Reader, the Text, and the Author*, Sheffield: Unpublished PhD Thesis, 1995.

Rogerson J. and Davies, P. R. *The Old Testament World*, Englewood-Cliffs: Prentice Hall, 1989.
Rorty, R. *Philosophy and the Mirror of Nature*, Princeton: Princeton University Press, 1979.
Sampson, P. "The Rise of Postmodernity," in: V. Samuel and C. Sugden, eds., *Faith and Modernity*, Oxford: Regnum Books, 1994, 29-57.
Samuel V. and Sugden, C. eds., *Faith and Modernity*, Oxford: Regnum Books, 1994.
Saussure, F. de. *Cours de linguistique générale*, éds., C. Bally et A. Sechehaye, Paris, Payot, 1955, reprinted in: *Cours de linguistique générale*, Paris: Payot, 1971.
Scott, J. "History in Crisis? The Others' Side of the Story," *American Historical Review* (1989).
Searle, J. R. *Speech Acts: An Essay in the Philosophy of Language*, Cambridge: Cambridge University Press, 1969.
Silverman H. J. and Ihde, D. eds., *Hermeneutics and Deconstruction*, New York: State University Press of New York, 1985.
Solomon, R. C. *Continental Philosophy since 1750: The Rise and Fall of the Self*, Oxford: Oxford University Press, 1988.
Southgate, B. *History: What & Why? Ancient, Modern and Postmodern Perspectives*, London: Routledge, 1996.
Stenger, W. R. *Narrative Theology in Early Jewish Christianity*, Louisville: Westminster, 1989.
Sternberg, M. *The Poetics of Biblical Narrative*, Bloomington: Indiana University Press, 1985.
Stout, J. "What is the Meaning of a Text?" *New Literary History* 14 (1982), 1-12.
Suleiman, S. R. and Crosman, I. eds., *The Reader in the Text: Essays on Audience and Interpretation*, Princeton: Princeton University Press, 1980.
Taylor, M. C. *Deconstructing Theology*, New York: Crossroad, Chico: Scholars, 1982.

———. "Text as Victim," in: T. Altizer, ed., *Deconstruction and Theology*, New York: Crossroad, 1982.

———. *Erring. A Postmodern A/Theology*, Chicago: Chicago University Press, 1984.

———. "Masking: Domino Effect," *JAAR* 54 (1986), 547-557.
Thiselton, A. C. *The Responsibility of Hermeneutics*, Grand Rapids: Eerdmans, 1985, with R. Lundin and C. Walhout.

———. *New Horizons in Hermeneutics*, Grand Rapids: Zondervan, 1992.

———. *Interpreting God and the Postmodern Self*, Edinburgh: T & T Clark, 1995.

———. *The Promise of Hermeneutics*, Carlilse: Paternoster, 1999, with C. Walhout and R. Lundin.
Tompkins, J. P. ed., *Reader – Response Criticism: From Formalism to Post-Structuralism*, Baltimore: Johns Hopkins University Press, 1980.
Vanhoozer, K. J. "A Lamp in the Labyrinth: The Hermeneutics of 'Aesthetic' Theology," *Trinity Journal*, Spring (1987), 25-56.

———. "The Hermeneutics of I-Witness Testimony: John 21.20-24 and the Death of the 'Author', " in: A. Graeme Auld, ed., *Understanding Poets and Prophets: Essays in Honour of George Wishart Anderson*, Sheffield: Journal of Old Testament Studies Press, 1993, 366-387.

———. *Is There A Meaning in This Text: The Bible, The Reader, and The Morality of Literary Knowledge*, Grand Rapids: Zondervan, 1998.
Vattimo, G. *La fin de la modernité. Nihilisme et herméneutique dans la culture post-moderne*, Paris: Seuil, 1987.
Veyne, P. *Comment on écrit l"histoire*, Paris: Seuil, 1971.
Via, Jr. D. O. *The Parables*, Philadelphia: Fortress, 1967.
Via, Jr. D. O. "The Parable of the Unjust Judge: A Metaphor of the Unrealized Self," in: D. Patte, ed., *Semiology and Parables*, Pittsburgh: Pickwick, 1976, 1-32.
von Rad, G. *Theologie des Alten Testaments*, 2 Vol., Munich: Kaiser, 1957-1960.
Vorster, W. S. "The Reader in the Text: Narrative Material," *Semeia* 48 (1989), 21-39.
Wachterhauser, B. R. ed., *Hermeneutics and Modern Philosophy*, New York: State University of New York Press, 1986.
Wachterhauser, B. R. *Hermeneutics and Truth*, Evanston: Northwestern University Press, 1994.
Wadsworth, M. ed., *Ways of Reading the Bible*, Brighton: Harvester Press, 1987.
Walhout, C. *The Responsibility of Hermeneutics*, Grand Rapids: Eerdmans, 1985, with R. Lundin and A. C. Thiselton.

Walhout, C. *The Promise of Hermeneutics*, Carlilse: Paternoster, 1999, with A. C. Thiselton and R. Lundin.
Warner, M. "The Fourth Gospel's Art of Rational Persuasion," in: M. Warner, ed., *The Bible as Rhetoric: Studies in Biblical Persuasion and Credibility*, Warwick Studies in Philosophy and Literature, London: Routledge, 1990, 153-177.
Warning, R. ed. *Rezeptionsästhetik*, UTB 303, Munich: Fink, 1988.
Watson, F. *Text, Church and World: Biblical Interpretation in Theological Perspective*, Edinburgh: T&T Clark, 1994.
Watson, F. *Text and Truth: Redefining Biblical Theology*, Edinburgh, T&T Clark, 1997.
Watson, F. ed., *The Open Text*, London: SCM, 1993.
Weinrich, H. *Le temps,. Le récit et le commentaire*, Paris: Seuil, 1973.
Wells, R. A. ed., *History and the Christian Historian*, Grand Rapids: Eerdmans, 1998.
Wenham, G. J. "The Coherence of the Flood Narrative," *Vetus Testamentum* 28 (1978), 336-348.
White, H. *Metahistory: The Historical Imagination in Nineteenth-Century Europe*, Baltimore: Johns Hopkins University Press, 1973.

____.
The Content of the Form: Narrative Discourse and Historical Representation: Baltimore Johns Hopkins University Press, 1987.
Wilder, A. N. *The Bible and the Literary Critic*, Minneapolis: Fortress, 1991.
Winquist, C. E. ed., *The Archaeology of the Imagination*, JAAR Thematic Studies 48, Chico: AAR, 1981.
Wittig, S. "A Theory of Multiple Meanings," *Semeia* 9 (1977), 75-103.
Wolterstorff, N. "John Locke's Epistemological Piety: Reason is the Candle of the Lord," *Faith and Philosophy* 11 (1994), 572-591.

____.
Divine Discourse: Philosophical reflections on the claim that God Speaks, Cambridge: Cambridge University Press, 1995.
Wright, N. T. *The New Testament and the People of God*, London: SPCK, 1992.
Wright, N. T. *Jesus and the Victory of God*, London: SPCK, 1996.
Wuellner, W. "Is there an Encoded Reader Fallacy," *Semeia* 48 (1989), 41-54.

INDEX

actantial model, (Greimas), 111
action, theory of, 29-30, 184
Alter, R., 169, 171
aneignung, 213
appropriation, 63, 76-77, 199, 211-217, 221, 225
Aristotle, 29, 47, 56, 114, 164-165, 181, 211
Aron, R., 173-174
Auerbach, E., 163
Augustine, 29, 129, 180
Austin, J.L., 50
author (s) (intention) (s), 28, 38, 45, 54-55, 57-59, 66, 75-76, 85-89, 96-97, 107, 110, 131, 158, 170, 185, 193-197, 199, 201-210, 216, 218-219, 224-225

Barr, J., 97-98
Barratt, D., 170
Barthes, R., 3, 5, 12, 91, 96, 111, 115, 133, 167, 170, 194, 201
Barton, J., 3
Barton, S.C., 220
Bebbington, D., 169, 173-174
Being and Time, 40-41, 207
Bentley, M., 169
Benveniste, E., 46, 62

Carr, D., 155, 163, 165-169, 173, 179-183, 185-186, 223
Carson, D.A., 3, 8, 123
Chatman, S., 155, 163, 167
Christian, 8, 11, 19, 22, 27, 73, 162
Christianity, 11, 26, 71-73, 161
Clark, S.H., 18
Clines, D.J.A., 3
code, 26, 47, 52, 56-60, 86, 92-96, 100, 111, 134-142, 148
cogito, 24-25, 33
Collini, S., 169, 219-220
confession of faith, 26, 64-65
configuration, 31-32, 37, 59, 68, 132, 148-149, 154, 158, 162, 164, 166, 168, 179, 183-184, 193, 199, 210-211, 218-219
Cooper, J.W., 10
Corinthians, 55, 160, 187
covenant(s), 61, 66, 72, 89, 125, 160, 220

Croatto, J.S., 195
cross, 67, 73
Crossan, J.D., 4-7, 13, 114-121, 124, 128, 142, 223

Davies, P.R., 176
death (of self, of text), 21, 73-74, 93, 122
demythologizing of Biblical text, 71, 74, 77-78
Derrida, J., 53-54, 115, 156
Descartes, R., 8-9, 24, 32
Destinateur and Destinataire, 87
dialectic, 22-23, 29-30, 39, 42, 44, 46, 48-55, 57, 61-62, 107, 112, 115, 122, 138, 159-160, 197, 202
Dictionary (theological), 97
Dilthey, W., 38, 40, 42, 45, 75-76, 105-108, 112
discontinuity, 119, 177, 179-181
discourse, 26, 28-29, 38, 44, 46-59, 62, 64-70, 77, 88, 92, 95, 97, 99-100, 103-104, 109-113, 123-126, 131, 135-136, 139-143, 148, 151, 153, 158, 160, 162-168, 174, 189, 194, 202, 205, 216
Dodd, C.H., 129
Dornisch, L., 132
Dutton, D., 210

Eagleton, T., 3
ego, 33, 213-214
ego cogito, 33
Ellingsen, M., 155
Emerson, R., 4
empiricism, 9
Enlightenment, 6-11, 13, 106
Ephesians, 55
Esprit, 20-22
Essays on Biblical Interpretation, 26
Evans, C.S., 155
event and meaning, 39, 46, 48-56, 61-62, 76. 107
evidence(d), 94, 154, 171-173, 175-176, 179, 206, 214, 223
existentialism, 17, 66, 168
explanation and understanding, 29-31, 34, 38-39, 42, 44, 56, 60-61, 85, 105-106, 108, 112

faith, 10-11, 26-27, 33-34, 68, 73, 79, 126, 130
Fallible Man, 23
fiction, 29-34, 148, 155, 160-200, 224
Finitude and Guilt, 21, 23
Finnegan's Wake, 89
Fish, S., 4, 6-7, 13, 115, 193-195, 201
Fisher, J. 159
Fisher, L., 204
Foucault, M., 170
Fowl, S.E., 3
France, R.T., 123
Freedom and Nature, 22
Frege, G., 51
Frei, H.W., 10, 12, 63, 78, 80, 125, 127, 169
Freund, E., 193
Furnish, V.P., 10

Gadamer, H-G., 8, 42-45, 106, 112, 212
Galatians, 55
Genette, G., 163, 207
Gerhart, M., 20
Gnosticism, 73-74
God, 9-11, 18, 28, 61, 65-70, 74-75, 79, 89, 103-104, 114, 117-129, 138, 141-142, 144, 150-152, 159, 196, 220
Gospels, 130, 133
Grenz, S.J., 7
"guess," 45-46
Gunton, C., 9

Halpern, B., 171
Harnisch, W., 115, 146-153, 186, 223
Harris, W.V., 190, 193-194, 209
Heidegger, M., 40-42, 45, 71, 112, 115, 163, 207, 213
Hemer, C.J., 171
hermeneutics, (Biblical), 1-2, 6, 12, 15-17, 25, 31-34, 60-73, 77-80, 88, 93-94, 102-105, 153, 162, 186-187, 190, 218-219, 221-224
Himmelfarb, G., 12-14, 156
Hirsch, E.D., 193
historian, 20-21, 81, 155, 170-177, 179, 184-185, 187-189
historical criticism, 81, 84, 133, 140, 221
historical narrative, 29, 159, 177-178
history, 16, 21, 28-30, 34, 39-40, 65, 72, 81-82, 88, 90-91, 103-107, 131, 155-156, 160, 163, 169-181, 183-190, 224
Hume, D., 9
Husserl, E., 20, 23-24, 71
Huyssen, A., 13

Ihde, D., 16, 22, 70, 155, 162-163
Ingarden, R., 151, 197

Ingraffia, B.D., 6, 11
interpretation theory, 37-61, 84-87, 199-202
Isaiah, 134
Jaspers, K., 20
Jauss, H.R., 193, 197, 201
Jenkins, K., 155-156, 169-170, 174-175
Jeremias, J., 129-130, 133
Jesus, (Christ), 26, 71, 73, 113, 115, 117-121, 123-124, 128-130, 133-136, 140-141, 144, 146, 149-154, 208, 223
Joy, M., 204
Joyce, J., 89

Kant, I., 9-10, 69
Kearney, R., 8, 12, 179, 208
Kellner, H., 173
kerygma,(tic), 26-27, 73-74, 77, 79, 130, 161-162
Kingdom of God, 61, 89, 114, 118-119, 122-125, 129, 141-142, 144, 220
Kittel, G., 97
Klemm, D.E., 18, 217

LaCocque, A., 34, 131, 154, 202-207
language, 2-3, 12-13, 24-25, 28, 30, 32, 37-38, 42, 46-52, 61-62, 67, 71-72, 74-75, 77-80, 90-93, 95-96, 98-104, 113, 119-121, 124-126, 132, 135-136, 138-139, 145, 147, 157-159, 166, 175, 194, 198
langue vs parole, 47, 90-91, 94-96, 99-102, 111, 139, 141
Lanser, S.S., 155
Lévinas, E., 181
Lindbeck, G., 62
linguistics, 38, 47-48, 50, 90, 94, 97, 102, 104
living hermeneutics, 16, 32, 34, 80, 96, 113, 131, 154, 186, 190, 218-219, 225
Locke, J., 8-9
Long, V.P., 169-170, 176-177
Longman, T., 177
Louw, J.P., 98
Luke, (gospel), 129, 144, 208
Lundin, R., 3, 163, 218
Lyotard, J-F., 6, 8, 12, 156

McCullagh, C.B., 169, 171-172, 175
McKnight, E.V., 3, 187. 195
Madison, G. B., 10-13, 173
Malbon, E.S. and Brown, F.B., 115, 117, 120
Marcel, G., 20, 23
Marcionism, 72
Marguerat, D., 172
Marin, L., 93, 133-139, 142
Marrou, H., 173-174
Matthew, (gospel), 118, 121, 127, 132, 144, 150, 160

meaning, (surplus), 121, 127, 152
Mercer, N., 6, 14-15
metaphor, 17, 25, 29, 55, 115, 117-118, 120, 142-144, 146-152, 157-159, 161, 186, 198, 212, 223
Metaphor, The Rule of, 29, 56-57, 123, 157, 198-200, 205, 224
methodologies, 39, 112, 128, 140, 152
Milbank, J., 220
mimesis, 31-32, 111, 163(I) (II), 164 (I) (II) (III), 182-183 (I-III), 193(III), 196(III), 197(I-III), 201(II), 210(III)-211(II-III)
modernism, 3, 6-8, 10, 12-16, 24, 82, 94, 113, 156, 190, 221, 224
Momigliano, A., 173
Mongin, O., 19, 34
Moore, S.D., 3, 7, 15, 194-195
Morgan, R., 3
Mounier, E., 20-21
Mullen, S.A., 170-172, 175-176

Narrative, 17-18, 25, 28-32, 37, 56-57, 65-66, 83-84, 111, 117, 121, 125-126, 130, 134-135, 137, 140-146, 148-154, 158-169, 171-172, 174-190, 193, 196, 198-202, 207, 211-213, 217, 221, 223-224
New Testament, 2, 3, 10, 27, 65, 72, 74, 98, 138, 141, 160, 172, 187, 220
Nida, E.A., 98,
Nietzsche, F., 10-12, 32, 115
non-sense, 14, 16, 37, 51, 67, 69-70, 121, 128, 146
Norris, C., 4, 8

Old Testament, 27, 47, 65, 72-73
Oneself as Another, 32, 34

Parable of the Sower, 132-133, 137
Parables, 25, 113-124, 126, 128, 130-135, 137, 139-144, 146-154, 186, 221, 223
Passion, the, 73
Paul, (letters), 55, 73
Penser la Bible, (Thinking Biblically), 34, 154, 202, 206, 224
Perrin, N., 124, 129-130, 141
Phaedrus, (Plato), 54
Pharisees, 129
phenomenology, 20, 24-25, 48, 71, 102, 104, 168
Plato, 44, 47, 54
play, (metamodel), 116-117
plot, 83, 111, 114, 126, 134, 143-145, 147, 159, 164, 172, 174, 178, 181-182, 199, 211
Poetics, (Aristotle), 114, 181
Poland, L.M., 118
polyvalence, 117, 119, 121

Pooley, R., 170
Porter, S.E., 3
post-modernism, 7, 11, 12-15, 34, 170, 224
Pound, E., 115
Poythress, V., 10
prefiguration, 1, 31-32, 158, 183, 210, 218-219
pre-modernism, 195
Prickett, S., 215-216, 225
prism as metaphor, 152, 186, 223-224

radical indeterminacy, 15, 17, 156, 185, 190, 221-222, 224
rational, (ist), (ity), 7-9, 13, 19, 69, 165, 182, 205
reader response theory, 193, 201
reader,(s), 3-5, 7, 27, 30-32, 46, 55, 58-61, 66, 72, 75-76, 79, 84, 87, 114-115, 118, 121, 126, 131, 138, 140, 144-145, 149, 158, 161-162, 164, 173, 189, 193-205, 207-225
reading, 4, 14, 54-55, 71-73, 99, 114, 125, 129, 131, 133, 151, 158, 161-162, 195-200, 203-207, 213-219, 224-225
Reagan, C.E., 38, 78, 113, 161
reality, 4-5, 7-8, 11-13, 23, 27, 31, 34, 39, 44, 54, 59, 73, 76, 91, 101, 104, 110, 113, 116, 121, 124-127, 139, 142-146, 148-151, 159, 161, 166-169, 172, 175-176, 178, 188, 198, 212-213, 218-220, 223, 225
reason, 8-15, 69
refiguration, 31-32, 143, 154, 158, 162-164, 183-184, 193, 196-197, 199, 210-213, 215-220, 225
Resurrection, 65, 67, 70, 73, 93, 195
Rhetoric, (Aristotle), 114
Ricoeur, P., (born), 19, (contributions to biblical hermeneutics), 28-34
Rogerson, J., 176
Romans, (letter), 55
romanticism, 39, 66
Ryken, L., 170

Saussure, F., 90, 101
Schaldenbrand, M., 161
Schleiermacher, F., 19, 38, 40, 45, 75, 105, 107, 112, 216
Schneiders, S.M., 214
Scott, J., 173
Searle, J.R., 50
self, 17, 21, 32-34, 60-61, 68-70, 78, 91, 103, 106-108, 121, 124-127, 138, 159, 172-173, 185, 213-214, 216-218, 220, 225
Semeia, 8, 16, 25, 115, 118, 126, 132, 178, 196
semiotics vs semantics, 47-48, 62, 158, 197
sense, 14, 16, 37, 53, 58, 67-70, 75-76, 80, 87-89, 95, 109, 114, 121-124, 128, 133, 136-137, 145-147, 151,

156, 178, 182, 209, 221, 223
sense and reference, 15-16, 34, 51-52, 61-62, 77, 87, 89, 101-104, 113-114, 121, 128, 132, 137, 142, 144, 149, 151, 196, 198-199
sharp boundaries, 12-13, 15, 17, 156, 185, 190, 221-222, 224
sign system(s), 51, 104, 116, 128, 138-139, 142, 158
Socrates, 181
Solomon, R.C., 8
Southgate, B., 156, 169
speech act(s), 28, 50-52, 111, 151, 202
Stenger, W.R., 155
Sternberg, M., 169, 209
Stout, J., 3
structuralism, 19, 25, 29-31, 57, 90-96, 98-99, 116-117, 133, 138, 140, 142, 221
Suleiman, S., 196
surplus of meaning, 121, 127, 152
Symbolism of Evil The, 23-24, 29
Synoptic gospels, 133, 146

taxis, 56
Taylor, M.C., 4-7, 11, 13, 58, 115, 156
Time and Narrative, 28-29, 30, 34, 154, 200, 207
tension theory, 66, 112, 127-128, 132, 140, 143, 145-149, 151-154, 161-162, 177, 203, 223
Terre Nouvelle, 20
theory of action, 29-30, 184
Thiselton, A.C., 3, 6, 8, 10-11, 163, 218
Thompson, J.B., 2, 43, 178, 203, 208, 211
Tompkins, J.P., 193
trinity of methods, 128
Truth and Method, 8, 42, 106

understanding and explanation, 39, 87, 108, 160, 174, 219

Valdés, M.J., 44, 161, 179, 182, 207
Vanhoozer, K.J., 17, 78, 80, 125, 151, 155, 160, 195-196, 208-209
Veyne, P., 173-174
Via, D.O.Jr., 123
von Rad, G., 64

Walhout, C., 163, 218
Wallace, M.I., 17, 63, 154, 187, 214, 218
Warner, M., 201
Watson, F., 3, 7
Wells, R.A., 155, 169-170
Wenham, G.J., 177
White, H., 166-167, 169-170, 173, 179
Wholly other, 126
Wittgenstein, L., 47, 71, 213
Wolterstorff, N., 8, 209
world of the text, 61-64, 66, 68, 70-71, 80, 126-127, 153, 164, 199-201, 211, 214-215, 217-219, 225
World War II, 20
Wright, N.T., 151
Yale school, 63, 222
Yeats, W.B., 115

Zugehörigkeit, 43

Destinée Media

Destinée Media publishes both fiction and non-fiction, and aims to provide culturally engaging publications that bring a fresh perspective to spirituality and culture.

At Destinée Media we seek to operate by faith in God within a Biblical/Christian worldview. We hope to inspire 'culture making' by promoting ideas that will contribute to Christ being understood as Lord of the whole of life, which is to be marked by redemption and renewal. We are committed to reflecting carefully on vital matters for the church, academy, and society, while aiming to keep a personal and intimate dimension of the Christian life in view.

Destinée Media is interested in people and shares in several key aspects of the L'Abri ethos, (www.labri.org) including being innovative, living truth in love, and supporting the arts.

We thank you for your interest in our materials and hope that you find them both relevant and challenging. Please share your thoughts with us:

www.destineemedia.com

destinēe

www.ingramcontent.com/pod-product-compliance
Lightning Source LLC
Chambersburg PA
CBHW021142080526
44588CB00008B/181